AN INVESTIGATION OF KOIMAOMAI IN THE NEW TESTAMENT

The Concept of Eschatological Sleep

AN INVESTIGATION OF KOIMAOMAI IN THE NEW TESTAMENT

The Concept of Eschatological Sleep

Paul Norman Jackson

Mellen Biblical Press Series
Volume 45

MELLEN BIBLICAL PRESS
Lewiston/Queenston/Lampeter

Library of Congress Cataloging-in-Publication Data

This volume has been registered with the Library of Congress.

ISBN 0-7734-2417-2

This is volume 45 in the continuing series
Mellen Biblical Press Series
Volume 45 ISBN 0-7734-2417-2
MBP Series ISBN 0-7734-2430-X

A CIP catalog record for this book is available from the British Library.

Copyright © 1996 Paul Norman Jackson

All rights reserved. For information contact

The Edwin Mellen Press
Box 450
Lewiston, New York
USA 14092-0450

The Edwin Mellen Press
Box 67
Queenston, Ontario
CANADA L0S 1L0

The Edwin Mellen Press, Ltd.
Lampeter, Dyfed, Wales
UNITED KINGDOM SA48 7DY

Printed in the United States of America

To my wife, Janet,

and my children, Garrett, Lindsey, and Meghan

TABLE OF CONTENTS

List of Tables	i
Foreword	ii
Preface	iv
Acknowledgements	vi

INTRODUCTION 1
   The Research Problem 1
   Presuppositions' Endorsement 10
   Hermeneutical Procedure 12
      Treatment Basis 12
      The Hypothesis 12
      Content Outline 14
      Complementary Themes' Relationship 18

PART ONE
THE HISTORICAL BACKGROUND OF THE
KOIMAOMAI DOMAIN

Chapter

I.   **NON-CHRISTIAN GREEK AND LATIN LITERATURE**   20
     Synonyms in the Semantic Field   21
     The Sleep of Slumber or Natural Process   27
     The Sleep of Death   29
     The Gods Hypnos and Thanatos   36
     Conclusion   37

II.   **LINGUISTIC EVIDENCE FROM THE HELLENISTIC PERIOD**   39
     The Frequency of the "Metaphor" Sleep for Death   39
     Sepulchral Art   40

Memorial Epitaphs and Inscriptions	41
The LXX and Diaspora Greek	44
The Pentateuch	44
Excursus on Sheol	45
Septuagintal Eschatology in a New Testament Parable?	48
The Books of the Kingdoms	51
The Regnal Obituaries	51
Two Prophets and Two Harlots	55
Jobian Thanatology	57
The Sleep of Death Expressed by Synonymous Phraseology in the LXX	65
Pseudepigraphical Citations	67
Philo and Josephus	69
Conclusion	71
III. THE SEMANTIC DOMAIN IN HEBREW AND ARAMAIC	74
Old Testament Witnesses	74
Major Semitic Terms Depicting the Sleep of Death	
שָׁכַב	74
יָשֵׁן	77
Minor Semitic Terms Depicting the Sleep of Death	81
Second Temple Judaism	82
Aramaic Targums	84
The Dead Sea Scrolls	86
Babylonian Talmud	88
Palestinian Talmud	90
Rabbinic Midrash	91
Conclusion	92

PART TWO
INTERPRETATIVE ANALYSIS OF THE NEW TESTAMENT USAGE OF KOIMAOMAI AND ITS EFFECT ON THE EARLY CHURCH

IV. THE NEW TESTAMENT TRADITION	96
Synoptic Gospels	100
Matthean Adoption of Ezekiel's Valley of Dry Bones	100
The Raising of Jairus' Daughter	104
The Lazarus Episode	111
Form Critical Analysis	112
Source and Redaction Critical Analysis	113
Historical Value of the Lazarus Pericope	115
Exegesis	117
The Sleep of Death in the Primitive Church	121
The First Christian Martyr	121

The Davidic Regnal Obituary Redivivus: A Key Element in a Lukan Missionary Speech	126
The Pauline Witness	128
The Thessalonian Correspondence	129
The Corinthian Correspondence	132
Late Pauline Texts Related to the Intermediate State	138
The Scoffers' Old Testament Allusion in 2 Pet. 3.1-7.	141
Conclusion	143

V.	**POST-BIBLICAL REFLECTION**	145
	The Apostolic Witness and the Early Church	146
	Clement of Rome and Ignatius	147
	Justin Martyr	149
	The Apocryphal Gospels	151
	The Church Fathers	152
	The Alexandrians	153
	Latin Representatives	156
	Subsequent Patristic Thought	158
	Memorial Epitaphs and Inscriptions	161
	Conclusion	164

CONCLUSION	165
The Meaning of Κοιμάομαι in the New Testament	165
The Meaning of Κοιμάομαι for Contemporary Christians	170
Significance for a Christian Understanding of Death	173

APPENDIX A
The Semantic Range of the Sleep-of-Death Metaphor in the New Testament   175

APPENDIX B
Κοιμάομαι as the Sleep of Death in the LXX   178

APPENDIX C
Ὑπνόω as the Sleep of Death in the LXX   183

APPENDIX D
Καθεύδω as the Sleep of Death in the LXX   184

APPENDIX E
Synonymy Correspondence between Greek and Hebrew Sleep-of-Death Terminology   185

APPENDIX F
Κοιμάομαι as Physical Sleep in the Homeric Period   186

APPENDIX G
Κοιμάομαι *as the Sleep of Death in Apostolic and Patristic Works*   188

APPENDIX H
Κοίμησις *in the 'Bosom of Abraham' Epitaph*   189

APPENDIX I
Jewish Epitaphs Found in the Necropolis   190

APPENDIX J
The "Εκοιμήθη ἐν Χριστῷ' Epitaph   191

APPENDIX K
The "Εκοιμήθη ἐν Κυρίῳ' Epitaph   192

SELECTED BIBLIOGRAPHY   193

INDEX OF ANCIENT SOURCES   222

INDEX OF MODERN AUTHORS   237

LIST OF TABLES

Table 1.	The Semantic Diversity of Κοιμάομαι in the Homeric Period	23
Table 2.	Polysemic Versatility of Κοιμάομαι in the Homeric Period	28
Table 3.	The Sleep of Death in the **Anthologia Palatina**	43
Table 4.	Regnal Résumés Excluding the Sleep-of-Death Formula in the Books of the Kingdoms	53
Table 5.	Grammatical Usages of Κοιμάομαι Reflecting Patristic Belief in the Intermediate State	160

FOREWORD

Despite a representative number of New Testament examples portraying death as being a sleep, many Christians believe that immediately after death they are transported to heaven to live eternally with the Lord. By believing this Platonic idea, Christians not only skip completely over the last two temporal events in the scheme of salvation-history—the parousia and bodily resurrection, but they also adopt Greek philosophical principles. The purpose of this work was to investigate the pagan and biblical teaching of the "sleep of death," especially as characterized by the term κοιμάομαι and its synonymous semantic field, in an attempt (1) to shed light on why Jesus' "sleep-of-death" words were misunderstood by his disciples and unbelievers and (2) to determine whether or not κοιμάομαι could help establish the reality of an interim period between death and resurrection. The subject of this work is critical because it deals with death, an issue both vexing and perennial for those in the pulpit and the pew.

The Introduction justified the investigation by explaining the research problem at length, endorsed the basic presuppositions, set forth hermeneutical procedures, and outlined the contents of the work. Diachronically and synchronically, Greek, Hebrew, Aramaic, and Latin equivalents were established. Chapter I compiled non-Christian Greek and Latin literature. Chapter II investigated the linguistic evidence from the Hellenistic period. Chapter III surveyed the semantic domain in Hebrew and Aramaic. Chapter IV reviewed the New Testament tradition. Chapter V comprised a brief look at the post-biblical reflection. The Conclusion set forth the meaning of κοιμάομαι in the New Testament, the meaning of κοιμάομαι for contemporary Christians, and its relative significance for a Christian understanding of death.

The principle conclusions reached in this study are related to the doctrine of thanatology in the New Testament. First, while the biblical tradition verbally assimilated the pagan notion of the "sleep of death," it conceptually departed from it with respect to its ontological model. Second, the "wholistic dualism" model is compatible with biblical anthropology, thanatology, and eschatology. Monism, therefore, is not the only ontological option for the postmortem state. Lastly, κοιμάομαι, in a predominant sense, theologically and functionally situates each deceased Christian in the pre-parousia disposition of the intermediate state in an intimate, conscious relationship with Christ.

Paul Norman Jackson
Southwestern Seminary 1992

PREFACE

This work is a dissertation which was accepted for the degree, Doctor of Philosophy, by the Committee for the Ph.D. Degree of Southwestern Baptist Theological Seminary of Fort Worth in the Fall term of 1992. The thesis was supervised by Dr. Bruce Corley, and was examined by Dr. Curtis Vaughan and Dr. Burt Dominey. The desire to pursue this topic arose while attending Dr. Bruce Corley's seminar on the Life and Letters of Paul. This discovery was odd because the text we discussed was found in the Gospel of John. In a conversation about the resurrection, Dr. Corley drew my attention to a pre-parousia theme, the intermediate state. Specifically, we talked about the conversation Jesus had with his disciples concerning the fate of their friend Lazarus in John 11. The question he posed was, "Why did Jesus cause obvious confusion when he told the disciples that Lazarus was asleep (κεκοίμηται)?" Another way to state this problem is, "Why were Jesus and the disciples not using the same dictionary (word bank) at the time he quizzed them?" While the disciples were thinking about convalescence, Jesus was referring to death. This illustration was enough to warrant an investigation into the term Jesus used to cause this breakdown in communication. So spawned the dissertation topic. Directly associated with this concept of the sleep of death is a point of eschatological confusion. Do Christians receive their resurrection bodies at death or at the parousia? This subject is of great interest mainly because of its universal appeal and application. The experience of death and the preaching of funerals is an important and perennial component of the pastoral and teaching ministries. The topic of death is also a highly interesting subject among lay people. The eschatological plight of the Christian, therefore, must be addressed biblically and compassionately.

If there is an intermediate state, why do so many Christians believe in a thanatological model appearing to be more Hellenistic than biblical—that is, the teaching of the separation of the soul and body at death and the immediate acquisition of heaven? Conversely, if there is not an intermediate state preceding bodily resurrection, why do people tend so carefully to the deceased as though physical bodies will have a postponed stake in the future or at least some earthly connection with the afterlife? While the Bible fails to mention the phrase "intermediate state" explicitly what exactly is intended by the Old Testament idea of the various Hebrew kings sleeping with their fathers and the New Testament idea of the sleep of death if they do not indicate a discernible intermediate state between death and resurrection? I wanted to explore more deeply these probing questions. It has been found after completing a diachronic and synchronic evaluation of the Greek term κοιμάομαι and its synonymous associates that the concept of the "sleep of death" evolved from a deceptive euphemism in the Homeric period to a bold metaphor of hope in the New Testament. Although the post-biblical era represents many writers who used the concept voluminously, several key figures blended Hellenistic/Platonic principles of centuries past with their theologies thus adulterating the pure biblical message of death, the intermediate state, and the resurrection of the believer. It is my desire that this work will serve to help the lay person, the pastor, and the teacher reevaluate current thanatological beliefs and, if need be, realign those beliefs with New Testament teaching.

Paul Norman Jackson
Union University 1995

ACKNOWLEDGEMENTS

Deep gratitude swells in my heart as I think of the many people who have given me constant encouragement and leadership throughout the process of completing this project. First and above all I wish to thank my wife. Most of our married life she has tirelessly and joyfully carried most of the domestic burden, including the rigors of managing three beautiful and energetic children, due to my seemingly "perennial" enrollment in school and now as I serve as Assistant Professor of Religion at Union University. Without her neither the dissertation nor the book would ever have been completed. I dedicate this book with all my love to her and to my children. I am also deeply indebted to so many loving relatives who have prayed, paid, and demonstrated tremendous patience for the completion of this project.

I am also thankful for the contributions of several professors at Southwestern Seminary: Dr. Bruce Corley, my dissertation supervisor, who not only suggested the idea for the dissertation's topic, but also provided "long distance" guidance for two years while I was pastoring in Colorado; Dr. Lorin L. Cranford, whose New Testament Critical Methodology Seminar set me in the proper direction for New Testament studies; and Dr. Thomas C. Urrey, who allowed me to serve as his grader for several years, and taught me to love the Greek New Testament in my early days at Southwestern. Special thanks also should be extended to Francene Purdom, a marvelous and gifted research librarian at the Fort Collins Public Library in Fort Collins, Colorado, who efficiently and gracefully acquired numerous inter-library loan materials for me. I am also deeply grateful to Dr. Louise Bentley, extraordinarily gifted and recently retired long-time Professor of English at Union University. She assumed the laborious task of helping me transform a dissertation into book form by meticulously and expertly checking grammatical forms and functions and pointing out other "typical" dissertation errors. She will be sorely missed at Union. I would like also to thank the library staff at the St. Thomas Catholic Seminary in Denver, Colorado for their valuable assistance in the research process. Lastly, I would like to thank my many Christian friends at the Fort Collins Southern Baptist Church, especially the late Zula Fryberger, for their heartfelt prayers and unsolicited financial support to enable me to be in a position to finish the dissertation. My family is equally grateful.

Paul Norman Jackson
Union University 1995

INTRODUCTION

The Research Problem

The plight of the Christian at the time of death elicits debate both exciting and polemical. Death's natural association with the unknown easily attracts speculation and fear. Satisfactory solutions, however, must be distinguished from the written biblical and extra-biblical sources in order to discover how pagans, Christian believers, and Jesus himself addressed this mystery. Existential proof of the precise experience of the Christian at death can only be fully ascertained a posteriori. Christians, therefore, are compelled to rely primarily upon the biblical witness for their presuppositions. Especially since the time of Oscar Cullmann's classic rendition of the problem in his slim but weighty book, *Immortality of the Soul or Resurrection of the Dead? The Witness of the New Testament*, debate has rumbled vociferously.[1] In his own words, "No other publication of mine has provoked such enthusiasm or such violent hostility." One respondent wrote, ". . . the French people, dying for lack of the Bread of Life, have been offered instead of bread, stones, if not serpents."[2] The present writer has encountered a similar volatile reaction while discussing 1 Thess. 4.13-18 in a church study group. A

---

[1] Oscar Cullmann, *Immortality of the Soul or Resurrection of the Dead? The Witness of the New Testament* (London: Epworth Press, 1958).

[2] Ibid, 5.

young man in attendance became visibly disturbed when the suggestion was made that his mother and other Christians were asleep in Christ until the resurrection. Adamantly, he held that when his mother died he and his pastor saw her spirit leave the body.

The debate has surfaced recently in discussions related to the resurrection of Jesus between Murray J. Harris and Norman Geisler. Although the charges levelled against Harris are in direct relation to the reality and nature of Jesus' resurrection, the condition of dead Christians is addressed as well.[3] Continuing in the tradition of Cullmann is the Catholic theologian Joseph Osei-Bonsu, who believes in the disembodied existence of the soul during the interim period between death and the resurrection of believers at the parousia of Christ. Osei-Bonsu claims that Cullmann cited the New Testament passages which indicated an interim state but failed to support them with exegesis.[4]

Scriptural opinions concerning the postmortem state of the believer seemingly oscillate between the unique, Lukan words of Jesus, "Today you will be with me in Paradise," and the Pauline admonition, "Those who have fallen asleep

---

[3] To understand the nature of the debate, see Murray J. Harris, *Raised Immortal: Resurrection and Immortality in the New Testament* (Grand Rapids: Eerdmans, 1983), and more recently, idem, *From Grave to Glory* (Grand Rapids: Zondervan Publishing House, 1990); Norman Geisler, "The Apologetic Significance of the Bodily Resurrection of Christ," *Bulletin of the Evangelical Philosophical Society* 10 (1987): 15-37; idem, "The Battle for the Resurrection," *Fundamentalist Journal* (March, 1989): 12-15; idem, "The Significance of Christ's Physical Resurrection," *Bibliotheca Sacra* 146 (1989): 148-70; idem, "'I Believe . . . in the Resurrection of the Flesh,'" *Christian Research Journal* 12 (1989): 20-22; and idem, *The Battle for the Resurrection* (Nashville: Nelson, 1989).

[4] For treatment, see his recent thesis, "Soul and Body in Life after Death: An Examination of the New Testament Evidence with Some Reference to Patristic Exegesis" (Ph.D. diss., University of Aberdeen, 1980), and his more current articles, "Does 2 Cor. 5.1-10 Teach the Reception of the Resurrection Body at the Moment of Death?," *Journal for the Study of the New Testament* 28 (1986): 81-101; "The Intermediate State in the New Testament," *Scottish Journal of Theology* 44 (1991): 169-94; and "Anthropological Dualism in the New Testament," *Scottish Journal of Theology* 40 (1987): 571-90.

(κοιμωμένων)."⁵ Historically, 2 Corinthians 5, in comparison with 1 Corinthians 15 and 1 Thessalonians 4, has proven to be a most troublesome passage with regard to the "when" of the Christian investiture of the spiritual, transformed body.⁶ This writer believes the same Paul, anthropologically and doctrinally, is reflected in each passage. A healthy group of scholars, however, support the idea of Paul's change in eschatology, thus paving the way for belief in the acquisition of the heavenly body at death.⁷ On the other hand, various objections have been

---

⁵In the Pauline corpus three eschatologically slanted passages, 1 Thessalonians 4, 1 Corinthians 15, and 2 Corinthians 5, some have seen a development of Paul's thought which supposedly reflects an influx of Hellenistic thought (See Albert Schweitzer, *Paul and His Interpreters* [London: 1912], 69-76). E. Earle Ellis rightly rejects any Hellenistic tampering and suggests this viewpoint has resulted from a misunderstanding of Pauline anthropology (See "II Corinthians v.1-10 in Pauline Eschatology," *New Testament Studies* 6 [Jan. 1960]: 211-24 = *Paul and His Recent Interpreters* [Grand Rapids: Eerdmans, 1961], 35-48.).

⁶Many scholars have argued that Paul's eschatological viewpoint shifted in his later writings, especially in 2 Corinthians 5. For a chronological list of these adherents, see M. J. Harris, *Raised Immortal*, 255, n. 2. Ralph P. Martin offers three suggested reasons why Paul wrote 5.2-4 in *2 Corinthians*, Word Biblical Commentary (Waco: Word Books, Publisher, 1986), 97-102. These motivations include: 1) shift of eschatology—W. L. Knox, *St. Paul and the Church of the Gentiles* (Cambridge: Cambridge University Press, 1939), 121-45; 2) the emphasis of the corporate body rather than individual resurrection—E. Earle Ellis, "II Cor. v.1-10 in Pauline Eschatology," 211-24; and 3) a polemic directed at incipient gnosticism in Corinth—F. G. Lang, *2 Korinther 5, 1-10 in der neueren Forschung*, BGBE 16 (Tübingen: J. C. B. Mohr, 1973), 183. The proposed idea of theological change is difficult to accept. This writer agrees with M. J. Harris, "2 Cor. 5:1-10: A Watershed in Paul's Eschatology?" *Tyndale Bulletin* 22 (1971): 32-57, that the eschatology expressed in 2 Corinthians 5 "cannot be deemed a temporary aberration in his thought" (56). Although one must allow room for ideas to develop in Scripture as the New Testament does cultivate Old Testament themes (see Heb. 1.1-2; Mt. 5.17; and F. F. Bruce, *The New Testament Development of Old Testament Themes* [Grand Rapids: Eerdmans, 1968], 17-21), one must be careful not to accept any idea which would suggest the apostle Paul was later correcting an earlier mistaken eschatological view. Instead of using the phrase "change or shift of doctrine," it would be better to see this supposed discrepancy as a "change of focus" based on the provenance of the letter, rather than revamping a mistaken view. The idea that Paul's thought developed in a manner that suggests correction is curiously Hegelian. See also B. F. Meyer, "Did Paul's View of the Resurrection of the Dead Undergo Development?," *Theological Studies* 47 (1986): 363-87. He identifies linguistic and conceptual touchstones linking 2 Cor. 5.2-5 with two other passages on final salvation at the parousia, that is 1 Cor. 15.50-55 and Rom. 8.18-27.

⁷See Harris, *Raised Immortal*, 98-100, for five popular exegetical conclusions about the passage. The exegesis of the pericope in question will be addressed below in Part Two, Chapter IV.

raised against this viewpoint in favor of donning the spiritual body at the parousia.[8] Harris lists ten proposed solutions to both supposed views.[9] The purpose of this work is to establish the reality of an "interim" period (German: *Zwischenzeit* or *Zwischenzustand*) based upon the scriptural use of κοιμάομαι and its synonymous semantic field as it refers metaphorically to the "sleep of death." Grammatically, the problem could be stated: "Is the 'sleep of death' punctiliar or linear?"[10] That death is described consistently in the Scripture as "sleep" warrants an investigation into the ontological status of its meaning. Metaphorically, if death can be seen as eschatological sleep, then there must be a measurable "elapsing of time" between the cessation of physical life and the parousia. Christ's coming the second time, and not until then, will prompt the resurrection of believers.[11] All believers will then experience fully what Jesus had already pioneered and established as a paradigm for all subsequent Christian death. Cullmann rightly suggests that the difficulty in properly understanding one's plight during death is related directly to one's personal predilections. The conflict is whether one mirrors Greek philosophical beliefs about death, like Socrates who heralded the belief in the immortality of the soul, or whether one mirrors biblical beliefs, such as Jesus, the Synoptic writers, or Paul, who advanced the idea of the resurrection of the dead. N. D. O'Donoghue sketches his understanding of the pervasive influence of the specific Greek belief of immortality of the soul. It

---

[8]Ibid., 255, n. 4.

[9]Ibid., 100-101. The intent of this study is not to reconcile the supposed inconsistency because it is not presupposed there is one.

[10]Robert E. Bailey, "Is 'Sleep' the Proper Biblical Term for the Intermediate State?" *Zeitschrift für die neutestamentliche Wissenschaft* 55 (1964): 164, points out that κοιμάομαι appears eight times in the aorist tense (1 Cor. 7.39, 15.6, 18; 1 Thess. 4.14, 15; Acts 7.60, 13.36; 2 Pet. 3.4), three times in the perfect (John 11.11; Matt. 27.52; 1 Cor. 15.20), twice in the present (1 Cor. 11.30; 1 Thess. 4.13), and once in the future (1 Cor. 15.51). This distribution should be sufficient indication to discourage any solution based on grammatical evidence alone.

[11]O. Cullmann, *Christ and Time: The Primitive Christian Conception of Time and History*, rev. ed., trans. Floyd V. Filson (Philadelphia: The Westminster Press, 1964), 3, refers to this tension between the "already" and "not yet" of salvation history as D-Day and V-Day.

antedated Christianity by four hundred years; it was prevalent during the time of Jesus; it appears in the prologue of John's gospel in the form of Middle Platonism; it was taken over by Christian philosophy as the handmaid of Christian theology; and caused deep division between both sides of the Reformation tradition.[12] One's anthropology and ontological conclusions will largely determine the essence of a proper thanatology. Is man a Hellenistic, dichotomous being or is he a Hebraic, psychosomatic unity?[13] If at one point there is realized death and at a future point a reciprocal resurrection, then it must follow that there is some measurable ontological state between these two events. This measurable period of time has been designated by theologians as the "intermediate state." While admitting to the apostle Paul's reticence of explicit teaching of the intermediate state, Earle Ellis rightly believes there are grounds to draw conclusions strongly pointing in that direction.[14] Ellis's use of the phrase "during death" clearly reveals his posture. Any "death talk" along Cullmannian lines creates high anxiety in the camp of "those with lenses ground in Athens"[15] because it is altogether unsavory for most Christians to believe that the dead "are sleeping," awaiting a future resurrection.

---

[12]N. D. O'Donoghue, "The Awakening of the Dead," *Irish Theological Quarterly* 56 (1990): 50. Also, as E. Earle Ellis has pointed out, even if with scholars like W. D. Davies, we see "two diverse strains in Paul's conception of resurrection" in a hellenized Judaism, the end result is the same ("II Corinthians v. 1-10 in Pauline Eschatology," 211). By the same author, see "*Sōma* in First Corinthians," *Interpretation* 44 (1990): 132-44; and see W. D. Davies, *St. Paul and Rabbinic Judaism: Some Rabbinic Elements in Pauline Theology* (London: S.P.C.K., 1958), 319.

[13]See E. Earle Ellis, "*Sōma* in First Corinthians," 141. While treating the anthropological concerns of the Apostle Paul in 1 Corinthians, Ellis has concluded that a reference to a specific group of Corinthians who say that "there is no resurrection of the dead" (15.12) and who also, in contradictory fashion, believed in some kind of substitutionary baptism with respect to departed believers, were early adherents to Platonic dualism.

[14]Ibid., 142-43. "One's corporate inclusion in Christ and, thus, one's corporate life continue after the ending of one's individual life. 'Whether we live or die, we are the Lord's, for to this end Christ died and rose to life in order that he might be Lord of both the dead and the living' (Rom. 14.8-9), and 'whether we are awake or asleep (in death) we may begin simultaneously to live with him' (1 Thess. 5.10). Thus while death is not an individual fulfillment of salvation, *during death* one remains under Christ's Lordship and in his care" (emphasis mine).

[15]Ibid.

Ellis's explanation attempts to solve the epistemological/ontological problem at this point:

> ... while the Christian dead remain in time, they do not count time. The hiatus in their individual being between their death and their resurrection at the last day of this age is, in their consciousness, a tick of the clock. For them the great and glorious day of Christ's Parousia is only a moment in the future. The 'intermediate state' is something that the living experience with respect to the dead, not something the dead experience with respect to the living or to Christ.[16]

Ellis's explanation, however, invokes another problem. How can the event death command two different ontological states simultaneously? Can a "sleeping Christian" be both temporal and transcendent? If Ellis is right, it seems that dead Christians are metaphysical schizophrenics, that is, having already experienced the resurrection, yet also being asleep from the perspective of οἱ ζῶντες οἱ περιλειπόμενοι. Ellis could be right if at death Christians enter into an ontological state of nontime, thus making ontology a subset of eternity. It is, therefore, not only a significant theological problem but also a weighty philosophical problem.

Recently, John W. Cooper accomplished this prerequisite.[17] His indispensable treatment is simultaneously pastoral and scholarly, historical and analytic, biblical, philosophical, and scientific. Cooper's model does not call for the jettison of every brand of anthropological dualism. It does, however, rightly reject dualism in the Platonic/Greek sense. "Wholistic dualism" is a view that Scripture teaches both the functional integration of human life and a disembodied intermediate state. His view sheds much light on the extremely difficult topic of postmortem affairs. This position is consistent with the traditional belief that a Christian is at no time separated from Christ, even during death (Rom. 8.38, Lk. 23.42, Phil. 1.23, etc.). Cullmann, therefore, is right in holding that "being with Christ" does not denote

---

[16]Ibid.

[17]John W. Cooper, *Body, Soul, & Life Everlasting: Biblical Anthropology and the Monism-Dualism Debate* (Grand Rapids: Eerdmans, 1989). The importance of Cooper's work will be crucial in Chapter IV.

resurrection of the body.¹⁸ This study will attempt not to treat resurrection per se; rather it will concentrate on that intermediate state of death between the conclusion of physical life and the parousia/resurrection.

The issue continues to be current because people die and funerals must be preached. Some sermons preached on the subjects of death and heaven, however, are launched from a biblical platform but are soon shrouded with the mists of Hellenism long before they reach their conclusion. Others attempt to deal with it honestly. Consider this excerpt from a sermon by Daniel Vestal entitled "Heaven" based on the exegetically difficult passage 2 Cor. 5.1-10, which is a current example of dealing with the problem:

> Verse 6 says, 'While we are at home in the body, we are absent from the Lord.' Verse 8 says, 'To be absent from the body is to be present with the Lord.' Death means I leave this dwelling place *which is the physical body*, and I enter into a new dwelling place *which is the immediate presence of Christ*. So from this side death is a departure, and from the other side death is an arrival. From this side death is a goodby, and from the other side death is a good morning. Death for the Christian is a transition, in a moment, in the twinkling of an eye, from one home to another. Death for the Christian is a journey from one abode to another.¹⁹

Although Vestal denounces any kind of soul sleep, his interim period is a disembodied/conscious state. The only question about Vestal's expository sermon is that his interim state is in heaven proper. Vestal's supposed eschatological disembodied spirit exists in spite of his quoting 1 Cor. 15.51-57, in which verse 51 and 52 declare: "Behold, I tell you a mystery. We shall not all sleep (κοιμηθησόμεθα), but we shall all be changed, in a moment, in the twinkling of an eye, at the last trumpet: For the trumpet of God will sound and the dead will be raised incorruptible, and we shall be changed" (emphasis mine).

---

¹⁸Oscar Cullmann, *Christ and Time*, 240. Even though Ellis agrees, he nevertheless points out that Cullmann falls into a body/soul dualism ("Sōma in First Corinthians," 143). Cullmann states: "Hence the dead likewise live in a condition in which the tension between present and future still exists. For them the question arises, 'How long yet?' (Rev. 6:10). Indeed, it is perhaps even more in place for them, in view of the fact that *they are out of the body*" (emphasis mine, ibid., 240-41).

¹⁹Daniel Vestal, sermon preached in the morning worship service at the First Baptist Church in Midland, Texas on June 1, 1980.

Cullmann believed that Paul was referring to an intermediate state of the dead in 2 Corinthians 5.[20] This study will answer Robert E. Bailey's question in the affirmative that "sleep" is the proper biblical term for the intermediate state.[21] Many authors, including Bailey, see the term "sleep" as a euphemistic device. Comparing this designation to non-Christian euphemistic instances of death allows little, if any, differentiation. If the Christian usage is seen as metaphorical, then a sharp distinction between the two becomes apparent. When the concept of the "sleep of death" is cast in metaphorical garb, an explicit comparison can yield an implicit comparison.[22] No euphemism is intended in the words of Pirké de Rabbi Eliezer concerning the death sleep:

> The sleep at night is like this world, and the awakening of the morning is like the world to come. . . . The awakening in the morning is like the future world. . . . To a man who awakes out of his sleep in like manner will the dead awake in the future world.[23]

---

[20]Those in the "intermediate state" school in this century are H. A. A. Kennedy, *St. Paul's Conceptions of the Last Things* (London: Hodder & Stoughton, 1904), 266-81; A. Schweitzer, *The Mysticism of Paul the Apostle* (New York: H. Holt & Co., 1931), 131; Kurt Deissner, *Auferstehungshoffnung und Pneumagedanken bei Paulus* (Naumberg: Lippert & Co., 1912), 54; Philippe H. Menoud, *Le sort des trépassés* (Neuchatel: Delachaux & Niestle, 1945), 39; J. N. Sevenster, "Einige Bemerkungen über den 'Zwischenzustand' bei Paulus," *New Testament Studies* 1 (1955): 291-96; J. A. T. Robinson, *The Body: A Study in Pauline Theology* (Chicago: Henry Regnery Company, 1952), 29, 78; M. E. Dahl, *The Resurrection of the Body*, Studies in Biblical Theology 36 (London: SCM Press, 1962), 43, n. 3; Jacques Dupont, *ΣΥΝ ΧΡΙΣΤΩ: L'union avec le Christ suivant St. Paul* (Bruges: Editions de l'Abbaye de Saint-André, 1952); H. Ridderbos, *Paul: An Outline of His Theology*, trans. John Richard de Witt (Grand Rapids: Eerdmans, 1975), 556-62; E. Earle Ellis, "Sōma in First Corinthians," 140-44; and Ralph P. Martin, *2 Corinthians*, 102-16.

[21]"Is 'Sleep' the Proper Biblical Term for the Intermediate State?," 161-7. Bailey concludes that the term is unsatisfactory because of its interpretative liabilities, even though he agrees with Otto Michel, ("Zur Lehre vom Todesschlaf," *Zeitschrift für die neutestamentliche Wissenschaft* 35 [1936]: 285-90), on his contention that the term "sleep" does not refer to the condition of the dead, any speculation pertaining to immortality, or an anthropological subset. To both it is concerned with the eschatological mystery of the sleep of death. See, however, J. G. S. S. Thomson, "Sleep: An Aspect of Jewish Anthropology," *Vetus Testamentum* 5 (1955): 421-33. Thomson posits that there are anthropological presuppositions that underlay the Jewish view of both physical sleep and the sleep of death. See also, Karel Hanhart, *The Intermediate State in the New Testament* (Franeker: T. Wever, 1966).

[22]For a good treatment of metaphor as rhetorical device, see Robert H. Stein, *The Method and Message of Jesus' Teachings* (Philadelphia: The Westminster Press, 1978), 15-17.

[23]Quoted in Thomson, "Sleep: An Aspect of Jewish Anthropology," 430.

The phrase, "death is like sleep," therefore, gives way to the phrase "death is sleep," if considered metaphorically.

This enigma finds its most sensitive setting in the life of the Christian community. As the concern of the Thessalonians in Paul's day, so contemporary believers are anxious about their loved ones who have encountered death. While laboring to console bereaving Christians, is it possible that many ministers, with honest yet blind compassion, have erroneously postured Socratic conclusions relating to death?

According to some preachers, the body is significantly demoted in stature at death. It is no longer "God's temple." It becomes an "inexorable prison" from which the soul, or spirit, has gained emancipation. Two questions about death become important. Is it possible to have a Christian dualism categorically different from the Platonic prototype? Does belief in the intermediate state require a monistic stance?

This investigation directly involves the subject matter emanating from the conversation that developed between Jesus and the disciples in Jn. 11.1-44, the episode of the raising of Lazarus; and the triple tradition account of the resuscitation of Jairus' daughter in Mk. 5.21-24a, 35-43, and parallels. In the Lazarus pericope Jesus announced in verse 11: "Our friend Lazarus has fallen asleep (κεκοίμηται), but I go to awake him out of sleep (ἐξυπνίσω)." The disciples replied in verse 12: "Lord, if he has fallen asleep (κεκοίμηται), he shall recover." John added an editorial note in verse 13: "Now Jesus had spoken of his death, but they thought he meant taking rest in slumber." This explanation is in anticipation of verse 14 where Jesus informed them plainly: "Lazarus is dead (ἀπέθανον)." Jesus, therefore, obviously generated a great deal of confusion for the disciples by referring to death as a sleep. Jesus was by no means attempting to depreciate the event or to offer a trite attenuation of the harsh reality of death. Jesus spoke metaphorically, not euphemistically, about death. This writer appraises Jesus' design in the Lazarus episode in the same manner as Sandra M. Schneiders: "This almost brutal announcement serves to correct any tendency to see death as illusory or unreal. Human death is brutally real. Referring to it as a sleep is not recourse to a euphemism to soften or disguise its reality."[24]

A similar thrust in the Synoptic account of the raising of Jairus' daughter depicts a grief-stricken wailing group of mourners causing a great tumult at the death scene. Each account casts Jesus as the object of the crowd's ridicule, hinging upon his mind-boggling pronouncement: "The child is not dead (ἀπέθανον), but sleeping (καθεύδει)." Here, Jesus was addressing the grievers' hollow anguish over the girl's apparent demise. The strongest clue betraying the crowd's unfamiliarity and confusion with regard to Jesus' words is found in the Lukan account. Not only does Luke report the crowd's resultant amusement, but he also supplied the reason: "And they laughed at him, *knowing that she was dead* (8.53, emphasis mine)." Jesus' use of the sleep imagery definitely invoked a major point of contention with the contemporary *vox populi*.

Although Lazarus and Jairus' daughter were dead Jesus characterized each of them as being asleep. Similarly, the witnesses in both cases reacted with incredulity and sarcasm and Jesus awakened both victims. The primary question here is directly correlated to the resultant confusion precipitated by Jesus' analysis of both predicaments. If this question is answered, it may shed light on another: Can we speak of believers "sleeping" in the intermediate state until the resurrection/parousia?

Presuppositions' Endorsement

The authority and primacy of the biblical witness over all other data and biblical evidence as the ultimate truth are foundational in this study. Although the semantic field of the "sleep of death" metaphor including κοιμάομαι and its synonyms is not peculiar to the New Testament, its meaning is unique within the

---

[24]Sandra M. Schneiders, "Death in the Community of Eternal Life: History, Theology, and Spirituality in John 11," *Interpretation* 41 (1987): 49.

biblical context as part of salvation history.[25] This recognition is essential because a number of theologians, ministers, and laity herald beliefs about death more akin to the hallmarks of Greek philosophical speculation than to the teaching of Scripture.[26]

A second presupposition is that all prior eschatological conclusions, directly or indirectly linked to the subject area, are subject to scrutiny. This study will systematically address these conclusions from a different perspective. The ontological status of each concept will be examined as to what constitutes its mode of existence. This distinction of thanatology is crucial because many thinkers deny it as a real category. The conclusions of a biblical thanatology will necessarily require that some conclusions of those, who deal with the complementary themes of parousia, resurrection, and judgment including Southern Baptists, undergo differing levels of reevaluation. Since the thesis deals with the pre-parousia state of a deceased Christian, its emphases will be seen as somewhat "pre-eschatological" in that the dead in Christ are still a critical part of the history of salvation.

---

[25]That the κοιμάομαι domain does occur with regularity in extrabiblical sources is reason to investigate the evolution of the field of words from its pristine usage until it was embraced and employed by biblical authors. See Appendix A for the semantic range of the sleep-of-death metaphor in the New Testament.

[26]According to Ellis, "Sōma in First Corinthians," 143, n. 63, a probable point of inception of the synthesis of Christianity and Greek philosophy is found in Clement of Alexandria and Origen. Clement envisioned Christ to be the full meaning of the Greek periphrasis (τῆς περιφράσεως τῆς Ἑλληνικῆς), Stromata 1.19.92.2). This expression apparently means that the whole of Greek culture was a circuitous route to experience God. Waldo Beach and Richard Niebuhr, eds. in Christian Ethics: Sources of the Living Tradition, 2d ed. (New York: The Ronald Press Company, 1973), 72, say: "Clement was the first Christian thinker who deliberately attempted to bring together the Christian religion and Hellenic philosophy. . . . He was not the last nor the most successful in his effort." Also see E. Molland, "Clement of Alexandria on the Origin of Greek Philosophy," Symbolae Osloenses 15/16 (1936): 57-85.

Hermeneutical Procedure
Treatment Basis

This treatment emerges from the analytical words of Jesus in the Lazarus and Jairus' daughter passages. Although Paul's letters antedate the Gospels in written form, his ideas are partially dependent upon the Jesus tradition. Jesus, therefore, supplied the *crux interpretum* of the sleep metaphor, setting the stage for subsequent Christian reflection in the New Testament and beyond. Jesus' position is the crucial fulcrum point which rectified the past and established the future exegetical guidelines. The initial task is the analysis of the prevailing beliefs of the past, from the time of Greek antiquity and Hellenism, through the LXX and Hebrew literature, leading up to and including the *Sitz im Leben* of Jesus. The teaching of Jesus will be examined in the early church and in the writings of the church fathers.

After consulting the history of incorporation of the sleep metaphor, each New Testament passage which contains the term κοιμάομαι will be inspected. Examination of synonymous phraseology and an exegesis will clarify the New Testament concept of sleep, using the best hermeneutical techniques available. Both primary and secondary, English and foreign sources will be employed. This methodology will serve to unveil the truth of the biblical witness even if contrary to popular dogma. In the spirit of A. C. Thiselton's thesis about hermeneutical procedures, this researcher desires to "fuse the horizons" of the biblical world and the modern world with respect to the contemporary application and implications of the eschatological sleep concept in the New Testament.[27]

The Hypothesis

The hypothesis is: The New Testament deployment, especially the use by Jesus in Jn. 11.11-14, of the term κοιμάομαι (or καθεύδω) when referring to death

---

[27]Anthony C. Thiselton, *The Two Horizons: New Testament Hermeneutics and Philosophical Description* (Grand Rapids: Eerdmans, 1980).

marks a significant watershed in the history of the interpretation of the concept in that the dead in Christ are asleep until the parousia/resurrection. Anthropologically, unlike the Greek dualistic assessment of man, the Judeo-Christian biblical tradition teaches that man is a psychosomatic unity.[28] When an individual dies, it is a total death. The Hebraic accent on unity and wholeness extends also into the New Testament; however, historically, Christians have had trouble adhering to this perspective. Paul E. Irion has rightly observed the following:

> Detours into dualistic understandings which substitute the concept of immortality of the soul for that of resurrection of the body have been persistent. This position envisions the spiritual essence of man as separable from the nonessential body. The spirit involves all that is good; while the body, as a part of the material world, is inferior, perishable, a necessary evil. So pronounced is the cleavage between the spiritual and the material that the very notion of resurrection of the body seems monstrous and anomalous.[29]

New Testament spokesmen, without using any pagan euphemism, metaphorically describe death as a sleep from which there is an eschatological arousal. The advent of this concept is coextensive and collinear with the mission and message of Jesus—the ultimate defeat of the last enemy, death. In this regard, death means life for the Christian. Jesus advanced his teaching not only by applying the sleep metaphor to a decedent, but also by stirring that individual back to life. These resuscitations were both a symbolic portrayal of Jesus' own impending death and resurrection and an earnest foreshadowing of our own.

---

[28]H. Wheeler Robinson's anthropological assessment is instructive at this point: "The Hebrew idea of the personality is an animated body, and not an incarnated soul" ("Hebrew Psychology," in A. S. Peake, ed., *The People and the Book* [Oxford: The Clarendon Press, 1925], 362). J. A. T. Robinson rightly concludes also that "man does not have a body, he is a body" (*The Body* [London: SCM Press, 1952], 14).

[29]Paul E. Irion, *The Funeral: Vestige or Value?* (Nashville: Abingdon Press, 1966), 154. In addition, see, M. E. Dahl, *The Resurrection of the Body*, 7-10; D. R. G. Owen, *Body and Soul* (Philadelphia: The Westminster Press, 1956), 53; John A. T. Robinson, *The Body*, 17-26; and Rudolf Bultmann, "New Testament and Mythology," in *Kerygma and Myth*, ed. Hans W. Bartsch, trans. Reginald Fuller, vol. 1 (London: S.P.C.K., 1953), 1-44.

Content Outline

This work employs two main sections: historical backdrop and interpretative analysis. The chapters in the first section will be devoted to an inquiry into the earliest contexts in which κοιμάομαι surfaced. The application of this strategy will help trace the static and dynamic features of κοιμάομαι through and within Hellenistic and Jewish sources up to the time in the New Testament. It is important to note that this philological study will take into consideration both the diachronic and synchronic aspects of word studies set forth by the Swiss scholar, Ferdinand de Saussure, and championed by Moisés Silva and James Barr. Procedure will emphasize Silva's methodology of lexical semantics.

This procedure will allow the concept of κοιμάομαι to be evaluated in its cultural context with a comparative analysis. A general examination of the religious beliefs in Greek antiquity will also be germane to a comprehensive articulation of the proposed thesis. It is of paramount concern that this foundation be established for deciphering the origin of New Testament reflection. Initially, to aid the accomplishment of this quest, an exhaustive study of literary sources will be done with the assistance of the Ibycus search of the *Thesaurus Linguae Graecae* (referred to hereafter as *TLG*) database for all the various, inflected forms of κοιμάομαι and other synonyms.[30]

Various types of Christian as well as pagan memorials, such as sepulchral art, epitaphs, and inscriptions, will offer additional aid.[31] Diachronic evaluation will also move the search into the annals of the LXX and Diaspora Greek produced

---

[30]*Thesaurus Linguae Graecae* CDROM database, version C (Irvine, CA: University of California at Irvine, 1987).

[31]Examples of these sources include: G. H. R. Horsley, ed., *New Documents Illustrating Early Christianity: A Review of the Greek Inscriptions and Papyri Published*, 5 vols. (Macquarie University: The Ancient History Documentary Research Centre), 1981-1989); Elsa Gibson, *The "Christians for Christians" Inscriptions of Phrygia* (Missoula, MT: Scholar's Press, 1978); and P. Jean-Baptiste, *Corpus Inscriptionum Judaicarum: Jewish Inscriptions from the Third Century B.C. to the Seventh Century A.D.*, vol. 1 (New York: Ktav Publishing House Inc., 1975).

15

during the Hellenistic period.[32] The works of Josephus and Philo will also be researched for any occurrences of κοιμάομαι.[33] For each particular epoch the Saussurean synchronic methodology will be applied.

The third chapter will require a somewhat chronological regression in order to consider the Hebrew literature. Beginning with the Old Testament, a study of Hebrew terms used for the sleep-of-death equation will be done.[34] The same method will be followed for the writings of Second Temple Judaism which include the Palestinian materials and Rabbinic texts.[35] Through the intertestamental period

---

[32]The search for κοιμάομαι in the LXX and the writings of Diaspora Greek will be aided by A. Rahlfs, ed. *Septuaginta*, 2d ed. (Stuttgart: German Bible Society, 1979); E. Hatch and H. A. Redpath, *A Concordance to the Septuagint and the Other Greek Versions of the Old Testament*, reprint ed. (Graz-Austria: Akademische Druck- und Verlagsanstalt, 1954); Abbey of Maredsous, Centre Informatique et Bible, ed. *A Concordance to the Apocrypha/Deuterocanonical Books of the Revised Standard Version* (Grand Rapids: Eerdmans, 1983); Lester T. Whitelocke, ed., *An Analytic Concordance of the Books of the Apocrypha*, 2 vols. (Washington, DC: University Press of America, 1978); and J. B. Bauer, ed., *Clavis Librorum Veteris Testamenti Apocryphorum*, repr. ed. (Graz: Akademische Druck- und Verlagsanstalt, 1972).

[33]For a concordance to the works of Philo see G. Mayer, *Index Philoneus* (Berlin: de Gruyter, 1974); for Josephus see K. H. Rengstorf, ed., *A Complete Concordance to Flavius Josephus*, 2 vols. (Leiden: E. J. Brill, 1973, 1975).

[34]An investigation of E. Hatch and H. A. Redpath, *A Concordance to the Septuagint*, s.v. "κοιμᾶν" reveals that κοιμάομαι translates ten Hebrew and two Aramaic words. See Appendix B for a list. By far, שָׁכַב lies beneath κοιμάομαι with greater frequency than any other Semitic term, the first Old Testament occurrence being in the story of the death of Jacob in Gen. 47.30 (κοιμηθήσομαι = וְשָׁכַבְתִּי). It also serves as somewhat of a technical term for the royal "lying down (sleeps) with his fathers" paradigm of death in 1 and 2 Kings, and as a somber description in Ezekiel 32 of the uncircumcised "lying" (dead) in Sheol. As κοιμάομαι shares a synonymous semantic field in the New Testament, so does שָׁכַב in the Old Testament. These Semitic relationships will be addressed in more detail in Chapter III. The New Testament "κοιμάομαι group" will be examined closer in Chapter IV. The common denominator that all biblical occurrences of the "sleep-of-death" metaphor share in meaning is "lying down" and/or "the cessation of activity." The two Hebrew Old Testament concordances which will be utilized are S. Mandelkern, *Veteris Testamenti Concordantiae*, repr. ed. (Tel Aviv: Schocken, 1969), and Gerhard Lisowsky, *Konkordanz zum Hebräischen Alten Testament*, 12th ed. (Stuttgart: Württembergische Bibelanstalt, 1958).

[35]Especially helpful are Marcus Jastrow, ed., *A Dictionary of the Targum, the Talmud Babli and Yerushalmi, and the Midrashic Literature*, 2 vols. (New York: Pardes Publishing House, Inc., 1950), and K. G. Kuhn, *Konkordanz zu den Qumrantexten* (Göttingen: Vandenhoeck & Ruprecht, 1960). To search for the subject of the sleep-of-death motif, C. G. Montefiore and H. Loewe, *A Rabbinic Anthology* (London: Macmillan, 1938), will also be utilized.

the Hellenistic ideas wrought by Alexander the Great merge with Jewish influence during the last third of the first century before Christ. This study will seriously weigh several associative strands of influence which provided the initial data for, and exerted a weighty influence on, the accepted common perspectives about death in New Testament times. For instance, one goal of the research is to calculate what elements were responsible for fashioning the mind-set of Jesus' hearers and of the recipients of first-century apostolic correspondence.

Part Two will turn to an interpretative analysis of the New Testament texts and their effect on the early church. Every important New Testament passage which contains the term κοιμάομαι, used as a metaphor for death, will be examined in the fourth chapter with the aid of the critical disciplines.[36] Intrinsically, the concept of the sleep of death appears to be accepted without debate outside the Gospel narratives. Jesus, however, ostensibly generated a great deal of ridicule and bewilderment when he chose to qualify death as a sleep.

Is there any difference between the use of the terms ἀπέθανον and κοιμάομαι in death contexts? As a corollary to that question, if it is determined that κοιμάομαι functioned as a specialized Christian designation for death, why do all non-Pauline (with the sole exception of 2 Pet. 3.4) and non-Gospel authors fail to employ it although appropriate to do so in their compositions? Thirdly, do the small number of texts, such as the parable of the Rich Man and Lazarus (not of John 11) in Lk. 16.19-31 and the details of life after death in 2 Cor. 5.1-10, corroborate or contradict the findings of the research?[37] Regardless, Jesus ushered

---

[36]One of the exegetical models which will be consulted is the one created by the Ph.D. seminar, New Testament Critical Methodology 651-771/772, 1987/88. This work, *Exegeting the New Testament: A Seminar Working Model* (Fort Worth: Scripta Publishing Inc., 1989), was published by Lorin L. Cranford. This work was an attempt to develop a work similar to Gordon Fee, *New Testament Exegesis: A Handbook for Students and Pastors* (Philadelphia: The Westminster Press, 1983). Both works contain useful bibliography pertaining to the exegetical task. The prior work is subject to revision, because it is in a state of flux, dependent on the work of future seminars.

[37]See Murray Harris, "The New Testament View of Life after Death," *Themelios* 11 (1986): 47-8. One must guard against trying to force the text to say something that is not meant. Craig Blomberg, *Interpreting the Parables* (Downers Grove, IL: InterVarsity Press, 1990), 203-8, points

in a novel concept of death that was only described euphemistically previously; Jesus' teaching on death served as a turning point in the attitudes and beliefs that accompanied the event of death itself.

Lastly, the fifth chapter will represent an analysis of the early church's reflection of the New Testament usage of κοιμάομαι. This procedure will include a combing of Lampe's standard patristic lexicon, in full awareness of its lack of scientific description, and patristic concordances in order to find occurrences of κοιμάομαι and/or legitimate synonyms in the writings of the church fathers.[38] The apostolic witness of the early church and the apocryphal gospels will also be appraised by a selected synchronic study.[39] This process will help answer the question, Was Jesus' idea about death embraced by the first Christians? The writings of first-century Palestinian and Rabbinic Judaism will also be inspected in search of an answer.

The Conclusion will state the proper meaning of "Κοιμάομαι in the New Testament" as resolved by the historical and interpretative research. The conclusions of the research will describe the unique position of the New Testament on the theme of death and its subsidiary function as a catalyst for early Christian thought and practice. Since this study casts the Bible in an authoritative

---

out that while Harris maintains that "the parable of the rich man and Lazarus was told to illustrate the danger of wealth and the necessity of repentance, not to satisfy our natural curiosity about man's anthropological condition after death," he disregards his own caution by adding, "it is not illegitimate to deduce from the setting of the story the basic characteristics of the postmortem state of believers and unbelievers."

[38]See G. W. H. Lampe, ed., *A Patristic Greek Lexicon* (Oxford: Clarendon Press, 1961-1968); E. J. Goodspeed, ed., *Index Patristicus*, rev. ed. (Naperville, IL: Allenson, 1960); H. Kraft, ed., *Clavis Patrum Apostolicorum* (Darmstadt: Wissenschaftliche Buchgesellschaft, 1963); E. J. Goodspeed, ed., *Index Apologeticus* (Leipzig: Hinrichs, 1912); and the invaluable *Biblia Patristica: Index des Citations et Allusions Bibliques dans la Littérature Patristique* (Paris: Centre National de la Recherche Scientifique, 1975, 1977).

[39]One of the best available works in this area is E. Hennecke and W. Schneemelcher, eds., *New Testament Apocrypha*, 2 vols., trans. R. McL. Wilson (London: Lutterworth Press, 1963). For important cross reference parallels between the canonical Gospels, and New Testament apocryphal gospels and patristic sources for occurrences of κοιμάομαι see K. Aland, ed., *Synopsis Quattuor Evangeliorum*, 13th rev. ed. (Stuttgart: Württembergische Bibelanstalt, 1990).

light as a viable canon for the exercise of contemporary faith, the research must evoke what "Κοιμάομαι in the New Testament" means for today. Ideally, a consequential addressing of the thorny problem of the state and immediate posthumous destination of the Christian will result.

Admittedly, the outline's scope is broad. The methodology of the research, however, is necessary in order for the proper meaning of "Κοιμάομαι in the New Testament" to be analyzed. The notion of the "sleep of death" must be studied in each relevant cultural arena so that the profundity of the New Testament posture can be clearly deduced.

Complementary Themes' Relationship

Without treating any theme beyond the grave, this work will address and challenge some of the accepted eschatological conclusions. It may serve as a preliminary checkpoint for properly approaching the themes connected with the eschatological doctrines of parousia, resurrection, and judgment. The main interest is thanatology—what does the New Testament mean by referring to death as sleep?

The problem has consistently been fertile soil for the critical tilling of scholars, primarily because of its rootage with the perennial themes of parousia, resurrection, and judgment. The proposed research will address a vital point of contention in Christian scholarship. Historically, the complementary themes of the parousia, resurrection, and judgment have produced a mountain of controversy. Logically one must grapple with the sizable problem that the circumstances associated with death presents before the others can be fully considered. The direction of many facets of the latter trilogy of doctrines hinges directly upon a viable, biblical anthropology and thanatology.

The solution to this problem finds its practical application in the discipline of pastoral care in the local church. Just as in New Testament times, Christians are concerned about loved ones who have preceded them in death. Perhaps the most circumspect service a minister can render is to reevaluate the empty religious language about death.

Therefore, equipped with Judeo-Christian, biblical truth, the minister can speak confidently and honestly about the plight of the deceased Christian. The preponderance of the biblical evidence demands that the minister offer the bereaved hope, comfort, and truth which stem squarely from such documents entitled, Κατὰ Λουκᾶν, Κατὰ Ἰωάννην, and Πρὸς Κορινθίους α'; not from the Φαέδω.

CHAPTER I

NON-CHRISTIAN GREEK AND LATIN LITERATURE

Although the representation is sketchy, both Greek and Roman literature provide illustrative samplings of the sleep-of-death formula. The writings under consideration in this section extend from as early as Homer in the eighth century B.C. to the Alexandrian period of the fourth century B.C.

The eighth century B.C., of course, is not the earliest time people grappled with the idea of death. Themes pertaining to the afterlife abounded in Egypt.[1] According to Harris our knowledge about Egyptian eschatology emerges from three basic sources: 1) the *Pyramid Texts* (2800-2500 B.C.); 2) the *Coffin Texts* (2134-1786 B.C.); and 3) *The Book of the Dead* (5th Dynasty, 2600 B.C.)[2]

---

[1]For a brief discussion pertaining to this subject, see Murray J. Harris, *From Grave to Glory*, 31-36. Detailed treatments pertaining to Egyptian eschatology include C. Andrews, *Egyptian Mummies* (Cambridge: Harvard University Press, 1984); E. A. T. W. Budge, *Osiris and the Egyptian Resurrection*, 2 vols. (London: Warner, 1911); S. G. F. Brandon, *The Judgement of the Dead* (London: Weidenfeld and Nicolson, 1967), 6-48; and A. H. Gardiner, *The Attitude of the Ancient Egyptians to Death and the Dead* (Cambridge: Cambridge University Press, 1935).

[2]Harris, *From Grave to Glory*, 31. Although Egyptian eschatological beliefs did not remain harmonious, they did espouse some brand of immortality of the soul reflected clearly in their anthropology.

Similarly, the Greeks also varied in their doctrine of the immortality of the soul.³ Over a period of time four stages contributed to the total development of this slippery doctrine: 1) the Homeric poems (the *Iliad* and the *Odyssey*), 2) the Orphic religion,⁴ 3) Plato (particularly in the *Phaedrus, Republic, Timaeus,* and *Phaedo*), and 4) Aristotle (primarily in *De Anima*⁵). Although the idea matured under the respectable influence of Plato, it became more complex and remained unaccommodating to the biblical view of the resurrection of the dead. Armed and steeped in the Greek philosophies of the past, for example, the Stoics and the philosophers of the Areopagus, whom the Apostle confronted (Acts 17.16-34), responded in three ways to this foreign idea of the resurrection. Harris identifies these negative reactions as "straightforward rationalization, outright mockery, or cautious curiosity."⁶

Synonyms in the Semantic Field

Semantically, κοιμάομαι does not command universal control over the image of the sleep of death in the ancient documents. Joining it are two words which recur with varying frequency in the Hellenistic, New Testament, and post-biblical literature. Καθεύδω (εὕδω, simple form) and ὑπνόω complete the trilogy of terms.

---

³For a brief treatment, see ibid., 36-43. Full blown works include E. Rohde, *Psyche. The Cult of the Souls and Belief in Immortality among the Greeks*, 8th ed. (London: Kegan, 1925); A. S. Pringle-Pattison, *The Idea of Immortality* (Oxford: Clarendon Press, 1922), 19-71; and C. H. Moore, *Ancient Beliefs in the Immortality of the Soul* (London: Harrap, 1931), 3-36.

⁴See Jane Ellen Harrison, "Orphic Eschatology," chap. in *Prolegomena to the Study of Greek Religion* (New York: Arno Press, 1975), 572-623. Also, on the issue of the immortality of the soul in the Orphic system, see J. M. Gonzáles-Ruiz, "Should We De-Mythologize the 'Separated Soul'?" in Edward Schillebeeckx and Boniface Wilkens, eds., *The Problem of Eschatology* (New York: Paulist Press, 1969), 82-96.

⁵Although Aristotle differed from Plato in considering the soul as a form of the body, one would be hard pressed to squeeze him into a materialistic mold. True to dualistic form, Aristotle believed, however, that the principle of thought known as the νοῦς was immortal and distinguishable from the body.

⁶Harris, *From Grave to Glory*, 41-3. For thorough treatments of Plato's views see R. L. Patterson, *Plato on Immortality* (University Park, PA: Pennsylvania State University, 1965) and R. S. Buck, *Plato's Phaedo* (New York: Bobbs-Merrill, 1955).

The largest representation of the group occurs in the Homeric and Hellenistic periods. The results of the κοιμάομαι word search provided by the *TLG* CDROM database are noteworthy. Comparatively, the LXX and New Testament reveal less frequent yet more pointed use of the word group in a general sense, κοιμάομαι being the most refined and technical with reference to the sleep of death.[7]

Counting words, however, is only a quantitative evaluation which provides a window through which linguists can begin conceptual studies represented by a particular word. The synonymous company of κοιμάομαι is of great interest because of the illuminating effects of its corroborative discourse, sentences, and paragraphs.

Diachronically, there is value in discovering the diverse or common manner, for example, in which Sophocles, Achilles Tatius, Nahum, Rabbi Johanan b. Zakkai, Matthew, Jesus, Origen, Tertullian, and John Chrysostom employed κοιμάομαι in each of their particular sleep-of-death treatments. The error of explaining one individual's usage of a word based on a previous author's usage of the same word will be avoided, if one stresses concept acquisition over short-sighted word meanings. Examining a particular concept invites the broader range of the synonymous association of other lexemes which convey the same theme.[8] The resultant interpretation, therefore, is based more on synchronic, contextual evidence rather than historical precedent. Transcending the brittleness of ordered

---

[7]See Appendixes A, B, C, and D for tabulations. Of the 209 occurences of κοιμάομαι in the LXX, seventy-four refer to the sleep of death. Appendix E shows that, of the seventy-four death sleep metaphors, שָׁכַב = κοιμάομαι sixty-four times.

[8]See Peter Cotterell and Max Turner, *Linguistics and Biblical Interpretation* (Downer's Grove, IL: InterVarsity Press, 1989), 21. It is important also to keep in mind the varying relationships between synonymous words. In the work cited a distinction is drawn between absolute, near and partial synonymy (156-61, see figure 4 on page 158 and figure 5 on page 163). Absolute synonymy by definition requires the dismissal of the secondary term because of its lack of uniqueness. As will be seen throughout this study, the triune Greek word group will exhibit mostly distinctive qualities of near and partial synonymy with some debatable absolute synonymy. Their major point of translational contact is shared between the overlapping visual and biological concepts of sleep and death. This investigation will attract other contexts which employ none of the word group, thus accentuating the versatility of the concept.

historical word study ushers one into the beneficial world of conceptual control. The same concept can be expressed by different individual lexemes or syntactical lexemic association, that is, a concept expressed by a combination of words rather than one.

Individually and in various combinations with each other, the concept of the sleep of death in the Homeric period was expressed by each of the three words under consideration. Intrinsically, κοιμάομαι is more diverse than its synonyms in nondeath contexts. Note the diversities below:

Table 1.--The Semantic Diversity of Κοιμάομαι in the Homeric Period

Author	Source	Translation
Hyperides	*Epitaphius* 41.2-3	still
Callimachus	*Fragments* 195.25-26	quench
Aristophanes	*Ecclesiazusae* 722	have sex
Euripides	*Rhesus* 137-38	appease
Euripides	*Andromache* 389-90	found refuge
Euripides	*Rhesus* 825-26	sleep
Pindarus	*Isthmia* 8.21	bed of love
Theophrastus	*Historia plantarum* 7.5.4.6-7	bug caught in the dung
Homer	*Odyssey* 4.574-75	lie down

The *TLG* search provided close to two hundred pages of the appearance of κοιμάομαι and its many perfective (prepositionally augmented) word forms. Even though alternate translations abound, they share an underlying association in basic meaning. The common denominator shared by the nondeath, death, and sleep-of-death images supported by the term κοιμάομαι and its cognates is the idea associated with "quelling a desire, cessation of activity, or lying down." Considering this wide range of translations, it is easy to see how κοιμάομαι could support the concepts of physical sleep as well as the sleep of death within its semantic domain.

Καθεύδω is more restricted to the idea of physical sleep.⁹ It is equivocally employed with reference to the entire scope of human life and death. Plato suggests the possibility that life is merely a sleep; attendant activities are dreams.¹⁰ Καθεύδω, albeit even more sparingly than κοιμάομαι, also was adopted for euphemistic service in death contexts. Just as in the case with κοιμάομαι, the resemblance of the body during sleep to the state of the body during death created a natural synonymous association between the two functions on a conceptual level to the Greek.

Divergently, Jesus makes several distinctions when he confronts and discusses the death event. Otto Michel correctly points out that Jesus draws a sharp contrast between sleep (καθεύδειν, κοιμᾶσθαι) and death (ἀποθνῄσκειν) in the first place.¹¹ Secondly, Michel believes Jesus contrasts the symbolic Old Testament understanding of the death sleep and the paraphrastic (*Umschreibung*) Greek view of death.¹² In the company of Jesus, though, the customarily assumed euphemistic manner of speaking is by no means universal. Keeping pace with a healthy Semitic anthropology, Jesus believes the death sleep to be a better form of life, while actual death (*Tod*) is that one death (*Sterben*) which is without promise.¹³

A clear example of how the death ideas of ancient Greece can grip the thinking of modern New Testament scholars is seen in Albrecht Oepke's treatment

---

⁹See Albrecht Oepke, "Καθεύδω," *TDNT*, 3:431-33. Oepke draws attention to the etymological uncertainty of καθεύδω expressed by E. Boisacq, *Dictionnaire étymologique de la langue Grecque*, 2d ed. (Heidelberg: C. Winter, 1923).

¹⁰Plato *Theatetus* 158b; quoted in Oepke, "Καθεύδω," 3:431. In addition, Socrates, in the *Apologia* 40d/e, postulates that death is only a deep sleep devoid of dreams.

¹¹Otto Michel, "Zur Lehre vom Todesschlaf," 285.

¹²Ibid. Michel used the word *Umschreibung* to describe the Greek circumlocutionary manner of speaking of death. They simply had no foundation for dealing with it.

¹³Ibid., 286.

of καθεύδω in the story of the raising of Jairus' daughter in Mark 5.35-43 and parallels.[14] Supposing that Jesus' pronouncement in verse 39, "the child is not dead but sleeping (καθεύδει)," means "proximate death," Oepke erroneously injects the mind-set of Athens and rabbinic understanding into the episode. He interprets Jesus' cryptic utterance by means of a Greek category.

> In terms of antique ideas, the most likely meaning is that the soul of the girl had left the body but was still in the vicinity and in the strength of God could be recalled by Jesus' word of power. The saying certainly does not teach that death in general is simply sleep.[15]

Although Oepke's euphemistic interpretation does not reflect the futility the Greek faced with the event of death, such an interpretation does advance dualistic tendencies.

The third term which completes the representation of the sleep-of-death category is ὑπνόω with its alternate noun and verb forms. Like καθεύδω, it refers predominantly to physical sleep. According to Horst Balz ὑπνόω heralds from the Indo-European *supnos* and its derived forms *suepnos* and *suopnos*.[16] Latin counterparts include *sopor* (deep sleep) and *somnus* (sleep).[17] Subsequently, *somnium* (dream) can be translated synonymously as "sleep." Prior to the LXX, ὕπνος is not translated "dream," even though in the fifth century of the Christian era the Greek lexicographer Hesychius of Alexandria used the word in his definition of ὄναρ.[18] On the other hand, when the LXX is considered, ὕπνος

---

[14]Oepke, "Καθεύδω," 3:436.

[15]Ibid. Michel, "Todesschlaf," 288, says this interpretation must be rejected on two counts: 1) there is not the slightest hint of a "hovering for three days spirit" in the story, and 2) the unclear relationship between "sleep" and "death" does not demand an interpretation that the dead "sleeps" first and later might be totally dead. More will be determined concerning this crucial story below.

[16]Horst Balz, "Ὕπνος," *TDNT*, 8:545.

[17]See Alois Walde and J. B. Hofmann, eds., *Lateinisches etymologisches Wörterbuch*, rev. 3d ed. (Heidelberg: C. Winter, 1914), s.v. "Somnus, sopio, sopor." Also see A. F. Pauly and G. Wissowa, eds., *Paulys Real-Encyclopädie der classischen Altertumswissenschaft* (Stuttgart: J. B. Metzler, 1916), s.v. "Hypnos," by A. Jolles.

[18]Ibid. Καθ' ὕπνον φαντασία.

frequently is translated "dream," especially in Genesis (20.3, 6; 31.10, 11, 24; 40.9; 41.17, 22), corresponding to חֲלוֹם each time.

Scarcity is the rule when attempts are made to find ὑπνόω underlying the sleep-of-death figure in the Homeric period.[19] The Hellenistic period, however, exhibits a dramatic increase in the frequency of the term for death but was not adopted consequently by Septuagintal, New Testament, early church, apocryphal, or patristic writers as a favorite metaphorical expression for death. Commencing with the LXX, κοιμάομαι by far captured the most attention with respect to its assignment to death passages. That the New Testament categorically omits ὑπνόω from any sleep-of-death context probably suggests an intentional demarcation from the prevalent belief in the Greek god Hypnos.[20]

Interestingly, all three of these words occur in contexts by themselves and in various combinations with each other in both death and nondeath contexts. In the Homeric period, though, no term demands prime focus of attention with respect to the concept of the sleep of death. This concerted struggle was implemented to deal with their crippling response to the reality of death. Popular religion could offer only lamentation; philosophers tried in vain to placate the fearful and

---

[19]Balz, "Ὕπνος," 8:548. To the examples provided below can be added Hesiod's description of man's gratifying manner of death in *Opera et dies* 116.

[20]Even though there are some *hapax legomena* in the New Testament peculiar to itself and most other terminology was commonly used by pagans before, during, and after its era, authors were extremely careful of any interpretative stigmas which could and should have been avoided. It should be remembered that concepts rather than words are sacrosanct. The iconography associated with Hypnos, or any other Greek god for that matter, was reason enough for its omission to prevent any thoughts of assimilation which might be invoked by its mention. On the Greek god Hypnos, see H. Schrader, *Hypnos, Winkelmann-Programm d. Archäologie Gesellschaft zu Berlin* (Berlin: Walter de Gruyter & Co., 1926), 85; H. J. Rose, *A Handbook of Greek Mythology*, 5th ed. (London: SPCK, 1953); and H. W. Haussig, ed., *Wörterbuch der Mythologie*, (Stuttgart: J. B. Metzler, 1965). Although the New Testament uses the word solely for physical sleep, the closest it comes to a death equation is the Lukan story of the somnolent Eutychus in Acts 20.9 and the Johannine Lazarus episode in John 11. In the Acts account, a deep sleep (ὕπνῳ βαθεῖ) overcomes Eutychus, causing him to fall to his death. In John 11, while Jesus refers to Lazarus' death as κεκοίμηται (verse 11), John reports that the disciples errantly thought Jesus meant the "sleep of slumber" (κοιμήσεως τοῦ ὕπνου, verse 13). It should be noted that the idea of both "death sleep" and "physical sleep" are found in John 11.

hopeless by suggesting the metaphysical proximity of death to sleep. What was sorely missing from their model was a God who was alive. Ironically, the statue erected "To the Unknown God" in Athens, referred to in Acts 17.16-34, was the one who would have solved their problem.

The Sleep of Slumber or Natural Process

Natural sleep is an appropriate picture of death. Insomniacs and narcoleptics aside, sleep was described as that phenomenon which brought much needed refreshment, relaxation, and rejuvenation.

Ὕπνος is used mostly in the Homeric period for natural sleep. Epithets are usually rendered adjectivally.[21] Literally, καθεύδω is used not only as a description of the human and animal sleep, but also as the passageway to the supra-sensual sphere of mental activity, as a derogatory remark aimed at sluggards and the slow-minded, and as an ambivalent term reflecting the totality of life and death.[22]

While καθεύδω and ὑπνόω are selected indiscriminately and profusely to describe physical sleep, κοιμάομαι is chosen equally to serve in the synonymous role. Κοιμάομαι does, however, have a larger polysemic field than the other two, alluded to above. Καθεύδω and ὑπνόω are both more restricted to the natural sleep field of interpretation. The chart below will demonstrate the wider range of meanings encompassed by κοιμάομαι.

---

[21]Scanning through a *TLG* search revealed the following adjectival modifiers: γλυκύς and νήδυμος (sweet)—*Greek Anthology* 7.260.7; ἱερόν (holy, sacred)—Callimachus *Epigrammata* 9.1; Βαθύν (deep)—Posidippus *Epigrammata* 7.170.5-6; and παγκρατής (all-powerful)—Sophocles *Ajax* 673-74.

[22]Oepke, "Καθεύδω," 3:431-33.

Table 2.--Polysemic Versatility of Κοιμάομαι in the Homeric Period[23]

καθεύδω	ὑπνόω	κοιμάομαι			
		physical sleep			
		death sleep			
		sexual intercourse[24]		bed of love[25]	
		lie down	rest	crouch	wait
		insobriety			
		soothe	assauge		relieve
		quiet	lull		hush
		quench	still	cease	appease
			found refuge		restrict

As can be seen by the chart, κοιμάομαι took on more meanings associated with the field collocation of lying down. Dormancy is a common denominator of all instances of κοιμάομαι. The major dormant inactivity is physical sleep. A diverse number of authors including comics, lyricists, doctors, philosophers, epigraphers, and historians used κοιμάομαι when referring to sleep in the Homeric period. For example, the medical doctor Hippocrates of the late Homeric period employed it fifty-eight times, more than any other writer. Appendix F charts all the instances of physical sleep the present writer found in the period under

---

[23]See Table 1 for examples of interpretations provided in Table 2.

[24]Κοιμήματα αὐτογέννητα—intercourse of the mother with her own child (Sophocles *Antigone* 861). These three terms used in the sexual sense include the activity fields of adultery, bestiality, rape, incest, pedophilia, and homosexuality. Lucianus *Dialogus Deorum* 10.4.12-13; 5.7-8, 14-15 ledgers the pedophilia of Zeus and refers to hermaphroditic and lesbian activity in 17.1.12-13 with the use of κοιμάομαι. Later in the patristic period, Gregory of Nyssa uses κοιμάομαι in a polemic deploring sexual immorality in *Contra fornicarios oratio* 9.215.1-10, 17-18; 216.2-3.

[25]Pindarus *Isthmia* 8.21. For comment on this type of language, see Frank J. Nisetich, *Pindar's Victory Songs* (Baltimore, MD: The Johns Hopkins University Press, 1980), 326.

29

consideration. While physical sleep was an activity from which one awakened, the sleep of death was a deplorable closure.

The Sleep of Death

Although κοιμάομαι and its many cognates occur with great regularity in non-Christian Greek texts, relatively few refer to the "sleep of death." Marbury B. Ogle notes:

> It is a striking fact and one, I think, not without significance, that the metaphor of the sleep of death, which is so common in modern poetry, seems to have found little favor with the Greek poets of the centuries from Homer to the Alexandrian period.[26]

The most ancient evidence combines two synonyms to express the sleep-of-death theme. Referring to the death of Iphidimas, Homer says that κοιμήσατο χάκεον ὕπνον, "he slept a(n) bronze/iron sleep" (translation mine).[27] Ensuing a discussion concerning Hypnos (Sleep), the brother of Thanatos (Death), Homer writes: "Calm me to sleep (κοιμήσον) the bright eyes of Zeus beneath his brows, so soon as I will lay by his side in love (translation mine)."[28] For Homer physical death is perpetual and devoid of eschatological arousal.

Euripides of fifth-century B.C. Athens also provides some clear citations. Rendered in choral meter, Hecuba says:

> Or in Pallas' town to the car all-glorious
> Shall I yoke the steeds on the saffron-glowing
> Veil Athene, where flush victorious
> The garlands that cunningest fingers are throwing
> In manifold hues on its folds wide-flowing,
> Or the brood of the Titans whom lightnings, that fell

---

[26]Marbury B. Ogle, "The Sleep of Death," *Memoirs of the American Academy in Rome* 11 (1933): 82. For a treatment of this idea, see ibid., 81-117; Otto Michel, "Todesschlaf," 285-90; J. G. Thomson, "Sleep: An Aspect of Jewish Anthropology," 421-33; and Paul Hoffmann, "4. Das Bildwort vom Todesschlaf," chap. in *Die Toten in Christus: Eine religionsgeschichtliche und exegetische Untersuchung zur paulinischen Eschatologie* (Münster: Aschendorff, 1966), 186-206.

[27]Homer *Iliad* 11.241. There is an unmistakable tone of defeat and permanence in this phrase.

[28]Ibid., 14.235-36.

Flame-wrapped from Cronion, *in long sleep quell* (κοιμίζει)?[29]

Hecuba also conveys this idea in the *Daughters of Troy*:

> Thou on whom Achaens heap
> Outrage, whom eldest I bare
> Unto Priam in that days that were,
> to thine Hades receive me *to sleep* (κοίμισαι).[30]

A third example in Euripides is an intriguing employment of κοιμάομαι used in the context of death. It refers to the "stilling" of the sword after it has accomplished its work of destruction rather than to the object of its wrath:

> Ho ye! I bid you, over-eager twain—
> Laertes' son!—*let sleep* (κοιμίσαι) the whetted sword;
> For at our feet dead lies the Thracian chief.[31]

Sophocles uses a form of κοιμάομαι with no synonymous accomplices in two clear, poetic prayers concerning the death event in the genre of Greek mythology. Functionally, both examples are cast in euphemistic tones so as to combat the Greek mythological fear of an inevitable and inconsequential death.

> O chariot race of Pelops old
> The source of sorrows manifold
> What endless curse hath fallen on us
> Since to his sea-grave Murtilos
> *Sank* (ἐκοιμάθη) from the golden chariot hurled
> Woe upon woe, of woes a world.[32]

> Thus much, O Zeus, I crave of thee;
> and Hermes I invoke, born guide of
> the spirits to the nether world, *to*
> *lay me soft to rest* (χθόνιον εὖ με κοιμίσαι)
> at one swift gasp, without a struggle when into
> my side I plunge this sword.[33]

---

[29]Euripides *Hecuba* 470-73. See Ogle, "The Sleep of Death," 83. Translation in G. P. Goold, ed., *Euripides*, vol. 4, trans. Arthur S. Way, Loeb Classical Library (Cambridge: Harvard University Press, 1978), 285.

[30]Euripides *The Daughters of Troy* 593-94. Translation in Goold, *Euripides*, 403.

[31]Euripides *Rhesus* 668-69. Translation in Goold, *Euripides*, 213.

[32]Sophocles *Electra* 508-9. Translation in E. H. Warmington, ed., *Sophocles*, vol. 2, trans. F. Storr, Loeb Classical Library (Cambridge: Harvard University Press, 1967), 165.

[33]Sophocles *Ajax* 831-32. Translation in Warmington, *Sophocles*, 71.

The interpretative versatility of κοιμάομαι is displayed as Philaenis laments her impending death by saying, "I Philaenis ill-spoken of by all men, *lie here* (κεκοίμημαι) in the extremities of old age. Not me, Oh vain passenger, the end of flexibility (translation mine)."[34]

The Greek Anthology, which dates from the seventh to the third centuries B.C., provides many clear examples of the sleep-of-death formula.[35] First, a young boy, Bianor, "saw carried away by the torrent a coffin in which *rested* (κοιμίζουσαν) still the remains of his parents."[36] A second example describes the sleep in proximity to the location. "The bridal song ended in wailing. And the fond anxiety of her parents *was set to rest* (κοίμισεν) not by marriage, but by the tomb."[37] As in John 11.11 and some Homeric references, the ensuing three accounts, a form of κοιμάομαι and ὑπνόω is used as a functional tandem in which the former refers to the act of dying and the latter to the ontological state of death. "But Therimachus, alas *sleeps* (εὕδει) *the long sleep* (τὸν μακρὸν ὕπνον) under the oak. The fire of heaven *laid him to rest* (ᾠκοιμήθη)."[38] Dripping with the

---

[34]Aeschrion the Lyricist *Epigramma* 7.345.1-2. An identical phrase appears also in *Fragmenta et tituli* 4.1-2. Since κοιμάομαι was used to describe many activities associated with lying down, such as sexual relations and physical sleep, it naturally follows that it could also support an easy transition to incorporate the event of death within its semantic field. In this account Aeschrion associates old age and death by bridging them with the euphemistic κοιμάομαι.

[35]The present writer realizes that some of the dates of the examples offered are uncertain and, therefore, might belong in Chapter II, which deals with the Hellenistic or Alexandrian period. The major concern is, however, to ledger sleep-of-death occurrences. There will be some inevitable overlapping between the late Homeric and early Alexandrian periods. That the concept was operative in both periods will diminish the criticism of anachronism.

[36]*The Greek Anthology* 9.278.pl, 1. Translation in E. Capps, T. E. Page, and W. H. D. Rouse, eds., *The Greek Anthology*, vol. 3, trans. W. R. Paton, Loeb Classical Library (New York: G. P. Putnam's Sons, 1925), 149.

[37]*The Greek Anthology* 7.183.3-4. Translation in Capps, *Anthology*, vol. 2, 105.

[38]Ibid., 7.173.3-4. Translation in Capps, *Anthology*, vol. 2, 99. A less common synonym for sleep, εὕδω (a special form of καθεύδω), forms a triad of emphasis in this story. It is found in Homer, Sophocles, and Theognis but not in the New Testament or LXX. It is employed by Homer, usually in reference to physical sleep, but was used to refer to the sleep of death as well (*Iliad* 14.482-83. See Ogle, "The Sleep of Death," 81.).

euphemism of dread a solemn exhortation is given to the living with the employment of a triple synonymy. Syntactically, the three words are grouped together with no semantic intervention as in the previous example: " . . . εὕδει κοιμηθεὶς ὕπνον . . " The whole thought translates, "Go noiselessly by, stranger, for the old man *sleeps* (εὕδει) among the pious dead, *wrapped* (κοιμηθεὶς) *in the slumber* (ὕπνον) *that is the lot of all*."[39] Another example resembles the Old Testament Elijah translation tradition. "Elias went to heaven in a fiery chariot and the great spirit took to itself Nonna while she was praying. Here dear Nonna *fell into* (κοιμήσατο) *the deep sleep* (ὕπνον), following gladly her husband Gregory."[40]

Also, in the *Greek Anthology* a highly ironic twist is described in an account of an ancient hunting trip which unfortunately ends in the death of both the hunted and the hunter. This cruel epigram relates the high price paid for bagging this particular game. After being shot by the hunter, "the eagle pierced his neck with the arrow which *had found a resting place* (κοίμισεν) in its own heart, and one missile drank the life-blood of two."[41]

---

[39]*The Greek Anthology* 7.419.1-2. Translation in Capps, *Anthology*, vol. 2, 227. Almost the exact phrase is found in 7.219.3-4 of the same work. Reference is made to a certain woman, Lais, "whose bloom was so lovely and delightful in the eyes of all; she who alone called the lilies of the grass, no longer looks on the course of the Sun's golden bitted steeds, *but sleeps the appointed sleep* (ἐκοιμήθη δ᾽ ὕπνον ὀφειλόμενον), having bid farewell to revelling and young men's rivalries, and lover's torments and the lamp her confidant."

[40]Ibid., 8.59.2, 60.1. Translation in Capps, *Anthology*, vol. 2, 422. Even if it were possible for a thematic intersection of an ancient Greek and Old Testament text to exist, the correspondence that the Greek author attempts to establish is askew from the Old Testament story of Elijah's "removal" in 2 Kgs. 2.1-11. Although there is some speculation about the mysteriousness associated with the death of Moses, only two biblical figures escaped death, Enoch and Elijah. Apocalyptically, these two remarkable exceptions escaped the burden of Sheol. Ontologically, these two "deathless" heavenly journeys avoid the same dualistic conclusions as do "death events" in the Old Testament. As Edmond Jacob rightly assesses: "To regard death as separation from God could have led to a dualistic assumption, but faith in the omnipotence of Yahweh was to make dualism impossible in Israel" (*Theology of the Old Testament*, trans. Arthur W. Heathcote and Philip J. Allcock [New York: Harper & Row, Publishers, 1958], 307). Because eschatology is usually regarded as a later development in Hebrew history, eternal life was not viewed as immortality of the soul, reward, or resurrection from the dead. The early emphasis was on the control of Yahweh and the contiguous nature of life and death.

[41]*The Greek Anthology* 9.223.6-7. Translation in Capps, *Anthology*, vol. 3, 117.

Καθεύδω is another synonym which was used in concert with the other sleep-of-death metaphors. Ogle includes what he describes as a "brutal *double entendre*" in the fifth century B.C. writings of the Athenian Aeschylus. Aeschylus causes Orestes, who has just swiftly executed Aegisthus, say to his mother, as he prepares to kill her: "After dying, *lie with* (συγκάθευδ') this one, since you love this man."[42]

The sleep-of-death theme also finds expression in some important Latin texts. The poet Lucretius clearly divulges his sentiments concerning death by saying: "Yes, you as you now *lie in death's quiet sleep* (*es leto sopitus*), so you will be for all time that is to come, removed from all distressing pain."[43] Severe pain, however, is detected in Lucretius's writings as he bemoans consistently the idea of life fading into the obscurity of death. Even though the cessation of physical pain characterizes the deceased, death is at best a dull and quiet sleep from which there is no arousal.[44] Keeping pace with the Greek expressions the Latin phrases

---

[42]Aeschylus *Choephoroe* 906. Translation found in Ogle, "The Sleep of Death," 82. Like κοιμάομαι, καθεύδω can also refer to sexual intercourse and death. The euphemistic substitution of "sleeping with" for "had sexual relations with" is not peculiar to the modern age. In this ancient example the "sleep of sex" and the "sleep of death" combine for an ironic, frightful climax. In relation to καθεύδω, it has been pointed out by Oepke that some argue if the view of the Platonic circle were that eschatological arousal was not a consequence of the death-sleep, then the account of Endymion, to whom Zeus granted eternal sleep, immortality and youth, would be nonsensical. What is overlooked, however, is that the theme of immortality is inferred from the death-sleep formula. The origin of the idea is biological not philosophical. The resemblance of sleep to death was responsible for popular perception. Κοιμάομαι was used, though, more often than other synonyms because it was more suitable to the tranquill imagery of the state of death (Oepke, "Καθεύδω," 3:433).

[43]Lucretius *De Rerum Natura* 3.904-5. Translation in G. P. Goold, ed., *Lucretius*, trans. W. H. D. Rouse, Loeb Classical Library (Cambridge: Harvard University Press, 1982), 259.

[44]Ibid., 3.909-11. Translation found in Goold, *Lucretius*, 231. Lucretius addresses the fear of death in numerous excerpts also. For these treatments, see ibid., 1.102-135, 2.45, 3.37-93; 830-1094, and 6.1182-83; 1208-12. In 3.830-1094 he offers a curious Jobian evaluation of death when he maintains that nothing is felt before our birth and nothing after death (see Job 1.21 and its midrash in 1 Tim. 6.6-10). The Platonic idea of an anthropological dichotomy is evident in 3.843-46 where he speaks of the "welding and wedding" together of body and spirit. Physical sleep is an indicative harbinger of an eternal schism between body and soul that occurs at death. The spirit is drawn apart through the body during sleep. If the spirit ever made a complete "jailbreak," the person died. This ancient understanding of the body-soul relationship is much like a chemical colloidal mixture where two nonblendable elements tend to separate when they are at rest not being stirred. Physical sleep, therefore, is dangerous in this sense because it could very easily

are equally euphemistic. The prevalent feeling can best be illustrated by a full quote from Catallus:

> soles occidere et redire possunt:
> nobis, cum semel occidit breuis lux
> nox est perpetua una dormienda.
>
> The sun can set and rise again
> But once our brief light sets
> There is one unending night to be slept through.[45]

Cicero attacks this hedging practice of euphemism when he says, "The dead do not exist, the living it will not touch. Those who minimize it are for making it clearly resemble *sleep (somnum).*"[46] Latin texts, therefore, also provide good examples of the sleep-of-death euphemism.

Although the frequency of the sleep-of-death theme in the Homeric period is not overwhelming, its sparce employment is adequate for the determination of some characteristic tendencies. Initially, death was characterized as sleep to sway the public interest of tolerable lamentation. The impersonal and serene philosophical expectation of the survival of the immortal soul stands in stark contrast with the courageous and joyful primitive hope of the resurrection of the dead. The hopeless referred to in 1 Thess. 4.13 concerns any group, such as the ancient Greeks, who attempted to hide their true feelings of dread under the cosmetic application of soothing euphemistic verbiage. Euphemistic treatments concerning death can never replace the faith exhibited by those who place their trust in the resurrected Christ. Faith allows an empty euphemism of deceit to be transformed into a glorious metaphor of hope. Although the pagan world had an

---

regress to the eternal death sleep. Also see "The Soul to Air, the Body to Earth" in Euripides *Supplices* 531.

[45]Catullus 5.4-6; quoted and translated in F. F. Bruce, *1 & 2 Thessalonians*, Word Biblical Commentary (Waco, TX: Word Books, Publisher, 1982), 96.

[46]Cicero *Tusculan Disputations* 1.91-92. Translated in G. P. Goold, ed., *Cicero*, vol. 18, trans. J. E. King, Loeb Classical Library (Cambridge: Harvard University Press, 1989), 109-11. In the same section Cicero makes reference to *sleep, death's counterfeit (habes somnum imaginem mortis)*. More examples can be seen in Virgil *Aenid* 6.278; 522, Horace *Odes and Epodes* 1.24.5-6, and Seneca *Hercules Furens* 106-9.

abundance of literature at their disposal to anesthetize their dismay, there is much evidence that it was unsuccessful.[47] The unsubstantiated claims for the belief in the existence of the immortal soul by Greek philosophy was a vain attempt to diffuse the sense of hopelessness created by the death event itself.[48] Secondly, the scarcity of this theme probably represents a literary convention rather than any popularity produced by a *consensus gentium*.[49] Certainly, the masses were driven to search for answers which were the most palatable in light of the futility precipitated by their fear of death. If one truly adhered to the doctrine of the immortality of the soul, then the fear of death would be unwarranted. That the outlook on death was extremely gloomy gave occasion for various philosophies of life to stress the *carpe diem* of Horace before his time.[50] Viable options were limited to two for the ancient Greek in the face of death: 1) the eternal sleep of dreamless slumber, or 2) the transmigration of the soul.[51] The absence of a bonafide "dying and rising" God in their model, however, deprived their system of an eschatologically confident foundation. Thirdly, as Ogle rightly notices, the sleep-of-death equation

---

[47]Bruce, *1 & 2 Thessalonians*, 96, quotes two examples before and after the Christ event: 1) Theocritus *Idyll* 4.42, says, ". . . hopes are for the living; the dead are without hope"; 2) Oxyrhynchus Papyri 115. A second-century A.D. letter of condolence states: "I sorrowed and wept over your dear departed one as I wept over Didymas, . . . but really, there is nothing one can do in the face of such things. So please comfort each other."

[48]For a discussion on the proofs Plato provided for the immortality of the soul, see E. Ehrmark, "Transmigration in Plato," *Harvard Theological Review* 50 (1957): 1-20. On this issue of the Greek belief in the hereafter, see W. Jaeger, "The Greek Ideas of Immortality," *Harvard Theological Review* 52 (1959): 135-47.

[49]Ogle, "The Sleep of Death," 84.

[50]This particular philosophy is prevalent today and fueled by the belief that death is the final act indeed.

[51]For a discussion of the Greek lines of influence on the Old Testament tradition and Judaism, see Otto Kaiser and Eduard Lohse, eds., *Death and Life*, trans. John E. Steely (Nashville: Abingdon Press, 1981), 12-30.

did not find acceptance in the tragedy. Seneca includes no examples in his plays.[52] Their tragedy was tragedy indeed.

The Gods Hypnos and Thanatos

Amidst the vast number of Greek and Roman gods of mythical lore existed a group designated "the denizens of the underworld," of whom Hypnos and Thanatos were major figures.[53] They were associated with unfortunate heroines and the unhappy early-dead, especially dead lovers, brides and bridegrooms. Subterranean scenery commonly showcased these two wiley characters. Known as twin brothers, they served as agents of the afterlife. Frequently, they were pictured carrying off dead bodies for embalming and burial.

While Thanatos functioned much like comtemporary ideas of the Grim Reaper, one of Hypnos' chief duties was to bring news of death and subsequently to ease the attendant pain experienced from the loss. Vivid fulfillment of this duty is seen in the love story of Ceyx and Halcyone. Halcyone unwittingly commited blasphemy by habitually referring to her husband as Zeus. On a trip to consult an oracle, the shipbound Ceyx was shipwrecked and drowned by a divinely-ordained storm. Worried about his tardy return, Halcyone diligently implored Hera about her husband's fate. Overcome with compassion, Hera sent Isis to the Cave of Sleep, which is located in the land of night. Poppies, the murmuring river Lethe, and Hypnos stretched out on a couch can be seen in the center of the cave. Innumerable shapes of empty dreams encompass Hypnos. After being aroused and informed, Hypnos dispatched his son Morpheus, that great imitator of reality, to shape himself into the likeness of Ceyx and tell Halcyone the truth.[54]

---

[52]Ibid., 83.

[53]Richard Y. Hathorn, *Greek Mythology* (Lebanon: The American University of Beirut, 1977), 95-96.

[54]Ibid., 121-22. This summary is typical of Hypnos' role and dates back to Hesiod. Hypnos was also depicted as one who craftily exercised power over the gods, even Zeus. On one occasion Hera bribed Hypnos with a bridal nymph if he would close Zeus' eyes. According to the designed

In another story Sophocles wrote about sailors who implored Hypnos to intercede on behalf of Philoctetes, a comrade who regrettably had to be marooned on an island because of a horrendous affliction.[55] Hypnos was invoked not only as the god who could provide release from pain, but also as the one who could render men helpless and give them over to their betrayers.[56] Functionally, one can see that Hypnos was not very far removed from death itself.

Although sleep usually was sweet and refreshing, sometimes it was a potential transitory precursor which easily could retreat into death. Accurately displaying the prevailing belief, Heraclitus saw sleep as a mode between life and death: "Man in the night kindles a light for himself, when he has died and yet lives. In sleep, when the vision of his eyes is quenched, he touches the dead; when he is awake, he touches the sleeping (translation mine)."[57]

Conclusion

The Homeric period depicts clearly the Greek context for the idea of the sleep of death. Based on the evidence produced, the reader can see that a desperate fusion was engineered between the concepts of sleep and death in the interest of calming the fears of a pagan world. Κοιμάομαι emerges as one of three terms chosen to communicate that association. As will be seen, the closer one moves

---

plan, Hera drew near to Zeus on Mount Ida. After voracious lovemaking Zeus fell into the power of sleep induced by Hypnos. This episode is known technically as the "Homeric Deception of Zeus" (see Homer *Iliad* 14.249-62).

[55]*Philoctetes* 827. For text and translation, see Warmington, *Sophocles*, 362-493. There is some question whether Philoctetes was praying to Hypnos for anesthetizing sleep or to Thanatos for a more permanent solution.

[56]D. M. Jones, "The Sleep of Philoctetes," *The Classical Review* 63 (1949): 85. For a brief discussion on the god Hypnos, see Balz, "Ὕπνος," 8:549-50, and Wilhelm Heinrich Roscher, ed., *Ausführliches der griechischen und römischen Mythologie*, vol. 1, part 2 (Leipzig: B. G. Teubner, 1884), s.v. "Hypnos," by B. Sauer. For a discussion and bibliography on Thanatos, see Rudolf Bultmann, "Θάνατος," *TDNT*, 3:7-25, especially section 1.

[57]Heraclitus *Fragments* 26. This thought is echoed later in Clement of Alexandria *Miscellanies* 4.22.

toward the unique New Testament message of the defeat of death; the disparity created by death grows worse and the utilization of the sleep-of-death metaphor intensifies in the pagan world. Even the Old Testament does not teach a highly developed doctrine of resurrection. Not until the New Testament era does κοιμάομαι begin to acquire a metonymic transfer of meaning.[58] Later, it becomes a more technical term for death in the writings of the early church fathers, particularly by Eusebius of Caesarea, St. Athanasius, and John Chrysostom.[59] It will be maintained that there is no such biblical teaching as the "soul" in the sense in which it is found in Greek thought. Biblical man is a unit. Beyond this fact, and more importantly, the Bible does not teach that a person, Christian or not, "houses" a divine element which will never die. There is no σῶμα σῆμα (tomb of the soul) of Platonic stock found in the Scriptures.

---

[58]On this idea of change in lexical stock, see Cotterell and Turner, *Linguistics and Biblical Interpretation*, 131-32. As κοιμάομαι was in this process of Christian adoption, it lost much of its polysemic versatility.

[59]Judging from their extravagant usage of the term, sleep appears much more than a metaphor. The semantic line of distinction was all but erased in the early church as the concepts of sleep and death were functionally absolute synonyms. The two terms were interchangeable for all practical purposes.

CHAPTER II
LINGUISTIC EVIDENCE FROM THE HELLENISTIC PERIOD

The Frequency of the "Metaphor" Sleep for Death

Diachronically, the presence of the sleep-of-death motif vigorously increases as one moves closer to the New Testament. Frequency is, however, not as crucial as the synchronic evaluation of the concept's meaning. Death continued to leave its calling card in the Hellenistic period as it did in previous times. The mood of extreme dissolution now characterized the popular thanatology. Although the reaction in the LXX was not as loathsome and paranoid as nonbiblical paganism, the transition from euphemism to metaphor with respect to the sleep of death had not yet taken place. The Old Testament certainly does exhibit a degree of hope beyond the grave, such as Ps. 16.10: ". . . because you will not abandon me to the grave, nor will you let your Holy One see decay," which is employed by Peter in Acts 2 to refer to the resurrection of Jesus Christ. Although the place and type of this envisioned relationship with Yahweh which the Psalmist projects is not clear, it nevertheless reveals at least a prophetic conditioning for the fully elaborated doctrine of resurrection in the New Testament. Hans Walter Wolff states the following in personal reference to Yahweh: "There is not only the alternative between this life and the shadowy existence in the world of the dead; there is a third possibility—a permanent, living fellowship with him."[1]

The aspect of resurrection is mentioned here only because it is closely related to one's thanatological outlook on the interim state. Spokesmen in the Hellenistic period, pagan or not, continued to refer to death as a sleep. Regardless of eternal aspirations or exasperations, the phrase "during death" is still an accurate description of the interim period which follows the cessation of biological life.

Sepulchral Art

Aesthetically, the sleep of death was expressed by means of sepulchral art. This means of architectural observation did not originate with the Greeks and was not initiated until the era after Alexander's conquests.[2] The figures in both the archaic and classical periods are depicted as stereotypical heroes or gods, or as snapshots of mere mortals still absorbed in either the joyful or sorrowful aspects of life.[3] The sleep of death concept acquired, however, a fresh image which projected a closer coordination between the activity fields of sleep and death in the Hellenistic period. These monuments depicted human figures stretched out in a supine position upon the cover of a sarcophagus as if swooning in a serene and silent sleep. Ogle remarks that the earliest examples of these decorated coffins were uncovered in the necropolis of Sidon, and it is generally acknowledged that the Phoenicians acquired this practice from the Egyptian anthropoid caskets.[4]

---

[1] Hans Walter Wolff, *Anthropology of the Old Testament*, trans. Margaret Kohl (Philadelphia: Fortress Press, 1974), 109.

[2] Ogle, "The Sleep of Death," 87.

[3] See Maxine Collignon, *Les Statues funéraires* (Paris: Leroux, 1911), 47-75, 126-39.

[4] Ogle, "The Sleep of Death," 87.

Memorial Epitaphs and Inscriptions

The literary epitaph accounts for the bulk of sleep of death occurrences in the nonbiblical Hellenistic sources. Outside of the epitaph the euphemism is due largely to Homeric reflection. A late fourth-century B.C. example emerges in a historical account of the death of one Alexander. Twice the identical line appears in different works: Κρυβέντος δὲ τοῦ ἀστέρος εἰς οὐρανὸν εὐθέως ἐκοιμήθη Ἀλέχανδρος τὸν αἰώνιον ὕπνον.[5] This can be translated: "Being hidden among the stars in heaven, Alexander immediately slept the eternal sleep."[6] Κοιμάομαι is a play on words in this last example in the genre of the funeral speech:

> It is extremely difficult to console those weighed down with woes like these. For woes are not *stilled* (κοιμάομαι) by word or law; but by each person's temper; and the measure of his love for the dead, governs the extent of his mourning (translation mine).[7]

The epitaph consists of inscriptions on tombs or gravestones in memory of the deceased. Epitaphs also include pithy compositions in prose or verse commemorating the deceased. Upon investigation these common phenomena betray a steadily deteriorating thanatology. The slender glimmer of masked hope projected in the Homeric period is now even more faint in the first century B.C. Note the disparity in the epigrammatical question: Τὶ πένθιμον ὕπνον ἰαύεις? G. Kaibel translates this phrase: "Why must you sleep your sorrowful slumber?"[8] An even harsher example comes from the first century A.D. Futility and despair rule as the sleep of death fades from euphemism to an actual correspondence between

---

[5]Historia Alexandri Magni *Recensio* α 3.33.8 and *Recensio* γ 33R.137.

[6]Also "being hidden in the ground" was synonymous with "being dead" (H. G. Liddell and R. Scott, eds., *A Greek-English Lexicon*, s.v. "Κρυβήτης").

[7]Hyperides *Epitaph* 41.2-3. Although the word for dead is not any form of κοιμάομαι, the presence of the word in the funerary oration is striking.

[8]Translation in G. Kaibel, ed., *Epigrammata Graeca ex lapidibus conlecta*, 204; quoted in H. Balz, "Ὕπνος," 8:548. Kaibel and Ogle suspect Phoenician persuasion in this epigram, but P. Hoffmann, *Die Toten in Christus*, 188-92, sees Egyptian and Akkadian influences. Also, see E. Peek, *Griechische Grabgedichte* (Berlin: Akademie, 1960), for examples.

the two: Τὸν φθιμένων νήγρετον ὕπνον ἔψων, translated, "the sleep of death from which there is no awaking."[9]

Ogle charts a flurry of illustrative examples from the *Anthologia Palatina*.[10] These efforts represent late nineteenth- and early twentieth-century linguistic scholars such as Johannes Geffcken, Ernst Diehl, Maxime Collignon, Hermann Dessau, and Carl Maria Kaufmann. Additionally, contemporary text critics and linguists have been able to enjoy an exciting and fresh investigation of Greek inscriptions and papyri edited by G. H. R. Horsley.[11] Horsley's examples are, however, continuations of the sleep-of-death motif already reviewed in the Homeric and Hellenistic periods with two exceptions. Although there may be some overlap, to the greatest extent they are either colinear or subsequent to Christian examples and will be discussed briefly in the last chapter. Table 3 charts a representative number of the uses of κοιμάομαι and its synonyms for the sleep-of-death image in this epoch from the *Anthologia Palatina*.[12]

---

[9]Translation in Peek, *Griechische Grabgedichte*, no. 284, 2; quoted in Horst Balz, "Ὕπνος," 8:548.

[10]Ogle, "The Sleep of Death," 83-85. A wide variety of inscriptions, epitaphs, and epigrams have been compiled by Johannes Geffcken, *Griechische Epigramme* (Heidelberg: C. Winter, 1916).

[11]Five volumes of *New Documents Illustrating Early Christianity* have been published, the latest in 1989. As long as newly discovered Greek papyri and inscriptions are published this series will continue.

[12]More examples of the sleep-of-death epitaph involving some form of κοιμάομαι can be gleaned from Theocritus *Idyll* 8.65-66; Posidippus *Epigrammata* 7.170.5-6; Parthenius Nicaenus *Narrationes amatoriae* 20.2.4-5; and Apollodorus of Corcyra *Fragmenta* 1.56.4-5.

Table 3.--The Sleep of Death in the *Anthologia Palatina*

Author	Source	Operative Terms
Idomeneus	7.725	ὕπνος
Leonidas of Tarentum	7.408	ὕπνος, κοιμάομαι, ἀναπαύομαι
Diotimus	7.173.3-4	ὕπνος, κοιμάομαι, εὕδει
Carphyllides	7.260.7-8	ὕπνος, κοιμάομαι
Philippus	7.405.4	κοιμάομαι
Statilius Flaccus	7.290.3	ὕπνος
Moschus[13]	3.103-4	ὕπνος

Of course, κοιμάομαι was still used heavily in this period to refer to physical sleep and sexual encounter. Several examples will be sufficient to illustrate the point. An ancient Rip van Winkle is referred to in the Hellenistic period. Pausanius depicts Epimenides the Gnossian, who is reported to have wandered off into a field and entered a cave where he subsequently slept for forty years before he awakened.[14] Secondly, in the interest of sexual jocularity, Timocles, a fourth-century B.C. comic, employs an effective word play device as he jokes about the difference of sleeping (κοιμᾶσθαι) with a maiden or a harlot (χαμαιτύπης).[15] This tendency continues even into the LXX.

---

[13]This example is a pastoral lament.

[14]Pausanius *Description of Greece* 1.14.4.3-5. In a third-century A.D. biographical work, Epimenides also is described as having taken a fifty-seven year nap (κοιμάομαι) in Diogenes Laertius *Vitae philosophorum* 1.109.6-7.

[15]Timocles *Fragmenta* 22.1-2.

44

The LXX and Diaspora Greek[16]

Alexandrian Jewry expressed the sleep-of-death concept with no hesitancy in the LXX and apocryphal writings. Appendixes B, C, and D chart the usage of κοιμάομαι, ὑπνόω, and καθεύδω, as they are related to this idea. By far, κοιμάομαι was the translator's number one option over all other synonymous phraseology and concepts to express the sleep of death. That κοιμάομαι was used frequently illustrates the point of its semantic popularity throughout the Hellenistic period. The question which confronts the interpreter is at what point, if at all, does the Septuagintal author part ways with the nonbiblical Hellenists, the Apocrypha, and from the Hebrew text with regard to the idea of death? Can it be shown that the Greek translator exhibited any theological tendencies which are not complementary with the Hebrew author?

The areas in which κοιμάομαι exerts the heaviest concentration is in Kings, Chronicles, Job, Psalms, and Ezekiel. These will receive the most attention. Passing comments will be offered for some of the less conspicuous entries. All other references can be checked in the proper appendix. A sufficient amount of evaluation will be completed in order to do a theological comparison of all the material in the Hellenistic period.

The Pentateuch

Κοιμάομαι refers to the sleep of death only two times in the Pentateuch: Gen. 47.30 and Deut. 31.16. The primary example in Genesis is in reference to the death of Jacob.[17] Although the writer of Genesis had already recorded the deaths of Abel, the wicked in the Noanic flood, the inhabitants of Sodom and Gomorrah, Sarah, Abraham, Rachel, and Isaac, Jacob is the first to be described as "resting"

---

[16]English translations consulted and occasionally quoted from the LXX are found in *The Septuagint Version of the Old Testament, With an English Translation and with Various Readings and Critical Notes* (London: S. Bagster and Sons, 1950).

[17]See Appendix B, n. 1.

(κοιμηθήσομαι) with his fathers.[18] Up to this point in the LXX, κοιμάομαι as only been used with reference to physical sleep and sexual intercourse of both humans and animals. Why is Jacob the first to receive this designation of the sleep of death?

Jacob was the fountainhead of the twelve sons who spawned the respective patriarchal tribes in Israel. Building on this idea, it should be remembered that in Sheol the "family-gathering" would continue as the true meeting place of the dead.

Excursus on Sheol

The popular expression "to be reunited with his fathers and with his people" signifies the coming together of members of the same clan in a common grave.[19] Although it has been pointed out by scholars that the term Sheol received little currency in the early writings, it appears that the concept was clearly present in their minds. That the idea of resurrection was not developed at this particular juncture of the patriarchal history and that death was common gave rise to a penultimate idea: the hope of rejoining after death those from whom the blessings of ancestry were initially received.[20] But as E. Jacob states: "It is, nevertheless, certain that the Old Testament never presents death as a liberation or as a gateway giving access to perfect felicity."[21] The Hebrew concept of corporate personality,

---

[18]Gerhard von Rad, *Genesis*, rev. ed., trans. John H. Marks, The Old Testament Library (Philadelphia: The Westminster Press, 1961), 414, identifies the writer in this section as the Yahwist. It could be that the Yahwist identified the Cave at Machpelah as the location where Jacob was "gathered unto his fathers" (Gen. 49.29-33).

[19]Edmond Jacob, *Theology of the Old Testament*, 303. The idea of Sheol was not unique among Israelites. Some scholars believe the idea of Sheol was borrowed from the Babylonians. A. Lods, however, *La Croyance à la Vie Future et le Culte des Morts dans l'Antiquité Israélite*, vol. 1 (Paris: Fischbascher, 1906), 209-10, rejected the idea and surmised that the common belief surfaced due to "the general laws of human imagination." Also see Andrew F. Key, "The Concept of Death in Early Israelite Religion," *The Journal of Bible and Religion* 32 (1964): 241.

[20]Otto Baab, *IDB*, s.v. "Father," 245.

[21]E. Jacob, *Theology of the Old Testament*, 300.

championed by H. Wheeler Robinson, is directly related to this idea.[22] Unity encompasses the past as well as the future. Depicted as sleep, Jacob's burial in the family sepulcher positions him immediately to enjoy his ancestral company and subsequently to await the arrival of his descendants.

Most scholars hold that no distinction was made between Sheol and the grave.[23] R. H. Charles, who was a pioneer in Old Testament eschatological ideas, believed that all of the graves of the clans were independently linking subsets belonging to a universal Sheol.[24] It is difficult to reconcile the ideas of the "grave" and "Sheol" unless one envisions Sheol as the "assemblage of all the graves."[25] The idea of death being sleep, therefore, was appropriate and accurate for the Hebrew mind-set, and the Greek translator bridged the idea into the LXX, only with more optimism. Although it was an early analytical strand of thought, the idea of death which dangerously approached the concept of annihilation was counterbalanced and finally overcome by "the synthetic view of the continuity between life and death."[26] According to the latter, more developed view, the

---

[22]H. Wheeler Robinson, *Corporate Personality in Ancient Israel* (Philadelphia: Fortress Press, 1964), 3. Robinson includes three other related aspects of this conception.

[23]On this idea, see A. Heidel, *The Gilgamesh Epic and Old Testament Parallels* (Chicago: University of Chicago Press, 1946), 174-91. For a more recent treatment of the equivocation of "Sheol" and the "grave", see M. L. Harris, "The Meaning of *Sheol* as Shown by Parallels in Poetic Passages," *Journal of the Evangelical Theological Society* 4 (1961): 129-35 and Robert Martin-Achard, *From Death to Life*, trans. John Penney Smith (Edinburgh: Oliver and Boyd, 1960), 36-47. On page thirty-eight Martin-Achard says: "Sheol is, in fact, a sort of vast grave of which the individual tombs are merely particular manifestations."

[24]For the historical development of eschatology in the Old Testament, see R. H. Charles, *A Critical History of the Doctrine of a Future Life* (London: A. & C. Black, 1913), 33. J. Pedersen refers to Sheol as the "Ur"-grave and Sheol manifests itself in every grave in the same way that Moab manifests itself in every Moabite (*Israel, Its Life and Culture*, I-II [London: Oxford University Press, 1926], 462).

[25]Ibid.

[26]The present writer believes this concept is one of the crucial gauges which will help redress the dualistic anthropological tendencies of ancient Greece which has been adopted and practiced by many modern Christians. See Lloyd R. Bailey, "Death As a Theological Problem in the Old Testament," *Pastoral Psychology* 22 (1971): 29-30.

existence of a person diminished to its lowest ontological point in Sheol. The dualistic model of Athens found no place in the Septuagintal idea of Hades (Sheol).

Anthropologically, upon death the Hebrew body was reduced as close to nothingness as possible without losing its basic identity. Early on the Hebrew person viewed death as a grim fate which meant the end of all human hopes and longings.[27] This model helps one to understand why the desperate King Saul was able to recognize and converse with Samuel after the prophet was summoned from Sheol by the medium at Endor (1 Samuel 28).[28] Samuel's appearance might lead one to suppose a Greek dualistic model. This assessment, however, is misguided. What is meant by "soul" in pagan Greek thought is by no means the biblical intention. Saul and the witch did not witness Samuel's soul but what D. S. Russell labels as his "shade" which was a duplicate of the once living prophet.[29] Treating this story as historical narrative, Cooper draws four conclusions which illustrate Israel's thanatology at this point: 1) it is clear that there is continuity of personal identity between the living and the dead; 2) although Samuel's appearance was highly unusual, he represents a typical inhabitant of Sheol; 3) although he was resting (sleeping), it was possible for him to wake up and engage in acts of conscious communication; and 4) Samuel is a "ghost" or a "shade," not a Platonic soul or a Cartesian mind.[30]

---

[27]Walther Eichrodt, *Man in the Old Testament*, trans. K. and R. Gregor Smith (London: SCM Press, 1961), 53. See 2 Sam. 14.14 for the popular expression of the somewhat pessimistic outlook on death.

[28]The principal texts on conferring with the dead in the Old Testament are Exod. 22.17; Lev. 19.31, 20.6, 27; 1 Sam. 28.3, 9-13; and Isa. 8.19, 19.3, 29.4.

[29]For an enlightening discussion on the subject, see D. S. Russell, *The Method & Message of Jewish Apocalyptic: 200 B.C.- A.D. 100*, The Old Testament Library (Philadelphia: The Westminster Press, 1964), 353-90. Also, see Hans W. Hertzberg's discussion in his *I & II Samuel*, trans. J. S. Bowden The Old Testament Library (Philadelphia: The Westminster Press, 1964), 215-21. Hertzberg points out that Samuel is referred to as a "godlike being" (אֱלֹהִים), not as a ghost (219).

[30]Cooper, *Body, Soul, & Life Everlasting*, 65.

The Old Testament term נֶפֶשׁ has been rendered by the Greek ψυχή and translated "soul" many times in the LXX. נֶפֶשׁ can also be translated "life," "appetite," "person," or "creature," thus displaying a polysemic range of meanings from which to choose. Instead of supposing Samuel, or any other Old Testament character for that matter, possessed some immortal quality such as the Greek idea of a soul, one rather should say that Samuel's "living principle" (נֶפֶשׁ חָיָה) had ebbed away leaving him at his absolute lowest degree of being during death. Death is the rupture of the center of vitality which constitutes life.[31] If this idea is true, then one can understand why the prophet was disturbed by the medium "bringing him up" (28.15). Biblical writers expressed an ontological, anthropological, and biological continuity between life and death by the notion of resting and being gathered to the ever-growing clan in Sheol.

Septuagintal Eschatology in a New Testament Parable?

With this model operative in the Old Testament, light can be shed on an important New Testament text erroneously related to the postmortem state as its primary emphasis. The episode of Lazarus resting in the bosom of Abraham and the Rich Man tormented in Hades in Luke 16.19-31 should not be seen as a lesson on the ontological state after death. It should, however, be seen initially as an admirable commentary on the results of ignoring Jesus' beatitude concerning mercy (the attribute which the love of riches can short-circuit) in Matt. 5.8.[32] The Matthean Jewish emphasis is clearly seen in the story as the poor beggar Lazarus

---

[31] Walter Brueggemann, *IDB*, Supplementary Volume, s.v. "Death, Theology of," 219-22, citation from 219. The present writer believes that, even though the Israelites were a little less pessimistic about death than the pagan world and had at best a very primitive idea of resurrection or afterlife, Brueggemann is incorrect to say that Israel's theology had no interest in it (220). Although it is the majority opinion that no more than a whisper of the resurrection can be claimed in the Old Testament, it is definitely "a clear and distinctly audible whisper" (Cooper, *Body, Soul, and Life Everlasting*, 72).

[32] For an excellent elaboration on this point, see Karel Hanhart, *The Intermediate State in the New Testament*, 193-99.

(not of John 11) finds comfort by being gathered to his father Abraham in Sheol.[33] While the stress is on the ethical import of the story it does not exclude eschatology. Ethics have definite eschatological significance, however, not in the pre-parousia sense. It would be chronologically inaccurate to think that at that particular moment, or even now, that Lazarus or the Rich Man had empirical eschatological evidence of either of the final double destinations.

This ethereal place of existence is supported by H. Wheeler Robinson:

> The dead are thus supposed to go on existing in some sense or other, even by the early thought of Israel. But it is an existence which has no attraction for the Israelite. . . . It is not his soul that survives at all; the dead are called 'shades' (rephaim), their abiding is called Sheol, and in many particulars it is like the Greek Hades.[34]

Joachim Jeremias remarks that Hades is almost always the Greek word for Sheol.[35] That both the righteous and the ungodly proceed to Sheol has led some to believe in its compartmentalization.[36] Perhaps the bosom of Abraham and Hades are two ways of referring to different sections in Sheol in Luke 16 as held by A. J. Mattill[37] and Joseph A. Fitzmyer.[38]

---

[33]Hartmut Gese, "Death in the Old Testament," chap. in *Essays on Biblical Theology*, trans. Keith Crim (Minneapolis: Augsburg Publishing House, 1981), 34-59, this citation 36.

[34]H. Wheeler Robinson, *The Religious Ideas of the Old Testament* (New York: Scribner's, 1913), 92.

[35]Joachim Jeremias, "Ἅδης," *TDNT*, 1:146.

[36]See Desmond Alexander, "The Old Testament View of Life after Death," *Themelios* 11 (1986): 43. The identification of the four sectors were gleaned from 1 Enoch 22.1-14. See M. A. Knibb, *The Ethiopic Book of Enoch*, vol. 2 (Oxford: Clarendon Press, 1978), 110-11: 1) the righteous (verse 9b); 2) the unpunished wicked from this life (verses 10-11); 3) the martyred righteous (verse 12); and 4) the punished wicked from this life (verse 13). Jacob, *Theology of the Old Testament*, 304-5, notes that any division of the righteous and the wicked in Sheol is not fully developed until the second century B.C.

[37]A. J. Mattill, *Luke and the Last Things* (Dillsboro, NC: Western North Carolina Press, 1979).

[38]Joseph Fitzmyer, *The Gospel according to Luke X-XXIV*, The Anchor Bible (Garden City, NY: Doubleday & Co., 1985), 1132. Fitzmyer maintains: "It may be that two different locales in Sheol are really meant." Mattill, Fitzmyer, and Joseph Osei-Bonsu run counter to R. E. Bailey, "Life after Death: A New Testament Study in the Relation of Body and Soul" (Ph.D. diss., University of Edinburgh, 1962), 420, and to William Strawson, *Jesus and the Future Life: A Study in the Synoptic Gospels* (Philadelphia: Westminster Press, 1959), 211.

Of importance are the conclusions of two Christian epitaphs from the Byzantine period published in 1976.³⁹ Although somewhat damaged, they both contain a formulaic allusion to the parable in Luke 16 discussed above. It reads: "Almighty God, the god of the divine spirits and Lord of all flesh, rest (ἀ[ν]άπαυσον) her soul in the bosom of Abraham and Isaac and Jacob. . . ." The thanatological idea appearing on this grave marker flourished in the Byzantine period. The sleep of death and the winnowing of the wicked from the righteous are complementary to the concept of the abode of the dead referred to as Sheol/Hades.

The only other pentateuchal example is found in Deut. 31.16. The Lord informs Moses that he is "going to rest (κοιμᾷ) with his fathers." The convergence of the dead is once again emphasized in Deut. 32.50, on Mount Nebo, as the Lord says: "There on the mountain that you have climbed you will die (מות) and be gathered to your people, just as your brother Aaron died (מות) on Mount Hor and was gathered to his people."⁴⁰ Privately, the Lord himself buried Moses (34.6) thus exhibiting not only his personal involvement in death but also his lordship over it.⁴¹

---

³⁹J. and L. Robert, "Bulletin épigraphique, 756, no.7," *Revue des études grecques* 89 (1976): 415-595; quoted in Horsley, *New Documents*, 1:98. The partial inscription also surfaces in J. G. Milne, ed., *Inscriptiones Graecae Aegypti*, vol. 1, *Inscriptiones nunc Cairo in museo* (Oxford: Oxford University Press, 1905; repr. Chicago: University of Chicago Press, 1976), 9243.6-12.

⁴⁰Just as in the death of Samuel, the most popular word for death (מות) is used to ledger the fact of Moses' death. Although the location of Moses' grave is uncertain, even the highly sceptical Martin Noth, *The History of Israel*, trans. Stanley Godman (New York: Harper & Brothers, 1958), 136, n. 2, refers to the solid tradition as to its whereabouts. A more spirited approach to the geographical problem is found in S. Schwertner, "Erwägungen zu Moses Tod und Grab in Dtn. 34.5-6," *Zeitschrift für die alttestamentliche Wissenschaft* 84 (1972): 25-46.

⁴¹Peter C. Craigie, *The Book of Deuteronomy*, The New International Commentary on the Old Testament (Grand Rapids: Eerdmans, 1976), 405, holds that even though the identity of the third person pronoun "he" is uncertain, the context suggests that God worked alone as grave digger and funeral director in this instance.

The Books of the Kingdoms

Before its heaviest employment as the sleep of death in Kings and Chronicles, κοιμάομαι occurs in Judg. 5.27.[42] *The Song of Deborah* celebrates the blessed Jael for driving a tent peg through Sisera's head. The poetic use of κοιμάομαι in this passage incorporates the ideas of falling, sinking, lying, and dying by the means of synonymous parallelism:

> At her feet he *sank*,
> he fell; there *he lay* (ἐκοιμήθη)
> At her feet he sank, *he fell*
> where he sank, there *he fell*—dead.

2 Sam. 7.12 (2 Kgs. 7.12, LXX) is the first reference appearing in the Books of the Kingdoms with Nathan's allusion to the death of King David.[43] This verse marks the inception of the "sleeping with your fathers" motif in the Old Testament.

The Regnal Obituaries

The Books of the Kingdoms cast a consistent formula for charting the deaths of the Hebrew kings which serve as summary statements of their lives. Most of the sleep of death reports in the LXX occur in Kings and their semisynoptic

---

[42]It is important to remember that the two books of Kings as are found in English translations, which were formerly undivided in Hebrew, comprised the fourth book of the Former Prophets. This fourth book was considered as the continuation of the third, the two books of Samuel. Some Septuagintal peculiarities include: 1) Lucian's recension of the LXX dividing the Kings and the books of Samuel at 1 Kgs. 2:11 which marked the end of David's reign; and 2) the designation "3 Reigns" and "4 Reigns" for the English "1 Kings" and "2 Kings" respectively. For a good discussion on the Hebrew and Greek texts of 1 and 2 Kings, and an informative bibliography, see G. H. Jones, *1 and 2 Kings*, vol. 1, The New Century Bible Commentary (Grand Rapids: Eerdmans, 1984), xiv-9.

[43]Appendixes B, C, and D reflect the reference in the Masoretic text. When cross-referencing between the Masoretic Text and the LXX, 1 Samuel=1 Kings; 2 Samuel=2 Kings; 1 Kings=3 Kings; and 2 Kings=4 Kings. References within parentheses represent the LXX. The textual problems that exist between the LXX and the Masoretic text nor the chronological problems will hinder the progress of this study because of the widespread usage of the death and burial formula in Kings and Chronicles. For an excellent treatment of the Septuagintal text of the Kings, see A. Rahlfs, *Septuaginta-Studien: I, Studien zu den Königsbücher* (Göttingen: Vandenhoeck & Ruprecht, 1904) and idem, *Lucians Rezension der Königsbücher* (Göttingen: Vandenhoeck & Ruprecht, 1911).

reflections in Chronicles.[44] Typically, this formula is cast as "X ("X" being the variable for any king) rested[45] with his fathers." Burke O. Long classifies it as a key element of the "Regnal Résumé" genre.[46] Although this concluding résumé is omitted at times, it normally incorporates the following components: (1) a citation formula, referring the reader to other sources for regnal information; (2) notice of death and burial of the king; and (3) notice of succession.[47] The second part (2) in Long's scheme is referred to as a "Death and Burial Formula" (*Todes- und Bestattungsformel*) as a more refined *kleinegattung*.[48] Some observations about this form are noteworthy. Initially, it has been noted correctly that this euphemistic formula not only is vitally connected with the community of families (*Gemeinschaftsgefühl der Familien*) but also with the faith that the deceased would still somehow survive in the grave.[49] Secondly, good and bad kings alike are classified in this manner, such as Hezekiah (2 Kgs. 20.21) and Manasseh (2 Kgs. 21.18) respectively. Thirdly, this phrase refers only once to a violent death, that of Ahab.[50] In the fourth place, the deaths of all the kings of Israel and Judah are not registered in this manner. In some instances either the reference to the death (he slept with his fathers) or the burial (they buried him) is missing (e.g., 1 Kgs. 14.20; 2 Kgs. 15.22). Sometimes both elements are missing or are replaced by a

---

[44] See Appendix B for explicit references.

[45] κοιμάομαι = שָׁכַב = *dormire*.

[46] Burke O. Long, *1 Kings: With an Introduction to Historical Literature* (Grand Rapids: Eerdmans, 1984), 259.

[47] Ibid.

[48] Also, see E. J. Smith, "Death- and Burial- Formulas in Kings and Chronicles Relating to the Kings of Judah," chap. in *Biblical Essays*, Proceedings of Die Ou-testamentiese Werkemeenskap (South Africa: Potchefstroom, 1966), 173-77.

[49] Ernst Würthwein, *Das Erste Buch der Könige*, Das Alte Testament Deutsch (Göttingen: Vandenhoeck & Ruprecht, 1977), 21.

[50] 1 Kgs. 22.40. R. H. Pfeiffer, *Introduction to the Old Testament*, 2d ed. (New York: Harper Books, 1948), 398.

death-event narrative as in the case of Elah, king of Israel (1 Kgs. 16.9-10). Those kings who died an unnatural death were not referred to as "sleeping with his fathers" with the exception of Ahab as the following table will illustrate.[51]

Table 4.--Regnal Résumés Which Exclude the Sleep-of-Death Formula in the Books of the Kingdoms

King	Disp.	Manner	Ref.	Kingdom
Nadab	evil[52]	murdered	1.15.27	Israel
Elah	evil	murdered	1.16.10	Israel
Ahaziah	evil	killed	2.1.1-16	Israel
Jehoram	evil	murdered	2.9.15	Israel
Zechariah	evil	murdered	2.15.10	Israel
Shallum	evil	murdered	2.15.14	Israel
Pekahiah	evil	murdered	2.15.25	Israel
Pekah	evil	murdered	2.15.30	Israel
Hoshea	evil	exilic death	2.17.6	Israel
Ahaziah	evil	murdered	2.9.27	Judah
Athaliah	evil	murdered	2.11.20	Judah
Amon	evil	murdered	2.21.23	Judah
Jehoahaz	evil	exilic death	2.23.34	Judah
Jehoiachin	evil	exilic death	2.24.15	Judah
Zedekiah	evil	exilic death	2.25.7	Judah
Josiah	good[53]	battle death	2.23.29	Judah

---

[51]Also see A. Alfrink, "שכב עם אבותי ו," *Oudtestamentische Studiën* 2 (1943): 106-18.

[52]The formulaic phrase "did evil in the sight of the Lord" consistently recurs in the "theological review" (*Theologische Beurteilung*) of almost all the wicked kings (Long, *1 Kings*, 262. For example, see 1 Kgs. 15.26; 22.52, and 2 Kgs. 15.9, 24, and 28). Where the explicit formula is absent, an unmistakable description of their wickedness is ledgered, such as sinning against the Lord (1 Kgs. 16.13), being guilty of conspiracy (2 Kgs. 15.15), or killing all the royal heirs to the throne (2 Kgs. 8.27).

Even though this writer is concerned mainly with the meaning of the "death notice," the location and character of the family tomb also is important. "Lying down with one's fathers" definitely meant to be dead. The family tomb was usually one of the caves embedded in the soft white limestone rock with which Palestine is inundated.[54] Scores of pocketed spaces were cut out in proximity to one another so the expired kings could actually "sleep" with each other in a community grave.[55] Being buried with one's fathers was not reserved solely for kings. In addition, sometimes disobedience precluded one from being buried with one's fathers, as in the case of the anonymous disobedient prophet from God in 1 Kings 13. Before his death by lion attack, another prophet in Nathanic style pronounced God's judgment on him in verse twenty-two: "You came back and ate bread and drank water in the place where he told you not to eat or drink. Therefore your body will not be buried in the tomb of your fathers." This ruling is another way of saying that the man of God would meet with a vicious death outside of his community.[56]

The *TLG* search uncovered an interesting sermon or treatise by a fourth-century ecclesiastical scribe named Epiphanius. The title of the work is "Epiphanius the Holy Bishop of Cyprus Concerning the Prophets, How *They Died*

---

[53]Josiah is the only "good king" not referred to as "sleeping with his fathers." While some "bad kings" like Manasseh and Jeroboam, who did evil in the sight of the Lord and led Israel to sin, are included as sleeping with the fathers, they nevertheless died a natural death. If ethical behavior were required to sleep with the Davidic fathers, David himself and Solomon would have to be omitted because of their actions which included murder, adultery, and idolatry.

[54]John Gray, *I & II Kings*, 2d rev. ed., The Old Testament Library (Philadelphia: The Westminster Press, 1970), 88.

[55]J. Robinson, *The First Book of Kings*, The Cambridge Bible Commentary (Cambridge: Cambridge University Press, 1972), 29. Jacob, *Theology of the Old Testament*, 302, also records that tombs commonly had the appearance of wells. They were usually several yards deep and had a door which accessed a burial chamber. This picture probably assisted in their idea of Sheol (see Job 33.18). On the importance of the "House of David" motif, see S. Yeivin, "The Sepulchres of the Kings of the House of David," *Journal of Near Eastern Studies* 7 (1948): 30-45.

[56]Gray, *I & II Kings*, 331. G. H. Jones, *1 and 2 Kings*, The New Century Bible Commentary, vol. 1 (Grand Rapids: Eerdmans, 1984), 267. This was a very serious threat to any Israelite.

(ἐκοιμήθησαν) and Where *They Lie* (κεῖμαι)".[57] The title of the message contains the word ἐκοιμήθησαν which is a key element in the summary statements concerning the kings' deaths discussed above. Epiphanius believed in the literal sleep of death as he interrelated the parousia of Christ, sleeping with the fathers, Elijah the prophet, and hallowed King David asleep (κοιμάομαι) in Babylon, in peace and gloriously buried in the royal tomb.

Although the Israelites believed in some kind of existence after death, the idea of resurrection remained a slimly attested possibility. The concept of the sleep of death is highly euphemistic in tone. Since a large number of the kings, with the remarkable exception of Josiah, were believed to be banned from sleeping with their fathers because they were evil and died an unnatural death, indicates that the textual recognition and assignment of the death sleep with the fathers was a significant honor. Not only was it an honor, but it also it signified a perpetuity still in effect until the parousia.

Two Prophets and Two Harlots

Besides the regnal obituaries, κοιμάομαι also is used in three death episodes, two of which were reversals. The first instance is found in 1 Kgs. 3.20 within the story of the scheming harlot who mistakenly rolled over and crushed her infant son during the night. Ἐπεκοιμήθη serves as the cause of death in verse 19—that is, she "slept" on him. In verse 20 the writer employs ἐκοίμισεν to depict the action of "laying down" the dead boy when she switched babies with the other prostitute. The fluidity of κοιμάομαι can be seen easily in this story as death, sleeping, and lying down are associated.

---

[57]Epiphanius Constantiensis *De prophetarum vita et obitu* 4.1t-2t; 6.10-11; and 16.20-17.1. The sermon is found within this major work translated *The Life and Death of the Prophets*. Epiphanius makes use of another Greek term for death which found wide currency in Homer. Κεῖμαι can be translated to lie "asleep," "idle," "inactive," "in weakness," "in infirmity," "in old age," "sick," "wounded," and "dead." See *Iliad* 19.32, where the word means "to lie unburied," and *Iliad* 5.685, *Odyssey* 17.296 in which κεῖμαι means "to lie uncared for, neglected."

The other two occurrences are miraculous resuscitations in the Elijah and Elisha cycles. Respectively, two women, one of Zarephath and one of Shunem, experienced the death of their sons. In 1 Kgs. 17.17-24 Elijah stretched himself and breathed three times upon a boy who had died and been laid (ἐκοίμισεν) on a bed. Verses 21 and 22 present a bit of a problem as the King James Version refers to the child's "soul" returning to the body. The New International Version, however, says that the boy's "life" returned. The word under consideration is נֶפֶשׁ. One may think of this living principle as a "soul" if the idea of Greek dualism is avoided.[58]

Similarly, in verse 32 in the story of the resuscitation of the Shunnamite woman's son in 2 Kgs. 4.8-37, κοιμάομαι is used in the context of death. Actually, the word translated "dead" is τεθνηκός, and the word "was laid" is κεκοιμισμένον.[59] These prophetic interventions are technically known as "resuscitations," because the first resurrection, which means rising to die no more in its fullest sense, is defined by Jesus Christ. Secondary resurrections will occur ensuing the parousia. Any person brought back to life by an Old Testament prophet or by Jesus himself died again, thus having the rare distinction of physically dying twice but being resuscitated and resurrected once.

Strikingly similar revitalizations also occur in the New Testament. In the form of a miracle story, Jesus and the Apostle Paul functioned as Elijah/Elisha

---

[58]In reference to 1 Kgs. 17.17, debate has surfaced over whether or not the boy was actually dead (T. C. Mitchell, "The Old Testament Usage of nšmh," *Vetus Testamentum* 11 [1961]: 177-87). There is no good reason not to suppose that the boy was dead. The main interest of this researcher is the anthropological ramifications of the circumstances of death, not the episode of resurrection. The Greek writer used the term ψυχή in the LXX. Although Alexandrian Jewry probably projected some dualistic tendencies, it is advisable for one to hold to the corporate idea of the individual in Hebrew thought.

[59]Ogle, "The Sleep of Death," 90, says that this picture is reminiscent of the sleeping figures of the sarcophogi featured in the Hellenistic sepulchral art.

revidivus.⁶⁰ Jesus raised the widow's son of Nain (Luke 7.11-17), Jairus' daughter (Mark 5.21-24a, 35-43 and parallels), and Lazarus (John 11.11-14). In addition, Paul raised Eutychus (Acts 20.7-12), who had fallen asleep during the Apostle's sermon and plunged to his death.⁶¹

Jobian Thanatology

Κοιμάομαι appears seven times out of twelve as the sleep of death in the book of Job. It is important to understand the overarching contextual problem of theodicy in which this concept is cast in Job.⁶² Reflecting upon his demise, Job curses the day of his birth in 3.1-13. In verse 13 κοιμάομαι functions as an element within a "Counter-Cosmic Incantation."⁶³ Hartley compares Job's lament in 3.3-13 with the creation account in Gen. 1.1-2.4.⁶⁴ Job attempts to extinguish himself by reversing his own creation by God through the means of a spell. If successful, Job "should have lain down (κοιμηθείς) and been quiet (ἡσύχασα), slept (ὑπνώσας), and been at rest (ἀνεπαυσάμην)" (3.13, translation mine). The four Hebrew and corresponding Greek synonyms provide a window through which peripheral sleep-of-death texts may be accessed. The question is now posed whether or not the sleep-of-death metaphor is found in any text governed by one of these synonymous terms.

---

⁶⁰For a recent literary critical discussion on the miracle genre, see Gerd Theissen, *The Miracle Stories of the Early Christian Tradition*, trans. F. McDonagh (Philadelphia: The Fortress Press, 1983).

⁶¹Detailed treatment concerning these related episodes will be pursued in Chapter IV.

⁶²For an excellent treatment of this theme in relation to the story of Job, see Gustavo Gutiérrez, *On Job: God-Talk and the Suffering of the Innocent*, trans. Matthew J. O'Connell (Maryknoll, NY: Orbis Books, 1988).

⁶³John E. Hartley, *The Book of Job*, The New International Commentary on the Old Testament (Grand Rapids: Eerdmans, 1988), 101-2.

⁶⁴See ibid., 102, for comparative chart. Hartley also finds a parallel of the desire to reverse the ordering of the universe in Jer. 4.23-26. On this topic, see M. Fishbane, "Jeremiah iv:23-26 and Job iii:3-13," *Vetus Testamentum* 21 (1971): 151-67.

Following the synonymous parallelism initiated by the Hebrew text, the Greek writer intended for all four words to reflect death in the same fashion. These four terms mirror the Hebrew שָׁכַב, שָׁקַט, יָשֵׁן, and נוּחַ respectively. While κοιμάομαι is used to translate שָׁכַב (sixty-four times) when referring to the sleep of death, it is never used for the other three. As has already been seen, however, κοιμάομαι is not the only word used in this way. Two other terms which will be added to the pool of the synonymous sleep-of-death phraseology are ἡσυχάζω and παύω. Both of these words are used interchangeably to translate שָׁקַט, which is rendered variously in nondeath texts as "peace" (e.g., the land had *peace* for eighty years, Judg. 3.30), "safety," "quiet," "rest," "silent," "unconcerned," and "subside."[65] Of all its occurrences it points to death only in Job 3.13 and can be taken as a synonym of שָׁכַב, thus allowing the semantic fields of ἡσυχάζω and παύω to intersect with κοιμάομαι at least in partial synonymy.

נוּחַ is usually translated with a form of παύω in the LXX. Like שָׁקַט, it is used primarily in nondeath situations. In addition to the verse under consideration in Job, there are three other instances in which the verb form of παύω refers to death as a rest:

> There (i.e., Sheol) the wicked cease from turmoil,
> and there the weary are *at rest* (Job 3.17).
>
> A man who strays from the path of understanding
> *comes to rest* in the company of the dead (Prov. 21.16).[66]
>
> As for you, go your way till the end. You *will rest*,
> and then at the end of your days you will rise to
> receive your allotted inheritance (Dan. 12.13).

נוּחַ/παύω also surfaces in Isa. 57.2. Several interesting features present themselves. First, the translation based on the Hebrew reflects a different source than the translation based on the LXX, as can be seen below.

---

[65]See Lisowsky, *Konkordanz*, s.v., "שָׁקַט" for tabulations.

[66]LXX has "giants" (γιγάντων) for the term "dead."

English translation based on Hebrew

Those who walk uprightly enter into peace;
they find *rest* as they lie in death/rest upon their couches.[67]

English translation based on LXX

His burial shall be in peace;
he has been removed out of the way.[68]

Secondly, the phrase "in death" is מִשְׁכְּבוֹתָם, which is translated "couch" or "bed" in forty-three out of forty-six cases.[69] It is evident that the Septuagintal author did not even consider the Masoretic text at this point. Sixty-four times the author chose a form of κοιμάομαι to translate שָׁכַב. In this case, the Masoretic text reading or one of the Greek versions should be selected over the LXX. The influence of this Hebrew noun can be seen since it is fairly certain that Jerome's translation is closer to the original Hebrew, as he renders מִשְׁכְּבוֹתָם with the Latin *cubile*, "the couch of death" or "bier." The same Hebrew noun appears in Ezek. 32.25[70] and in 2 Chr. 16.14 with reference to King Asa lying dead in the death vault.[71]

מִשְׁכָּב also appears in the apocryphal writing of Sirach composed in Hebrew during the first third of the second century B.C. The Greek translator used the noun κοίμησις to translate מִשְׁכָּב in Sir. 46.19 and 48.13. In this respect, κοίμησις is a *hapax legomenon* in the LXX. This fact is interesting in the first place

---

[67]The phrase "rest upon their couches" is an alternate translation of מִשְׁכְּבוֹתָם.

[68]The *Vorlage* of this verse is in question because the LXX has: "His burial shall be in peace; he has been removed out of the way."

[69]See Lisowsky, *Konkordanz*, s.v. "מִשְׁכָּב." Ogle, "The Sleep of Death," 91, points out that Aquila was closer to the original: Ἐλθέτω ἐν εἰρήνῃ, ἀναπαυσάσθωσαν ἐπὶ κοιτῶν αὐτῶν. The versions of Symmachus and Theodotion are essentially the same as Aquila's. Also consult the translation of L. Fillion, *La Sainte Bible commentée d'après la vulgata*, 8th ed. (Paris: Letouzey, 1925), 482: "Il (le juste) entrera dans la paix, il reposera sur sa couche (funèbre)."

[70]Κοιμάομαι as the sleep of death surfaces nine times exclusively in "Sheol's Hall of Fame and Shame" in Ezekiel 31 and 32. See Appendix B for references.

[71]This passage, 2 Sam. 3.31, and Luke 7.14 are the only three passages in the Bible to refer to a "bier."

because, as has been shown, the underlying Hebrew term surfaces in Isa. 57.2, Ezek. 32.25, and 2 Chr. 16.14 but not translated with the Greek noun seen in Sirach. Secondly, as Ogle points out, this use of κοίμησις would not have been customary when the early portions of the LXX were written.[72] Thirdly, the presentation of κοίμησις is significant because the euphemistic comprehension of the sleep of death is inching ever closer to the full-blown New Testament idea of a metaphorical connection between the concepts of sleep and death. This theme is also expressed synonymously in Sir. 46.20. In this instance the Vulgate retains *dormire*, while ὑπνόω and ישׁן now serve as the Greek and Hebrew counterparts.[73]

In a related text, the Hellenistic Jewish writer of 2 Macc. 12.45 describes a sacrifice designed by Judas for those slain in battle who "rest" (κοιμάομαι) in godliness. The vital nature of this verse resides in the thematic continuation of the death sleep idea and especially in the interpretation of the term *dormitionem acceperant*, which is pointedly used in alliance with the noun *dormitio* in the special sense of "death."

This first example in Job 3.13 is important initially because the registry for "sleep-of-death" terminology has grown to five. Secondly, the use of four words to capture Job's deep desire to have been "still born" expresses the intensity of the lamentation. Job offers this jeremiad as the only solution to his misery.[74] The vigorous ambition to be in Sheol is another revealing factor which displays Job's severe melancholy because Sheol was thought of as a place of gloom, despair, and darkness.[75]

---

[72]Ogle, "The Sleep of Death," 92.

[73]Ὑπνόω never translates שָׁכַב and κοιμάομαι never translates ישׁן in the LXX, yet both combinations express the sleep of death. See Appendix E for tabulations.

[74]Hartley, *The Book of Job*, 102.

[75]Norman C. Habel, *The Book of Job*, The Old Testament Library (Philadelphia: The Westminster Press, 1985), 110.

The second incident involving κοιμάομαι as the sleep of death is in Job 14.12. Like the previous example, both κοιμάομαι and ὕπνος occur corresponding with שָׁכַב and יָשֵׁן, respectively.[76] Crucial to this discussion is the discovery of the differences in the theological stock of the Masoretic and Greek text traditions. This divergence has been convincingly demonstrated by those who see an exegetical methodology employed by the Greek translator. This method is built on a theological interpretation of a Hebrew text comparable to that behind the Masoretic text.[77] Recognizing the existence of this principle will equip one to understand the Greek author's use of κοιμάομαι more clearly.

Although Job dabbles with the possibility of resurrection in this verse, the main thrust is aimed in the direction of the nature of death, which Job compares with the possibility of either the water in the sea or a large lake running dry.[78] For Job it was just as inconceivable for someone to return from the dead as it was for the Jordan River or the Dead Sea to evaporate. Eschatology was, therefore, not Job's primary interest. By denying the oblique category of resurrection as an available avenue of escape from his personal crisis, Job exposed the painful prospect of his condition. Death was permanent.[79] All of this preceding viewpoint

---

[76]See Appendixes B and C.

[77]See Harry M. Orlinsky, "The Hebrew and Greek Texts of Job 14.12," *Jewish Quarterly Review* 28 (1937-38): 57-68.

[78]Trying to evaluate Job's thanatology at this point is aided by the fact that Is. 26.19 and Dan. 12.2, the most unambiguous resurrection passages in the Old Testament, employ similar phraseology for resurrection. Life, not death, is what is difficult for Job at this point. From the viewpoint of the Masoretic text, no concept of resurrection was operative when Job was written. The author, therefore, stacks words associated with the idea of "awakening from sleep" in order to express the proposed reversal. On this idea, see J. G. Thomson, "Sleep: An Aspect of Jewish Anthropology," 420-33. It should be pointed out, however, that some theologians believe Israel did have a resurrection theology. For this position, see Francis I. Andersen, *Job*, Tyndale Old Testament Commentaries (Downers Grove, IL: InterVarsity Press, 1976), 55.

[79]Habel, *The Book of Job*, 242. L. Bailey, *Biblical Perspectives on Death* (Philadelphia: Fortress Press, 1979), 54, emphasizes the "mortality-accepting" tone present in Israel's canonical literature. Marvin Pope, *Job*, 3d ed., The Anchor Bible (Garden City, NY: Doubleday & Co., 1983), 108, compares Job 14.12b with a line from Sophocle's *Electra* 138: "But from the all-receptive lake of Death you shall not raise him, groan and pray as you will."

is, however, based upon the Hebrew expectation. When the Greek text is examined one finds that its author was much more optimistic with respect to eschatology. A comparison between the translations of the Hebrew and Greek texts of Job 14.14 illustrates this difference.

> (MT) If a man dies, will he live again?
> All the days of my service would I wait,
> Until my relief should come.
>
> (LXX) For if a man dies, he will live,
> Having completed the days of his life;
> I will abide until I be born again.[80]

While the Hebrew merely raises the question concerning life after death, the Greek expresses it as factual. This emphasis is supported and exerted by the presence of κοιμάομαι in verse 12. While this term is used to accentuate a reformed Greek thanatological idea of the sleep of death, its Hebrew counterpart, שָׁכַב, leans more toward the idea of the sleep of death with no subsequent arousal.

The Greek translator inserts κοιμάομαι into the mouth of Zophar, one of Job's counselors, to exhibit the same thanatological beliefs as Job in 20.11. Κοιμάομαι tones down the harsher concept of the sleep of death twice in a major segment in which Job caustically and vigorously addresses the theme of suffering as compared with the prosperity of the wicked (21.13, 26).[81] Verse 13 is peculiar because the Greek translator breaks the normal pattern of using κοιμάομαι exclusively for שָׁכַב. Instead, κοιμάομαι is employed to translate the Aramaic נחת. The introduction of ἀνεπαυσάμην in 3.13 is revealing because now the idea of "rest" and "death" are paralleled. Later in 3.23a θάνατος and ἀνάπαυμα are in a predicate complement

---

[80]Comparison based upon translations and comment by Donald H. Gard, "The Concept of the Future Life according to the Greek Translator of the Book of Job," *Journal of Biblical Literature* 73 (1954): 137-38. Gard examines other death passages which pertain to the future life. For more extensive coverage of this subject, see idem, *The Exegetical Method of the Greek Translator of the Book of Job*, SBLMS (Philadelphia: Society of Biblical Literature, 1952). Also, consult H. S. Gehman, "The Theological Approach of the Greek Translator of Job 1-15," *Journal of Biblical Literature* 68 (1949): 231-40.

[81]Homer Heater, *A Septuagint Translation Technique in the Book of Job*, CBQMS (Washington, DC: The Catholic Biblical Association of America, 1982), 44-45.

construction. At this point the Masoretic text and LXX are slightly divergent. As is the case with many anaphoric translations in Job, the author is paraphrasing with the difficult appearance of ἀνάπαυμα.⁸²

The verb ἀναπαύσει occurs with ἐκοιμήθησαν in 21.13b and the whole verse is translated, "And they finish their life in prosperity and 'lie down' (ἐκοιμήθησαν) 'in the rest' (ἀναπαύσει) of Hades." The Masoretic text is translated: "They finish their days in prosperity and peacefully go down to Sheol." According to Heater, the translator takes ἀνάπαυμα from 21.13b and plugs it into 3.23a where the Hebrew is totally ignored.⁸³ The "rest in Sheol" is, therefore, pressed into service as the same concept of θάνατος in 3.23a. Even though the translator elected to go above and beyond the call of translational duty, נָחַת (go down) and שָׁכַב (lie down) are in the same semantic field of intention. Perhaps the Greek translator was surprised by the absence of שָׁכַב.

The last two usages of κοιμάομαι appear in verses 19 and 20 in a section devoted to the impending requital of the wicked in Zophar's third discourse of 27.13-23. Κοιμάομαι is used in a death text in verse 19 and clearly alludes to the death of the rich man. Lying down in death was his last act: "He lies down (κοιμηθήσεται) wealthy, but will do so no more." It is better to take the reading of the LXX on the second phrase because the Masoretic Text "he is not gathered" contradicts the foregoing verses.⁸⁴

A larger textual problem exists in verse twenty. Hatch and Redpath shows no Hebrew equivalent for the aorist passive participial form κοιμηθέντι. Alexandrinus retains the reading, while it is omitted by Vaticanus and Sinaiticus which both supply the variant συναντήσονται translated as "come upon him."⁸⁵ There is no

---

⁸²Ibid. Here the theology of the translator is usurping authority.

⁸³Ibid. Comparison based upon Heater's translation.

⁸⁴Hartley, *The Book of Job*, 358, n. 10; Pope, *Job*, 193-94; and Habel, *The Book of Job*, 387.

⁸⁵M. Dahood, "Hebrew-Ugaritic Lexicography VII," *Biblica* 50 (1969): 342.

Hebrew word to support κοιμηθέντι in this verse. Theologically, the Greek author, therefore, may have been attempting to draw a thematic parallel with κοιμάομαι in verse 19.

Some conclusions can be drawn from the assignment of κοιμάομαι in Job's thanatology. Grammatically, the six appearances of κοιμάομαι in Job as the death sleep are equivalent to שָׁכַב each time except in 21.13 where the Aramaic נָחֵת is used. Κοιμάομαι and שָׁכַב still prove to be as consistently coordinated with each other as previous citations. This equivalency is not surprising because, for the greatest part, the Greek text of Job has been shown to be an extremely loyal translation of the Hebrew.[86] Many of the textual studies by Harry Orlinsky have demonstrated that the translator labored to coordinate the Hebrew into Greek with meticulous care except when theology differed. It is the conclusion of the textual critics that there was a common *Vorlage* behind both the Hebrew and Greek texts and that its subsequent rendering into Hebrew and Greek are skewed at the point of the possibility of the afterlife. While the Hebrew writer is somewhat Stoic in his response about death being the ultimate panacea of Job's ills, the Greek author offers the prospect of resurrection as the answer to the problem.[87]

Theologically, while the scent of the pagan pessimism which surrounded the prospect of death lingers in Hebrew Job, Greek Job offers a more optimistic sleep of death without the dualistic tendencies of Athens. The theological bias of the Greek translator is an issue which is debated sympathetically today. Even so, there appears to be no divergence in theology between the Masoretic text or the

---

[86]Confer the diverse treatments by H. Orlinsky, "Studies in the Septuagint of the Book of Job," *Hebrew Union College Annual* 28 (1957): 53-74; 29 (1958): 229-71; 30 (1959): 153-67; 32 (1961): 239-68; 33 (1962): 119-51; 35 (1964): 57-78. Greek Job is not, however, without its problems. For these difficulties, see idem, "Some Corruptions in the Greek Text of Job," *Jewish Quarterly Review* 26 (1935-36): 133-45. Although Orlinsky has provided these important textual studies, textual critics should still consult the dependable textual apparatus developed by E. Dhorme, in *A Commentary on the Book of Job*, trans. H. Knight, repr. ed. (Nashville: Nelson Press, 1984).

[87]Gard, "Concept of a Future Life," 143.

LXX which would affect the concept of the sleep of death in Job with the exception of the positive eschatological expectancy in the LXX. The concept of Sheol (Hades) is congruent with the idea of death being a sleep, which to the greatest degree at this point, in comparison with the rest of the Old Testament, is an eternal sleep. Although this dissertation is not acutely interested in the subsequent idea of resurrection, one's concept of resurrection determines to a great deal what one's thanatology will be. Although death and Sheol were welcomed by Hebrew Job, ontologically it remained the lesser of two evils. The Greek writer, on the other hand, strives to incorporate the hope of the resurrection into the equation by engaging concepts associated with κοιμάομαι, the "not final" sleep of death.

The Sleep of Death Expressed by Synonymous Phraseology in the LXX

The same trio of Greek terms which banded to convey the notion of the sleep of death in the Homeric period repeat their efforts in the Hellenistic period with even more force. While the applicability of κοιμάομαι by far exceeds καθεύδω and ὑπνόω, they materialize in some dynamic texts which appear more grammatically forceful. Bipolar thanatological perspectives are present as the two-termination adjective αἰώνιον is utilized both in prophetic and apocalyptic narratives.

Jer. 51.39 (28.39 LXX) contains the pregnant clause ὑπνώσωσιν ὕπνον αἰώνιον ("they sleep an eternal sleep"). Ὕπνον functions as a cognate accusative in a convincingly gloomy forecast concerning the death of Babylon. This poetic statement is echoed in verse 57 of the same chapter. Comparatively, the translator of Dan. 12.2 casts καθεύδω in a highly positive light:

> Multitudes who *sleep* (καθεύδω) in the dust of the earth *will awake* (ἐχεγερθήσονται); some to *everlasting* (αἰώνιον) life, others to shame and some to *everlasting* (αἰώνιον) contempt.[88]

---

[88]See the New Testament echo of this verse in John 5.28-29.

Remarkable is the synonymous use of καθεύδω and the antonymous use of αἰώνιον in comparison with the texts cited in Jeremiah.[89] The fact that Daniel was probably written later and is extremely apocalyptic in tone lends some assistance for evaluating the neutrality of αἰώνιον. Whether taken negatively or positively, death is nevertheless described as a sleep. Another valuable area of sleep-of-death inquiry in the LXX is in relation to the Psalms. These occurrences are crucial for two reasons. Psalms played a prominent role in the worship of the early Christian church, and all three of the synonyms under consideration for the sleep of death are tapped equally to voice the idea. Ogle falsely attributes Ps. 3.5(6) and 4.8(9) to the death sleep.[90] It is easy to determine this difference when a comparison is made with the true sleep-of-death passages:

13(12).3b: Give light to my eyes, or I will *sleep* (ὑπνώσω) in death.[91]

41(40).8b: He will never get up from the place *he lies* (κοιμώμενος).

76(75).5a: Valiant men lie plundered, they *sleep* (ὕπνωσαν) their last *sleep* (ὕπνον).[92]

88(87).5a,b: I am set apart with the dead, like the slain *who lie* (καθεύδω) in the grave.

---

[89]Compare Sir. 46.19; the memorial inscription of Antiochus I of Commagene whose body εἰς τὸν ἄπειρον αἰῶνα κοιμήσεται (Wilhelm Dittenberger, ed., *Orientis graecae inscriptiones selectae*, Supplementum Sylloges inscriptionum graecarum [Leipzig: S. Hirzel, 1903-1905]; and the inscription κοιμᾶται τὸν αἰώνιον ὕπνον (J. G. Milne, *Inscriptiones Graecae nunc Cairo*, 14.929).

[90]Ogle, "Sleep of Death," 90-91. These verses may be the basis for the common children's Platonic bedtime prayer which runs: "Now I lay me down to sleep, I pray the Lord my soul to keep. If I should die before I wake, I pray the Lord my soul to take." Although physical sleep certainly emulates physical death, the writer of these psalmic verses is emphasizing the sustaining power of God to awaken the physical sleeper. Psalms suggests no apocalyptic arousal of any death sleepers. For the patristic evaluation of the death sleep in Psalms, see Athanasius *Expositiones in Psalmos* 27.69.42,3-27.521.36,7 passim. Basilius *Homiliae super Psalmos* 29.296.35-6, and Eusebius of Caesarea *Commentaria in Psalmos* 24.72.18-22 compare the dead Thessalonian Christians to King David sleeping with his fathers. Κοιμάομαι appears many times throughout these excerpts.

[91]In a cognate sense, the Hebrew is expressed more powerfully with the prefixing of the noun with the article ה. The phrase הַיְשַׁן הַמָּוֶת can be translated "I sleep the sleep (repeated because of the ה) of death."

[92]Ὕπνωσαν is based on the Hebrew נום in this instance.

67

The last example of the sleep of death in the LXX is a *hapax legomenon*. Nah. 3.18 is the only example in the Minor Prophets that utilizes the sleep-of-death phraseology under investigation.[93]

Pseudepigraphal Citations

Κοιμάομαι appears sporadically in the pseudepigraphal literature while the sleep-of-death metaphor is well attested. The most frequent use of κοιμάομαι is in the *Sibylline Oracles* which are dated from 2 B.C. to A.D. 4. Five appearances of various forms of κοιμάομαι occur in the same work, *Oracula*, but are not in reference to the sleep of death. The idea of the sleep of death and immortality, however, is presented by the *midrashic* pre-Christian Jewish writing, *Life of Adam and Eve*, probably written sometime in Palestine toward the close of the first century A.D.[94] The contents of Adam and Eve 3.1-4 suggest an imperishability. Kaiser explains that this conviction is based on the first page of the Mosaic law (Gen. 1.26-27 and the *Imago Dei*).[95] The supposed logic undergirding this assumption hinges on the conditional assertion, if God is imperishable, then so is man. The rare noun κοιμήσεως and the verb ἐκοιμᾶτο surface in a section concerning the burial of Adam's body.

> While living, she herself wept about her *death* (κοιμήσεως), because she did not know where her body was to be placed. For while the Lord was in Paradise when they buried Adam, both she and her children *slept* (ἐκοιμᾶτο), except for Seth, as I said.[96]

---

[93]See Appendix B, n. 9. While Ralph Smith, *Micah-Malachi*, Word Biblical Commentary (Waco: Word Books, Publisher, 1984), 90, considers the possibility that this sleep reference may mean that the king of Assyria's officers are dead, it at least means that they are deactivated.

[94]This work survives in Latin and Greek texts which assuredly are based on a Hebrew original. The Latin text appears with the title "The Life of Adam and Eve" while the title "The Apocalypse of Moses" reflects the Greek text (D. S. Russell, *The Old Testament Pseudepigrapha: Patriarchs & Prophets in Early Judaism* [Philadelphia: Fortress Press, 1987], 15).

[95]Otto Kaiser and Eduard Lohse, *Death and Life*, 20-30.

[96]*Adam and Eve* 42.5-6; 7-9. For text, see James H. Charlesworth, *The Old Testament Pseudepigrapha*, vol. 1 (Garden City, NY: Doubleday & Company, Inc., 1985), 295.

Clearly, death is categorized as sleep here. At the conclusion of this work, however, a curious anthropological clue is uncovered as the writer says: "Therefore after she prayed, she looked up to heaven, rose, beat her breast, and said, 'God of all, receive my spirit.' And immediately she gave up her spirit to God" (42.8). The ideas in this writing are undoubtedly composed under the influence of Greek ideas.[97] A significant point is that Adam's body is buried in the earthly Paradise. Whether there is any connection between the body on earth and that which is in Paradise is hazy. Supposedly, the heavenly body awaits the resurrection but is coexistent with the physical body until that time.[98] This distinction is hard to determine because Jewish writings are either in step with traditional ideas about Sheol or lean heavily in the direction of Greek idealism.[99]

The same work offering a topographical description of Sheol also contains the most explicit chapter concerning thanatological beliefs during this period. Esdras 7 contains the question and its answer concerning the intermediate state. An extended quote illustrates the point:

> Now, concerning death, the teaching is: when the decisive decree has gone forth from the Most High that a man shall die, as the spirit leaves the body to return again to him who gave it, first of all it adores the glory of the Most High. And if it is one of those who have shown scorn and have not kept the way of the Most High, and who have hated those who fear God—such spirits shall not enter the habitations, but shall immediately wander about in torments, ever grieving and sad, in seven ways.[100]

---

[97]D. S. Russell, *Between the Testaments* (Philadelphia: Fortress Press, 1960), 155.

[98]Ibid.

[99]Cooper, *Body, Soul, & Life Everlasting*, 83. He lists the most systematic and comprehensive appraisal of this literature by H. C. C. Cavallin, *Life after Death: Paul's Argument for the Resurrection of the Dead in 1 Corinthians; Part 1; An Enquiry into the Jewish Background* (Lund: Gleerup, 1974). Cavallin investigates the Apocrypha, Pseudepigrapha, diaspora materials, Rabbinica, Targums, and tomb inscriptions. This methodology is the same this writer is following for the investigation of κοιμάομαι in order to acquire any insights which will shed light on the monist-dualist problem encountered in the postmortem state.

[100]2 Esdras 78-80, Revised Standard Version. This translation is provided by E. Isaac in J. Charlesworth, ed., *The Old Testament Pseudepigrapha*; quoted in Cooper, *Body, Soul, & Life Everlasting*, 90-91.

Elements emerging from this thanatology include a dualistic model and consequential judgment.

The sleep-of-death metaphor is exercised with a deeper interest in the Pseudepigrapha than in the LXX. Personal consciousness is a consistent characteristic attending an individual during death. Several of these are important for this study. While the righteous are enduring "long sleep" in 1 Enoch 100.5, the souls of the righteous are joyfully anticipating a terminus to the interval period in 1 Enoch 102.4-5.[101] Notice the arresting similarities shared by the next four quotes from the Pseudepigrapha, the Old Testament, and the New Testament:

Jub. 23.31: Their bones will rest in the earth, and their spirits will have great joy.[102]

2 Esd. 7.32: The earth shall give up those who are asleep in it, and the dust those who dwell silently in it; and the chambers shall give up the souls which have been committed to them.[103]

Dan. 12.2: Multitudes who sleep in the dust of the earth will awake: some to everlasting life, others to shame and everlasting contempt.

Jn. 5.28-29: Do not be amazed at this, for a time is coming when all who are in their graves will hear his voice and come out--those who have done good will rise to live, and those who have done evil will rise to be condemned.

From this comparison it is easy to see how important and illuminating noncanonical documents are for a complete picture of the sleep-of-death metaphor in the New Testament.

Philo and Josephus

While κοιμάομαι appears in the writings of Josephus (A.D. 37-100) in relation to the idea of physical sleep, it is never used for the sleep of death. That Josephus was a historian certainly would grant him the opportunity to be aware of postmortem issues. Wedding his anthropology and thanatology, Josephus delineates

---

[101]Michel, "Zur Lehre vom Todesschlaf," 287, reports that the common words for the sleep of death in the pseudepigraphal writings are κοιμάομαι and καθεύδω, which are both equated with life to God.

[102]Revised Standard Version translation.

[103]Revised Standard Version translation.

the concept of the immortality of the soul as he places the following oration in the mouth of the Zealots' leader at Masada as an incentive to commit suicide:

> For from of old . . . we have been continually taught by those precepts, ancestral and divine-- confirmed by the deeds and noble spirit of our fathers that life, not death, is man's misfortune. For it is death which gives liberty to the soul and permits it to depart to its own pure abode, there to be free from all calamity; but so long as it is imprisoned in a mortal body and tainted with all its miseries, it is, in sober truth, dead, for association with what is mortal ill befits that which is divine. True, the soul possesses great capacity, even while incarcerated in the body; for it makes the latter its organ of perfection, invisibly swaying in and directing it onward in its actions beyond the range of mortal nature. But it is not until, freed from the weight that drags it down to earth and clings about it, the soul is restored to its proper sphere, that it enjoys a blessed energy and a power untrammelled on every side, remaining, like God himself, invisible to human eyes.[104]

In addition, Josephus was conscious of the teachings of the Sadducees of New Testament fame, who denied the resurrection. Making a subjective evaluation on the debate, he likened the Sadducees to Epicurean materialists whose thanatological model also was stamped with an annihilistic trademark.[105] Death was extinction for them.

Philo (20 B.C. - A.D. 50), on the other hand, retains some intriguing usages of κοιμάομαι which may offer a clue for the personal interpretation of his thanatology. In the natural sense, the word appears twice in his *Legum allegoria* in relation to the sexual plottings of Potiphar's wife planned for Joseph in Genesis 39. In *De somnia*, κοιμάομαι is employed heavily in reference to physical sleep.

A penchant for Platonic dualism is unquestionably sprinkled throughout much of his writings. It should be remembered that in the Hellenistic period Philo probably comes closer to having a philosophical viewpoint more than any other writer. Dualism, it appears, fits nicely into his allegorical model. Philo takes κοιμάομαι and negates it with an α privative in order to create a term which can

---

[104]Josephus, *The Wars of the Jews* 7.8.7; quoted in E. E. Urbach, *The Sages—Their Concepts and Beliefs*, trans. Israel Abrahams (Jerusalem: The Magnes Press, 1975), 222.

[105]For the doctrinal comparisons see, Josephus *The Jewish Wars* 2.8.2 and *Antiquities of the Jews* 18.1.2; quoted in Cooper, *Body, Soul, & Life Everlasting*, 84. This Sadducean belief probably was not peculiar, but an imported innovation from Zoroastrianism (F. F. Bruce, *New Testament History* [Garden City, NY: Doubleday & Co., 1972], 74).

be translated "sleepless," or "unsleeping." A touch of Platonism can be seen in citations referring to this mind that never sleeps.[106]

The sleep-of-death motif emerges in his allegorical rendition of the book of Genesis:

> A man may counter the arguments just mentioned by saying that according to it the wise man will never be melancholy, never *fall asleep* (κοιμηθήσεται), in a word never *die* (ἀποθανεῖται)."[107]

Belief in the immortality of the soul is standard for Philo. This Platonic concept can be seen clearly in his comments on Gen. 2.17 which says: "But you must not eat from the tree of the knowledge of good and evil, for when you eat of it you will surely die." In his allegorical attempt to interpret this "penalty-death" he says:

> That one is in the course of nature in which soul is parted from body; but the penalty-death takes place when the soul dies to the life of virtue, and is alive only to that of wickedness. That is an excellent saying of Heracleitus, who on this point followed Moses' teaching, "We live," he says, "their death, and are dead to their life." He means that now, when we are living, the soul is dead and has been *entombed in the body* or in a sepulchre; whereas, should we die, the soul lives forthwith its own proper life, and is released from the body, the *baneful* corpse to which it was tied (emphasis mine).[108]

Conclusion

While the LXX, Apocrypha, and Pseudepigrapha provide a diverse, fairly distributed representation of the sleep of death concept, the LXX by far contains the most instances. Particularly in Job, the Greek translator has attempted to recast the pessimistic tone of the Masoretic text with regard to death. The Greek author definitely found some Hebrew ideas offensive to him and exercised

---

[106] Compare the "unsleeping mind" in *De mutatione nominum* 5.1-2; the "eye that never sleeps" in ibid., 40.3; the "unsleeping senses" in *De Abrahamos* 162.1-2; the "unsleeping wakefulness" in *De Josepho* 147.2-3; the "unsleeping eyes of the soul" in *De vita Mosis* 1.289.2-3; and the "vigilant eye" in ibid., 1.185.1-2.

[107] *De Plantatione* 177.2-3. Translation in T. E. Page, E. Capps, and W. H. D. Rouse, eds., *Philo*, vol. 3, trans. F. H. Colson and G. H. Whitaker, Loeb Classical Library (New York: G. P. Putnam's Sons, 1930), 305. See similar phraseology also in ibid., 177.7.

[108] *Legum allegoria* 1.105-8. Translation in T. E. Page, *Philo*, vol. 10, 217-19.

measures to express them in more palatable terms. While the theological intentions of an author can be debated, it does not alter the primary interest of this thesis—that is, death is viewed as a sleep, whether or not eschatological arousal is the case. The notion of the sleep of death in the Homeric and Hellenistic period denotes the condition of death, not the act.

The LXX is also important in the respect that it was the Bible of the disciples and the early Christian church. The data reviewed in this chapter must have exerted a heavy influence on early Christian thinking, especially when they heard Jesus' words or read Paul's letters which both incorporated the terminology and attendant concept in question. Structurally, there must be clues which will reveal the early Christians' mind-set which controlled their responses. Chapter IV will provide the opportunity to explore more deeply the ramifications of the leverage the LXX wielded on their interpretations. The transformation process from euphemism to metaphor has begun.

The apocryphal and pseudepigraphal writings present a wide spectrum of thanatological beliefs, ranging from annihilationism to the permanent separation and survival of the immortal soul from the body.[109] An extremely important commonality that they share with the writings in the LXX is that the antithetical posture of Greek idealism and Gnosticism is acutely absent. To them, mind/soul is not the measure of all things as it is with idealism or phenomenalism. This writer is in agreement with Cooper's assessment that these writings share a common denominator of what he designates as "wholistic dualism."[110]

Those who strive to avoid dualism, such as E. Earle Ellis, may be overreacting to the supposed influential power of Hellenism. In actuality, this writer believes Ellis wants to be monistic, but his model nevertheless demands a dualistic

---

[109] For the best treatments of this literature, see George Nickelsburg, Jr., *Resurrection, Immortality, and Eternal Life in Intertestamental Judaism* (Cambridge: Harvard University Press, 1972); idem, *Jewish Literature between the Bible and the Mishnah* (Philadelphia: Fortress Press, 1981); and Donald Gowan, *Bridge between the Testaments* (Pittsburgh: Pickwick Press, 1976).

[110] Cooper, *Body, Soul, & Life Everlasting*, 103.

interpretation because a deceased individual cannot entertain two ontic states which eclipse the intermediate state simultaneously. While it is not denied that Hellenism definitely influenced the writers of the intertestamental period, it does not necessarily follow that any kind of dualism is categorically tainted. As Cooper maintains, anthropologically one can retain the functional integration of human life consistent with the Hebrew mind and thanatologically not be required to dismiss a postmortem dualism. Something does happen at death, which evidently is anthropologically flawed and foggy, yet is not over until the resurrection. Christians can embrace a dualism which is not Platonic, that is, not a body-demeaning, soul-glorifying paradigm.

The intensity of sleep-of-death terminology mushroomed in the Hellenistic period. In addition, a notable shift occurred in the Apocrypha, Pseudepigrapha, and LXX which demarcated its writings from the pessimistically profane. During this age the concept of immortality achieved a new prominence in Jewish texts. Murray J. Harris has conveniently compiled lists representing three categories of thought in regard to the immortality of the soul: 1) texts which offer exclusive reference; 2) texts which are juxtaposed devoid of any attempt to harmonize the two; and 3) texts which seek to harmonize through appeal to the concept of an "intermediate state."[111] Although some of these writings are not considered canonical, they nevertheless serve as key touchstones for the New Testament interpretation of this metaphor. Once one entertains the New Testament documents, the sleep-of-death semantic field is drastically reduced to episodes describing physical sleep or death, while κοιμάομαι is used to the greatest extent as a metaphor for death.

---

[111] Murray J. Harris, *From Grave to Glory*, 70-74.

CHAPTER III

THE SEMANTIC DOMAIN IN HEBREW AND ARAMAIC

Old Testament Witnesses

Instead of a rehearsal of all the Old Testament writings reviewed in Chapter II under the heading of the LXX, a careful examination of the Hebrew and Aramaic semantic field which conveys the sleep-of-death motif will be conducted.[1] Other Old Testament texts which deal with the concept of the discarnate state will be analyzed in order to determine whether any similarities exist within the established synonymous semantic field.

Major Semitic Terms Depicting the Sleep of Death

שָׁכַב

It has already been validated that שָׁכַב is the principal term used in sleep-of-death contexts. It is also the case that κοιμάομαι is used to translate this term almost exclusively in sleep-of-death passages in the LXX. שָׁכַב exhibits the same kind of polysemic versatility as does κοιμάομαι. שָׁכַב is translated eighty-two times as "lie down," including one time in Job 38.37 as "tip over."[2] Some of these

---

[1]See Appendix E for Semitic synonymous terminology which parallels the Greek synonymous semantic pool in relationship to the sleep-of-death concept.

[2]Hiphil stem.

instances occur in death contexts such as the resuscitations performed in the Elijah/Elisha cycles treated in Chapter II. Technically, this writer has included them because occasionally the rhetorical device of paronomasia was employed to communicate forcefully the message of the text. These word plays usually are not detected in English. It is certain, however, that the written or spoken word would have easily culled the necessary word associations sharply into focus in the Hebrew mind. Consider the cognate expression in 2 Chr. 16.14 in reference to the death and burial of King Asa: וַיַּשְׁכִּיבֻהוּ בַּמִּשְׁכָּב ". . . they laid him on the bier." Functioning in synonymous parallelism with this phrase is the expression which precedes it in the same verse. It also contains a cognate phrase וַיִּקְבְּרֻהוּ בְקִבְרֹתָיו translated "they buried him in a tomb." These two phrases working together paint a vivid thanatological picture which includes the objects "tomb" and "bier" and the actions of "burial" and "lying down." The idea of the sleep of death can easily be deduced from this image.

Although lying down implies physical sleep, שָׁכַב is translated only seven times in this manner in the New International Version. The term is rendered nine times in reference to rape; twice regarding acts of bestiality; four times simply associated with rest; and twice it assumes the noun form "bed" (2 Sam. 13.5 and 2 Kgs. 4.21). The semantic agility of שָׁכַב is masterfully revealed in 2 Samuel 11. Irony and the infliction of guilt appear to be the motive of the writer in the sad tale of David and Bathsheba's adultery shadowed by Urriah the Hittite's display of noble devotion. In four separate verses the term alternately relates the "sleep of sex" with "the sleep of slumber." Though David "slept" (v. 4) with Bathsheba, Urriah would only "sleep" (v. 9) at the entrance of the palace.

Questionable occurrences aside, שָׁכַב appears as the sleep of death fifty-eight times, mostly with the major pattern sentence שָׁכַב עִם אֲבֹתָיו found heavily in

Kings and Chronicles.³ G. R. Driver's inquiry into the phrase yields some interesting points.⁴ In the first place, the term שָׁכַב means both "to be dead" and "to lie in the grave" in the pure sense of the word.⁵ Although this technical phrase at one time may have been associated with a deposit in the family grave, Driver explains that this usage is not true in the biblical sense. Joseph and Moses are reported as "about to sleep with their fathers" yet not in the family grave.⁶

Sometimes inclusion in the family grave is categorically repudiated. Compare the parallel reports of the death of Ahaz in 2 Kgs. 16.20 and 2 Chr. 28.27. Both references incorporate the facts of Ahaz "resting with his fathers" and being buried in the holy city. The chronicler, however, makes a point that "he was not placed in the tombs of the kings of Israel."

Secondly, שָׁכַב עִם אֲבֹתָיו is equivalent to death. Contextually, the phrase is never in the company of the most common word for death, מוּת, or any of the synonyms in its semantic field. Thirdly, this specialized locution is used as the common lot of kings unless they met with a violent death. The only exception provided by the Old Testament is Ahab, who died an ignominious death but still "rested with his fathers."⁷ Nicholas Tromp's conclusion is correct:

> ... the fixed formula is an indirect *testimonium pietatis*: in Israel an untimely death was considered a certain consequence of a bad life. Simply "to die," applied to kings in Kings

---

³For further explanation of the definitions of sentences in this manner, see Cotterell and Turner, *Linguistics and Biblical Interpretation*, 190-92. This repetitive Hebrew phrase can also be considered a favorite-pattern sentence.

⁴G. R. Driver, "Plurima Mortis Imago," in *Studies and Essays in Honor of Abraham A. Neuman* (Leiden: E. J. Brill, 1962), 137-43.

⁵See Appendixes B and D for the tabulation of the times שָׁכַב is used to express the sleep of death. Also, see Francis Brown, S. R. Driver, and C. A. Briggs, eds., *A Hebrew and English Lexicon of the Old Testament* (Oxford: Clarendon Press, 1979), s.v. "שָׁכַב," 1012, 4.a-c; and A. Alfrink, "L'Expression שָׁכַב, 106-18.

⁶See Gen. 47.30 and Deut. 31.16.

⁷See Table 4 in Chapter II for the manner of death of the wicked kings. Also, see Alfrink, "L'Expression שָׁכַב," 106-18.

and Chronicles, as a rule implies a violent death; said of other persons, however, it does not connote a judgment about the way of death.[8]

Whether or not one received an honorary obituary is a small factor relating to the thanatological thrust of this chapter. The existence of an interim state, however, can be deduced from this formula.[9] In addition, some form of judgment can take place either during the interim period or ensuing the parousia of Christ as various Scriptures, canonical or not, have warranted without damaging the plausibility of a measurable *Zwischenzustand*.

יָשֵׁן

יָשֵׁן is the specific activity which occurs between שָׁכַב and יָקַץ. Etymologically, it is debated whether the term originated from one or two roots.[10] If it is the case that there is one channel of interpretation which carries the meaning "be still" or "sleep," then it must support all the occurrences of the word in the Niphal stem, rendered "grow old."[11] This translation reflects a plausible maturation of the primary meaning of "be quiet, still." A second channel of interpretation is derived from the Ugaritic stem **ytn**, translated "old." It is possible that this term could explain the occurrence of the Niphal stem in Hebrew. Regardless, either track casts no new light on the meaning of the term and its various forms in the Old Testament.

---

[8]Nicholas Tromp, *Primitive Conceptions of Death and the Nether World in the Old Testament* (Rome: Pontifical Biblical Institute, 1969), 170. This entire book is a valuable source for research in the area of thanatology.

[9]The phrase "to sleep with one's fathers" represents one type of several evolutions of the phrase "to be gathered to one's people" (ibid., 168-69). For a comparative study, see A. Alfrink, "L'Expression נאסף אל עמיו," *Oudtestamentische Studiën* 5 (1948): 118-31. Alfrink has determined that this phrase represents the genuine wording of an ancient idiom which refers to the reunion of any particular decedent with appropriate predecedents. This special terminology appears only in the Pentateuch.

[10]J. Schüpphaus, *TDOT*, s.v. "יָשֵׁן," 6:438.

[11]See Lisowsky, s.v. "יָשֵׁן" and Ludwig Köhler and Walter Baumgartner, eds., *Lexicon in Veteris Testamenti Libros* (Leiden: E. J. Brill, 1958), s.v. "יָשֵׁן."

יָשֵׁן is used less frequently than שָׁכַב for the sleep of death. The most frequent usage, as is the case with its synonymous semantic field, pertains to physical sleep.[12] The major difference יָשֵׁן displays is the absence of symbolism in its stock expression with respect to physical sleep. שָׁכַב means to "lie down" in the greatest number of its pericopae. This generality encompasses, therefore, a larger interpretative field. In this sense יָשֵׁן is less fluid than שָׁכַב.

Adjectival modification, however, affords the term to be used in sleep-of-death contexts. In the first place it is somewhat surprising that יָשֵׁן is not used in connection with the deaths of the Hebrew kings memorialized in Kings and Chronicles. The proclivity to use שָׁכַב reveals the authorial intention not to mix formulas by introducing a new term in the form critical sense. It has already been pointed out that κοιμάομαι never translates יָשֵׁן in any sleep-of-death context. Even so, it is questionable if the Hebrew author's use of שָׁכַב is exactly equivalent to the Greek author's use of κοιμάομαι in the LXX. It appears that "sleeping" is intended more in the LXX than in the Masoretic text even though κοιμάομαι no doubt can incorporate with ease the translation to "lie down."

The clearest examples of יָשֵׁן as the sleep of death is found in Jer. 51.39, 57 under the popularly supposed influence of the Canaanite fertility cult which advanced the opinion of the yearly death and resurrection of the deity.[13] This sleep, however, is devoid of eschatological arousal in this imprecation reserved especially for a pernicious and Yahweh-hating Babylon. The phraseology used in Jeremiah concerning an everlasting sleep is reminiscent of the pagan posture

---

[12]For example, the term occurs in two renowned passages: 1 Kgs. 18.27 and 19.5. Respectively, these citations depict Elijah musing that the god of the Baal prophets is "asleep," and Elijah "sleeping" under a broom tree after fleeing from Jezebel.

[13]Schüpphaus, "יָשֵׁן," 6:441; Thomson, "Sleep: An Aspect of Jewish Anthropology," 427-31. For more on this topic, see J. Wijngaards, "Death and Resurrection in Covenantal Context (Hos. 6.2)," *Vetus Testamentum* 17 (1967): 227-28; Harris Birkeland, "The Belief in the Resurrection of the Dead in the Old Testament," *Studia Theologica* 3 (1949): 60-78; Robert Martin-Achard, *From Death to Life*, 84; and Friedrich Schwally, *Das Leben nach dem Tode* (Giessen: J. Ricker, 1892), 5-74.

already encountered in the Homeric and Hellenistic eras. Even though there are hints of the resurrection in the Old Testament, "the attitude of the majority of the Old Testament texts toward death is relatively neutral."[14] Only two highly apocalyptic references account for the most unambiguous teachings of resurrection in the Old Testament.[15] Dan. 12.2 contains יָשֵׁן in the description of "those sleeping in the dust." Interestingly, the Greek word normally employed to transmit this word in the LXX, ὑπνόω, is replaced by καθεύδω, the term employed later in the Synoptic sleep-of-death account of the raising of Jairus' daughter.[16]

Is. 26.19 pairs with the Danielic passage to emphasize resurrection. There is no major sleep-of-death term used synonymously in this verse. Semantically, the phrase "you who *dwell* in the dust" functions as a parallel sleep-of-death expression. The term שָׁכֵן is a close synonym of שָׁכַב. John Day advances the idea that the verse alludes to the time of ultimate deliverance from Sheol.[17] He translates טַל אוֹרֹת as "dew of light" in synonymous contrast to New International Version's "dew of the morning." Sheol is regularly portrayed as a place of concentrated darkness (see Pss. 88.6, 12; 143.3; Job 38.7) and emergence from it is characterized by "coming into the light."[18] The antithesis of light and darkness

---

[14]Helmer Ringgren, *Israelite Religion*, trans. David E. Green (Philadelphia: Fortress Press, 1966), 239. For general treatments of the subject, see G. Quell, *Die Auffasung des Todes im Alten Testament* (Leipzig: Hinrichs, 1925); Gerhard von Rad, "Alttestamentliche Glaubensaussagen von Leben und Tod," *Allgemeine evangelische-lutherische Kirchenzeitung* 4 (1938): 826; Edmond Jacob, "Death and the Future Life," chap. in *Theology of the Old Testament*, 299-316; and R. P. Féret, "La mort dans la tradition biblique," in *Le mystère de la mort et sa célébration* (Paris: Editions du Cerf, 1952), 133.

[15]This is the conclusion of F. B. Huey, "The Hebrew Concept of Life after Death in the Old Testament" (Th.D. diss., Southwestern Baptist Theological Seminary, 1961). While not denying the possibility of peripheral, vague references, Dan. 12.2 and Is. 26.19 are clearer than any other in the Old Testament.

[16]Dan. 12.2 marks the only time that καθεύδω is used for the sleep of death in the LXX.

[17]John Day, "טַל אוֹרֹת in Isaiah 26.19," *Zeitschrift für die alttestamentliche Wissenschaft* 90 (1978): 268.

[18]See Clement J. McNaspy, "Sheol in the Old Testament," *The Catholic Biblical Quarterly* 6 (1944): 331-32.

is also seen in Prov. 20.20. The writer uses בְּאֶשׁוּן, a substantive of יָשֵׁן, in a verse translated: "If a man curses his father or mother, his lamp will be snuffed out in *pitch* darkness." Tromp, however, translates בְּאֶשׁוּן as "sleep." He renders the second half of the verse: "His lamp shall go out in the sleep of darkness."[19] The juxtaposition of light and the sleep of death also appears in Ps. 13.3(4), where the psalmist says: "Give light to my eyes, or I will sleep in death" (פֶּן־אִישַׁן הַמָּוֶת). [20]

Equally interesting is the difficult citation in Ps. 90.5-6 which features the variant substantive form, שֵׁנָה.[21] The verse is translated: "You sweep men away in the sleep of death; they are like the new grass in the morning—though in the morning it springs up new, by evening it is dry and withered." This English translation, however, does not capture the striking Hebrew word order which serves to accentuate the awful and rash picture of death the psalmist has in mind. Violence collars the individual by death, as זְרַמְתָּם vividly qualifies שֵׁנָה at the outset of the verse.[22] The divergence between light and darkness is again displayed as man is likened to green grass which appears vivacious in the morning but regrettably dries up and withers in the evening.

Resurrection is mentioned here only because it warrants the idea of an intermediate state. Resurrection is meaningless if individuals go to heaven immediately after death. If light is associated with life either before or after death, then the darkness must be a characteristic of that period which ensues and elapses

---

[19]Nicholas Tromp, *Primitive Conceptions of Death*, 185, n. 44.

[20]See this writer's comments pertaining to Job 3.13, which holds a similar expression, in Chapter II, pages 85-90.

[21]See Appendix C for the three occurrences of שֵׁנָה represented by ὑπνόω in the LXX for the sleep of death.

[22]זְרַמְתָּם is a *hapax legomenon* in the Qal stem. The noun form of this verb is זֶרֶם and is used seven times in Isaiah in reference to a violent storm (4.6, twice in 25.4 and 28.2, 30.30, and 32.2).

during death.²³ In embryonic form, Is. 26.19 provides an important paradigm for future intermediate state elaborations in the New Testament.²⁴ On the appointed apocalyptic Day of the Lord, the Rephaim (shades) will be aroused and be reinstated to life in transformed physical bodies. While investigating the possible presence of a bonafide doctrine of resurrection in the Old Testament, it must be mentioned that some scholars do not find individual resurrection taught even in the two references under consideration.²⁵

Minor Semitic Terms Depicting
the Sleep of Death

נום appears twice as the sleep of death; in Ps. 76.5(6) (ὑπνόω, LXX) and Nahum 3.18 (κοιμάομαι, LXX). Both references are cast in correlation to the image of the battlefield. The reference in Psalms contains another sleep of death synonym already examined, שֵׁנָה:

Valiant men lie plundered,
    they sleep (שֵׁנָה) their last sleep (נום);
Not one of the warriors can lift his hands.

---

²³See the informative section pertaining to darkness as a part of the scenery of death/Sheol in Tromp, *Primitive Conceptions of Death*, 140-44.

²⁴Cooper, *Body, Soul, & Life Everlasting*, 89-90.

²⁵Both sides are represented in the quest for the resurrection in the Old Testament. For example, André Feuillet, "Le drama d'amour du Cantique des Cantiques remis en son contexte prophétique," *Nova et Vetera* (1987): 81-127, views Dan. 12.2 only as the awakening of Israel; R. Brandscheidt, "Psalm 102. Literarische Gestalt und theologische Aussage," *Trierer theologische Zeitschrift* 96 (1987): 51-75, holds that the psalm was prayed by a postexilic person in Jerusalem who recognized that the Lord who led his people out of exile would also secure the conversion of people to Zion; and Peter Welten, "Die Vernichtung des Todes und die Königsherrschaft Gottes," *Theologische Zeitschrift* 38 (1982): 129-46, believes that Dan. 12.2 says nothing directly about resurrection. It merely insists that death has no portion in the universal kingdom, a New Testament doctrine that was anticipated by the the Old Testament. On the other hand, James M. Lindenberger, "Daniel 12.1-4," *Interpretation* 39 (1985): 181-86, maintains that the theme of the eventual triumph of Yahweh led many to focus on the "resurrectional" aspect of the pericope; and Michael S. Moore, "Resurrection and Immortality: Two Motifs Navigating Confluent Theological Streams in the OT (Dan.12.1-4)," *Theologische Zeitschrift* 39 (1983): 17-34, joins the author's thesis that the belief in resurrection is a development of prophetic thought and that immortality was a concept that was elaborated in the wisdom tradition. The two ideas coalesced under apocalyptic influence, as seen in Dan. 12.1-4.

Nahum rings the death knell for Ninevah as he poetically parallels two terms for the sleep of death:

> O king of Assyria, your shepherds slumber (נָמוּ);
> your nobles lie down to rest (יִשְׁכְּנוּ).

Sleep here is not a figurative locution for nonchalance and idleness. The dispersion of the people, the destruction of the kingdom, by means of indifferent rulers suits neither the context nor Nahum's prophetic message.[26] A message of death is certainly intended. Secondly, through parallelism the term used in Is. 26.19 for "dwelling" in the dust surfaces again. Out of 111 times in the Qal stem, שָׁכֵן refers to the sleep of death only six times. The word almost always is translated "dwell" or some other synonym which suggests "living" or "abiding." Even in sleep of death contexts this translation can be retained:

Ps. 94.17: Unless the Lord had given me help,
I would soon have *dwelt* in the silence of death.

Job 26.5: The dead are in deep anguish,
those beneath the waters and all that *live* in them.

Pss. 16.9 and 139.9 also more subtly convey the idea of the sleep of death.

Second Temple Judaism

Much care must be taken when dealing with Semitic materials which are outside of the scope of the Old Testament because of their problematic chronological relationship with the New Testament and their overall intrinsic veracity. Roughly, the writings which will be considered date from the period 200 B.C. to A.D. 200.[27] Although Sanders is not concerned primarily with isolating

---

[26]C. F. Keil, *The Twelve Minor Prophets*, trans. James Martin, Commentary on the Old Testament, vol. 10, part 2 (Grand Rapids: Eerdmans, 1978), 41.

[27]Basically, the method of dating and material identification found in E. P. Sanders, *Paul and Palestinian Judaism* (Philadelphia: Fortress Press, 1977), will be followed. In addition, Sanders's newly released book, *Judaism: Practice and Belief, 63 b.c.e - 66 c.e.* (Philadelphia: Fortress Press, 1992), contains a section pertaining to death and the nether world which sheds light on early eschatological beliefs in Palestine.

any particular source of the Apostle Paul's ideas, this writer is interested in the seedbed of postmortem ideas which fully bloomed in the New Testament. It will be critical to assess properly which materials were in a chronological posture to exert any influence on New Testament eschatology, especially with regard to the sleep-of-death concept expressed by κοιμάομαι and שָׁכַב, and their respective semantic pools.

The Tannaitic (or "traditionalist") literature will be examined first for the presence of the sleep-of-death motif. This includes the Aramaic Targums which will be searched even though there is some hesitation among scholars to accept their antiquity.[28] Convincing demonstrations have been offered, however, that some New Testament texts and themes are illuminated by the Targumic materials.[29] The equally important Dead Sea Scrolls comprise the second major division of this literature to be considered. Besides the writings of the Pseudepigrapha, which were considered in Chapter II, the Dead Sea Scrolls represent some of the earliest Semitic examples and, therefore, are extremely important for New Testament exegesis. In addition, the Mishnah (A.D. 70-200), which denotes in the most significant sense the collection made by R. Judah ha-Nasi, the Tosefta, and the Tannaitic or halakic midrashim will be examined as well as the Gemara (2d-6th century A.D.[30]

---

[28]See Anthony D. York, "The Dating of Targumic Literature," *Journal for the Study of Judaism* 5 (1974): 49-62. It should be noted that Sanders dates the Aramaic Targums much later than does Martin McNamara or Jacob Neusner. Targumic influence on New Testament writings is debatable.

[29]For example, see R. Le Déaut, "Targumic Literature and New Testament Interpretation," *Biblical Theology Bulletin* 4 (1974): 243-89, Martin McNamara, *Targum and Testament* (Grand Rapids: Eerdmans, 1972), and idem, *The New Testament and the Palestinian Targum to the Pentateuch* (Rome: Pontifical Biblical Institute, 1966). One of the clearest introductions to the ancient Jewish writings is found in McNamara, *Targum and Testament*, 1-16.

[30]Hermann L. Strack, *Introduction to the Talmud and Midrash* (Atheneum, NY: The Jewish Publication Society of America, 1931), 3. R. Judah ha-Nasi is more commonly known as "Judah the Prince" or simply "Rabbi." This important reference work now appears as G. Stemberger and Hermann L. Strack, eds., Introduction to the Talmud and Midrash, trans. Markus Bockmuehl (Edinburgh: T. & T. Clark, 1991).

Collectively, these sources should reveal some exegetical traditions or patterns of religious beliefs which will be germane to New Testament exegesis of sleep-of-death texts. Certainly, Jesus and Paul knew of the Tannaitic elements of Jewish eschatology as well as those eschatological keystones of Old Testament Judaism. New Testament exegesis, therefore, should reflect upon this channel of influence while rightfully avoiding any Marcionitic tendency to divorce Christianity from Judaism.[31]

Aramaic Targums

In a secondary sense, שָׁכִיב is translated "dead" or "deceased" in the Targumic literature.[32] Primarily, the term means "lying down" or "dangerously ill." A definite shift occurs in these writings in that שָׁכַב becomes a substantive form expressing literally the event of death. Attendant words for sleep are not coupled with this term in order to render a phrase "the sleep of death." For example, *Tg. Yer. Deut.* 25.5 runs, "When brothers live together and one of them dies and leaves no son, the wife of the *dead* one (שָׁכִיב) should not marry another man. . . ."[33] Plural forms of שָׁכִיב are found in *Tg. Ruth* 1.8 and this interesting reference to a Jobian-type of death wish in *Tg. Qohelet* 4.2: "And I praised *the deceased* (שְׁכִיבֵי) who had already died and had not experienced the punishment which came into the world after their death, more than the living who endure in misery until now."[34] Both of these occurrences advance no euphemism whatsoever. שָׁכַב is literally synonymous with death in these examples.

---

[31]See especially John Bright, *The Authority of the Old Testament* (Grand Rapids: Baker Book House, 1967), 60-79.

[32]See Marcus Jastrow, *Dictionary of the Targumim*, s.v. "שָׁכִיב שְׁכִיבָא."

[33]Translation based on Bernard Grossfeld, *The Targum Onqelos to Deuteronomy*, The Aramaic Bible (Wilmington, DE: Michael Glazier, Inc., 1988), 73. For similar phrase, see *Tg. Ps.* 31.13.

[34]Translation based on Peter S. Knobel, *The Targums of Job, Proverbs, Qohelet*, The Aramaic Bible (Collegeville, MN: The Liturgical Press, 1991), 30-31.

85

This substantive also appears in a later exposition of the Mishnah called the Gemara.[35] Amidst a response to a question concerning whether burial is a disgrace or a means of atonement, this term is used again to refer to the deceased several times.[36] Secondly, in *Sanh.* 109b, the Aramaic phrase בי שכיבי can be translated "in the cemetery." This Gemaric phrase parallels κοιμητήριον, "sleeping room," "cemetery," or "grave."[37] Of course, these translations represent later developments of the sleep-of-death concept which will be investigated fully in Chapter V, "Post Biblical Reflection."

שָׁכַב functions with the same polysemic versatility in the Targums as it does in the Old Testament and other Jewish literature. The term is translated "sleep" in the physical sense in *Tg. Onq. Deut.* 24.12, but it stands for sexual intercourse both in *Tg. Gen.* 26.10 and *Tg. Onq. Lev.* 15.24. As the Old Testament utilizes שָׁכַב in contexts which described brutal rapes, so do the Targums. *Tg. Zech.* 14.2 and *Tg. Is.* 13.16 both employ the Hithpael verb אִשְׁתַּכַּב to convey the idea of being ravished.[38]

An investigation of synonymous terminology in the Targumic tradition reveals some noteworthy illustrations. Semantically, Chaldaic נוּח operates much like κοιμάομαι in the Homeric period. Variously, it refers to water ceasing to run, a

---

[35] The Gemara combines with the Mishnah to form what is known as the Talmud. They are expositions (hence Amoraim) of the Mishnah. During the period A.D. 250-420 the Mishnah was elaborated in the Jewish schools of Palestine and Babylonia. These writings, therefore, follow the Tannaitic period and would not influence the New Testament writings as those redacted A.D. 70-200.

[36] *Sanh.* 46b.

[37] For Christian definition, see Chrysostom *De coemeterio et de cruce* 1. Διὰ τοῦτο καὶ αὐτὸς ὁ τόπος κοιμητήριον ὠνόμασται, ἵνα μάθῃς ὅτι οἱ τετελευτηκότες καὶ ἐνταῦθα κείμενοι οὐ τεθνήκασιν, ἀλλὰ κοιμῶνται καὶ καθεύδουσιν. F. F. Bruce, *1 & 2 Thessalonians*, 96 says: "It is probably from the 'optimistic' nuance of κοιμᾶσθαι that the Jewish and Christian term κοιμητήριον, 'cemetery,' was derived."

[38] The range of activities associated with lying down continues into this period.

storm subsiding, leaving a person alone, setting an object down, a pain being relieved, or the convalescence of the sick.[39]

Keeping the versatility of these terms in mind, perhaps one can understand why the disciples misconstrued Jesus' use of κοιμάομαι in Jn. 11.11. If Jesus used a popular Aramaic word underlying κοιμάομαι which the disciples regularly associated with one of its nondeath interpretations, specifically convalescence, then the disciples' response in verse 12 is warranted: Κύριε, εἰ κεκοίμηται σωθήσεται, "Lord, if he is convalescing he will recover" (translation mine). Hebrew נוח in the Niphal stem surfaces in the Talmud and in two midrashim setting forth this idea exactly.[40] In *Yer. Ber.* 5.9d, one finds the phrase: "I am confident that the son of ... will recover (יִחְיֶה) from his illness."

A textual variant of Jn. 11.12 reveals that someone possibly was trying to be an interpreter as σωθήσεται is replaced with ἐγερθήσεται in ℘[75].[41] Σώζω can be translated "recover" and thus exist harmoniously in its context. This response reflects what the disciples truly thought, not what Jesus wanted them to think.

The Dead Sea Scrolls

According to K. G. Kuhn, שָׁכַב and its synonymous entourage are used sparingly in the Qumran material.[42] The best example is found in 1QH 6.34:

Hoist a banner,
   O you who lie (שָׁכַב) in the dust!
O bodies gnawed by worms,
   raise up an ensign for [the destruction of wickedness]!

---

[39]Various stems in the Aramaic language serve to express these notions.

[40]See the midrashim *Gen. Rab.* s.13 and *Yal. Chr.* 1072 for similar phraseology.

[41]In light of the author's theological intentions in the passage, one can easily see the emphasis of the death and resurrection motif. The disciples' failure to penetrate this reference is not surprising due to their overall denial of any messianic equation which included death as part of Jesus' experience. This writer is in agreement with R. Bultmann that this is not a case of Johannine misunderstanding (*Das Evangelium des Johannes*, 16th ed. [Göttingen: Vandenhoeck & Ruprecht, 1959], 304).

[42]See the appropriate listings in his *Konkordanz zu den Qumrantexten*.

[The sinful shall] be destroyed
    in the battles against the ungodly.[43]

One characteristic of the Dead Sea Scrolls evident here is their strong proclivity to imitate biblical style. "Lying in the dust" is almost a mirror image of the phrase found in Dan. 12.2. The only notable difference is that the Danielic passage employs יָשֵׁן instead of the more common שָׁכַב to offer a clue concerning the postmortem condition. The meaning, however, is the same. This concept of the sleep of death strides hand in hand with the complementary Qumranian theme of self-abasement:

Behold, I was taken from dust
    and fashioned out of clay
as a source of uncleanness
    and a shameful nakedness,
a heap of dust
    and a kneading with water. . .
a creature of clay returning to dust.[44]

Equally, an allusion to Dan. 12.2 and Is. 26.19 can also be detected in another posthumously flavored text from the Hymnbook which invites the reader to make an anthropological assessment:

. . . that bodies gnawed by worms may be raised from dust
    to the counsel of Thy truth,
and that the perverse spirit (may be lifted)
    to the understanding which comes from thee;[45]

Upon examination of the material, Vermes believes that the Qumran community did not project any essential fixation on the idea of the resurrection.[46] And what is more, Nickelsburg maintains that the intention expressed in the

---

[43]Translation found in G. Vermes, *The Dead Sea Scrolls in English*, 2d ed.(Baltimore, MD: Penguin Books, 1975), 172.

[44]1QH 19.

[45]1QH 17.

[46]Vermes, *The Dead Sea Scrolls*, 51. Also, George Nickelsburg, *Resurrection, Immortality, and Eternal Life in Intertestamental Judaism*, 144, says: "The published Scrolls of Qumran are remarkable in that they contain not a single passage that can be interpreted with absolute certainty as a reference to resurrection or immortality." For elaboration of differing viewpoints, see the references alluded to in Nickelsburg's work.

Scrolls is not one which refers to the resurrection or the postmortem state. Since the potential persecution did not materialize and lead to the inevitable deaths of the godly, such categories are precluded from being germane to the discussion.[47] This writer feels this interpretation attempts to ignore intermediate state possibilities. Concepts like sleeping in the dust, being worm food, and being dead are all indicative of an intermediate state. Vermes does say:

> But it is not impossible that the phraseology is metaphorical. On the other hand, considering the beliefs and expectations of the sect as a whole, it is difficult to conceive that the members would have denied their dead brethren and saints of the past a full share in the eternal joys of the Messianic Kingdom.[48]

While the cautions of potential exegetical pitfalls should be heeded when treading through apocalyptic material, one should equally allow the eschatological message to include assertions which are not relegated to the purely symbolic. This tendency of overstating euphemism is one reason why the concept of an intermediate state has not been easily accepted.[49]

Babylonian Talmud[50]

None of the references in the Talmudic corpus pertaining to the sleep of death are found in the Mishnah per se. Only the Amoraim (namely, the Gemara) reflect this expression. Most of the time שָׁכַב, any substantival variant, or synonymous parallel is cast as a technical term for the deceased.[51]

---

[47]Nickelsburg, *Resurrection*, 151. The emphasis is one of imminent deliverance in the highly apocalyptic-oriented Scrolls.

[48]Vermes, *The Dead Sea Scrolls*, 51.

[49]The same problem exists concerning the exegesis of the Revelation.

[50]For the text utilized in this section, see I. Epstein, ed. *The Babylonian Talmud*, trans. I. Epstein, parts 1-6 (London: The Soncino Press, 1948), and I. Epstein, ed., *Hebrew-English Edition of the Babylonian Talmud*, vols. 1-6, trans. Maurice Simon (London: The Soncino Press, 1960.

[51]For concordance searches, see the appropriate entries in Jacob Levy, *Neuhebräisches und Chaldäisches Wörterbuch über die Talmudim und Midraschim* (Leipzig: F. A. Brockhaus, 1876) and Haim Joshua Kassovsky, *'Otsar Leshon ha-mishna, Concordantiae totius Mischnae*, 2 vols. (Frankfurt: Y. Kauffmann, 1927).

89

Chaldaic שָׁכַב accounts for many death references in the Gemaric tradition. These references come into focus roughly between the second and sixth century A.D. The first example involves a stock expression commonly occurring throughout the Talmud. The urgency of transmitting a certain bit of information is seen in *Yebam.* 46a and *B. Metz.* 73b as shown in the phrase: "I might have died (שָׁכַב) without telling you this thing." This peculiar translation for שָׁכַב surfaces also in *B. Metz.* 85a and *B. Qam.* 91b in reference to premature death and in *B. Bat.* 26a amidst a fatherly lamentation for his dead son.

The substantive שְׁכָבָא is translated as "asleep," "dead body," or "corpse."[52] *Sanh.* 48b yields the most artistic stroke of the term's use. Therein is described the post-mortem practices of the inhabitants of Harpania, an extremely poor town. The dead (שְׁכָבָא) were covered by day with large sacks and in the night they removed the grave clothes.[53]

Synonymous Chaldaic נוּחַ also is employed to portray death in the Talmud. Three times in *B. Metz.* 86a the sleep-of-death motif is alluded to clearly. In this work the souls of various rabbis are pictured as having attained rest the day each one died. In addition, *Ketub.* 84b refers to the specific location where someone died, and *Ketub.* 104a contains the terse phrase: "He is dead."

The last synonym to consider is the Chaldaic verb נוּם. This word can be translated, "be in a comatose condition," "be dying,"[54] or "death sleep."[55] Apocalyptically, the sleep-of-death concept is unmistakable in *Erub.* 65a: "Soon will come the days which are long and yet short, when we shall have a long sleep." If erroneously tapped, the reference to the comatose victim in *Qidd.* 17b

---

[52]German: *Eine Leiche, ein Verstorbener.* Confer *Mo'ed Qat.* 27b and *B. Bat.* 91a.

[53]Levy, *Neuhebräisches*, s.v. "שְׁכָבָא."

[54]Also, see *Mo'ed Qat.* 28a and QKidd. 72a for rabbinic discussions on death and dying using the term נוּם.

[55]Jastrow, *Dictionary of the Targumim*, s.v. "נוּם."

and others like it might be responsible for some interpretations of the supposed death scene involving Jairus' daughter, in Mk. 5.21-24a, 35-43 and parallels, which suggest that she was not dead but merely in a coma.[56] That this reference is clearly Gemaric disqualifies it from exerting any exegetical influence on New Testament texts. Of course, ones viewpoint could be altered if this idea had been prevalent in oral tradition long before it was redacted, therefore rendering it available for the New Testament idea bank. On the other hand, the juxtaposed idea of a coma can also be refuted by Luke's remark in 8.53: καὶ κατεγέλων αὐτοῦ εἰδότες ὅτι ἀπέθανεν. The crowd's ridicule was the result of Jesus' supposed misguided diagnosis. In fact, the crowd knew (εἰδότες) beyond reasonable doubt that she was truly dead.[57] By the employment of καθεύδω, Jesus' determination was that she was not dead "finally" in the apocalyptic sense.

Palestinian Talmud[58]

Much of the same exegetical tradition continued in Palestine with some interesting additions. While *y.Sanh.* 29b used the substantive שְׁכָבָא to refer to death, *y.Ber.* I.3c includes the feminine form of the word in a model rabbinic prayer which figuratively viewed lying down (שְׁכִיבָה) and rising up in the morning

---

[56]The latest model which offers this interpretation is found in James Brooks, *Mark*, The New American Commentary (Nashville: Broadman Press, 1991), 94. Although Brooks is not clear whether or not he thinks the girl was dead, interpretations which follow these lines of thought are mere attempts at sidestepping the anthropological/thanatological problems associated with this episode. More will be said in refutation of this hyper-euphemistic stance in Chapter IV, "The New Testament Tradition."

[57]See John Nolland, *Luke 1-9:20*, Word Biblical Commentary (Dallas: Word Books, 1989), 415-23. While he does not elaborate on the crowd's response, he does say on page 421 that "Since the advent of Jesus, the ultimacy of death is broken" (also, see K. Kertelge, *Die Wunder Jesu im Markusevangelium: Eine redaktionsgeschichtliche Untersuchung*, Studien zum Alten und Neuen Testament [Munich: Kösel, 1970], 117).

[58]It should be noted that this version of the Talmud differs from the previous one in that it is substantially concerned with the opinions of the Amoraim resident in Palestine. As far as importance is concerned, a certain Rabbi Wasserman explained that while the Babylonian Talmud is the Major League of rabbinic interpretation, the Palestinian (or Yerushalmic) represents the Minor League exposition.

(*Sichlegen und Aufstehen*)[59] as a harbinger for death and the apocalyptic day of resurrection. This word progressively evolved in meaning from "the couch" to "sleep" and finally as "the dead." An extremely interesting concept is projected in the last example found in *y.Git.* 44d. Rabbinic tradition taught that there were two kinds of mats "to sleep" upon. One was for resting in physical sleep and the other was for the vault of heaven, evidently referring to death.

Rabbinic Midrash

Several rabbinic interpretations of the Hebrew Bible are helpful in the quest to observe שָׁכַב and its relevant death synonyms' *modus operandi* in this genre.[60] Most noteworthy is the rabbinic elaboration on the death of Jacob in *Gen. Rab.* 96.[61] Interestingly, some comments are based upon the first sleep-of-death appearance of שָׁכַב in the Hebrew Bible. This midrash, however, is fashioned indirectly to the postmortem description of sleeping. The emphasis of the explication is directed toward the effect death has on one's power to rule.[62] Comparing the strong personages of Moses, David, and Jacob, this midrash teaches that dominion does not follow the mighty to the grave. For example, the trappings of Sheol eradicate any designation of power, as in the case of King David:

---

[59]Levy, *Neuhebräisches*, s.v. "שְׁכִיבָה." These sources were translated from entries in Levy's concordance.

[60]On the whole phenomenon of Midrash, see Addison G. Wright, "The Literary Genre Midrash," *Catholic Biblical Quarterly* 28 (1966): 105-38, 417-57, and A. W. Greenup, *Sukka, Mishna and Tosefta* (London: SPCK, 1925).

[61]This particular written work can be dated A.D. 400-500. For further comment on this midrash, text, and translation, see Jacob Neusner, *Genesis Rabbah: The Judaic Commentary on Genesis. A New American Translation*, vol. 3 (Atlanta: Scholars Press for Brown Judaic Studies, 1985).

[62]Idem, *A Midrash Reader* (Minneapolis: Fortress Press, 1990), 77.

So too with David: 'Now King David was old' (1 Kings 1.1). What is stated about him when he lay dying? 'Now the days of David drew near, that he should die' (1 Kings 2.1). What is said is not *'king* David,' but merely 'David.'[63]

The theme of abasement is characteristic of the intermediate state. This idea is consistent with the idea of Sheol being a place of extremely low ontological intensity. Death, by ruling and binding, is in need of some stronger power to break its shackles. Eschatologically, the requirement is met by the full-blown doctrine of the resurrection in the New Testament.

Closer to the notion of the sleep of death are two prayers offered for the Hebrew fathers who are asleep in the ground. *Mek. Besha.* 3 and *Yal. Ex.* 260 both make reference to the sleep of death with the employment of שָׁבַב.[64]

The Hebrew synonymous term נוּחַ is used in *Yal. Gen.* 42 in another sleep-of-death allusion: "When Noah arose, they remained (נוּחַ) in their graves."[65] As before the rabbinic accent is on the cessation of activity.

Conclusion

In retrospect, the sages' anthropological perspectives are vitally linked to and depend upon the Old Testament. Preparation for the New Testament assumptions concerning the intermediate state has been made complete by the precursory investigation of Old Testament thanatology. While Rabbinic literature is important, the ultimate "midrash" on the Old Testament is the New Testament. It is not that what the rabbis believed was erroneous. Jesus himself, the Apostle Paul, a Christianized Jew, and the remainder of the New Testament corps of writers, including Luke in a guarded sense, were all cognizant of and governed a certain extent by the Old Testament witness.

---

[63]*Gen. Rab.* 96.1, h-i; quoted in Neusner, *A Midrash Reader*, 77.

[64]See Jacob Neusner, *Mekhilta Attributed to R. Ishmael: An Analytic Translation*, vol. 1, *Pisha, Beshallah, Shirata, and Vayassa* (Atlanta: Scholars Press for Brown Judaic Studies, 1988). "Mekhilta Attributed to R. Ishmael" is the first scriptural encyclopedia of Judaism.

[65]Translation from Jastrow, *Dictionary of the Targumim*, s.v. "נוּחַ."

Anthropologically, the Old Testament casts mankind in a functionally wholistic mold, namely, a psychomatic unity. During the highest expression of life the person is a functioning integration of the material and nonmaterial. On the other hand, during the lowest expression of life, which the Bible calls death, preparation for a future ultimate transformation is implemented. During death a measurable intermediate time is elapsing when life is at its lowest possible frequency.

As a provisional conclusion at this juncture it is still maintained that any model which posits any kind of continuation of life after death is in some way dualistic. Every brand of anthropological dualism is not automatically dismissed. The Greek dualistic design of the immortality of the soul, however, should be avoided. Dissatisfaction arises not because of the idea of a soul, but because of the idea of the immortality of that soul in a pre-existent state. The concept of the immortality of the soul completely denigrates the total biblical view of man. If Plato's concepts are correct, then the subsidiary biblical teachings associated with pneumatology, hamartiology, thanatology, and eschatology will be severely skewed ontologically and chronologically. Subscription to undetected Greek philosophical influences causes an eschatological shift of events associated with death to take place only in the minds of many well-meaning Christians. Keeping the record straight, the full experience of heaven is subsequent to the resurrection of the dead. Resurrection completely fits the Christian for heaven, not death. With respect to the resurrection, Jesus is still the πρωτότοκος and only-born (μονότοκος?) from the dead at this moment. Resurrection remains a prerequisite for the final, uninterrupted experience of heaven.

Life is a power and sleep is, as E. E. Urbach holds, "the narcotization of this power."[66] Similarly, death is not the reciprocal of life, rather it is an eschatological sleep characterized by "extreme enfeeblement."[67] This diminished mode of existence is wholly in step with the concept of Sheol and its "weak"

---

[66] E. E. Urbach, *The Sages*, 216.

[67] Ibid.

(רְפָאִים) occupants.⁶⁸ With respect to a great number of works, many candidates for canonicity were disqualified because of the detection of foreign influences not consistent with those deemed reliable. As radioactivity contaminates a landfill, so do the rubrics of Greek philosophy contaminate biblical anthropology and thanatology. This group includes a large number of apocryphal and pseudepigraphical writings, along with the works of Philo and Josephus. As has been demonstrated, some extraneous works do set forth eschatological ideas which are consistent with the biblical record and thus can be accepted as a functional canon for faith and practice.

Christian eschatology has suffered greatly due to the atrocious Platonic doctrine of the preexistence of souls.⁶⁹ In the beginning was the Godhead, not the Godhead and a sea of disorganized souls looking for a suitable body in which they could be downgraded temporarily. Zoroastrianism and a host of Greek philosophical systems all have formed an alliance broadcasting the doctrine of the immortality of the soul which is diametrically in opposition to the biblical sense of the resurrection of the dead.

The rabbinic writings provide a tamer view of the body-and-soul equation. The sages drew no distinction between souls that were never attached to a body. Souls are created by God. Urbach provides a series of notable distinctions between the sages and Greek philosophy. The Tanna does not 1) address mankind as body and soul, but as an integrated whole; 2) teach the antithesis between matter and idea; 3) use the term "immortalilty" in reference to anything in the temporal world; or 4) teach the transmigration of souls.⁷⁰ For the most part, the rabbinic material emphasized the intermediate state rather than the final

---

⁶⁸Confer Isaiah 14 and Ezekiel 32.

⁶⁹Plato remarked that it was the express business of philosophers to drive a wedge between body and soul, "to pry the soul loose and isolate it from the body" (*Phaedo* 67).

⁷⁰E. E. Urbach, *The Sages*, 224 and 234-35.

postjudgment destinations, although some form of judgment could take place in Sheol.[71]

The Rabbis undoubtedly adopted שָׁכַב and its respective semantic group to function as a technical term for the act of death and the designation of defunct persons. Although some evolution took place before this terminology actually shifted from euphemism to metaphor, it is plausible to say that the oral ideas were operating in the tradition early enough to have a concerted influence on the New Testament tradition.

The Targums, for example, are extremely important, not only for the study of the New Testament but also for the analysis of the works of Rabbinic Judaism. Samuel Sandmel asserts the Targumic manuscripts facilitated the Mishnah and the halakhic midrashim of the Tannaim, such as Mekhilta, Sifra and Sifre, as significant sources.[72]

It makes sense that the Gemaric tradition provides the sleep-of-death equations in the Talmudic tradition as opposed to the Mishnah. The Mishnah basically deals with the legalistic aspects of Jewish life, namely, halakic comments as opposed to the Gemara, which provides the nonlegal, or haggadic, interpretations. That the Tosefta provided no sleep-of-death examples should not be cause for alarm. By definition it literally means "supplement" and is lightly referred to by some rabbis as "the Mishnah that did not make it." Summarily, the Hebrew and Aramaic semantic team of sleep-of-death terminology is well represented in the material so that the stage is now ready for a consideration of the New Testament tradition.

---

[71]Samuel Sandmel, *Judaism and Christian Beginnings* (New York: Oxford Press, 1978). Sandmel points out that both hell and paradise were temporary abodes which preceded the awesome consummative apocalyptic Day of judgment in the future. Sometimes rabbinic interpretation placed paradise in Sheol. If this is true, then the groundwork is laid for understanding the whereabouts of Jesus during his sojourn in the grave (E. O. James, *The Tree of Life* [Leiden: E. J. Brill, 1966], 79; quoted in Cooper, *Body, Soul, & Life Everlasting*, 97, n. 38).

[72]P. E. Kahle, *Recent Progress in Biblical Scholarship* (Boars Hill, Oxford: Lincombe Research Library, 1965), 43.

CHAPTER IV
THE NEW TESTAMENT TRADITION

Death acquires a completely new orientation once one enters the pages of the New Testament because of the person and work of Jesus Christ. To review the ontological problem at hand, note these questions. Do Christians have an immortal soul which will continue after death? Three Greek terms are utilized to communicate precisely the concept of immortality. Paul used all three in 1 Corinthians 15: ἀθανασία (verse 53); ἀφθαρσία (verse 42); and ἄφθαρτος (verse 52). Categorically, these terms are never used in conjunction with the term ψυχή.[1] Even when the concept of immortality is brought into service it never refers to man in his present state. Immortality is something which Christians attain after the resurrection. Holding to this scenario, however, does not negate the fact that something mysterious does happen to the Christian at the time of conversion which allows the effects of eschatology to be realized temporally.

At this juncture, two presuppositions which have direct bearing on the subject need to focus sharply. First, that which occurs during spiritual transformation according to the Pauline prescription of 2 Cor. 5.17 is extremely crucial for any

---

[1]Murray J. Harris, "The New Testament View of Life after Death," 47. Also, see idem, *From Grave to Glory*, 260-69, and F. F. Bruce, "Paul on Immortality," *Scottish Journal of Theology* 24 (1971): 457-72. Without exception, there is no biblical precedent for binding the qualitative terms "immortal" or "immortality" to the term "soul" (Harris, *From Grave to Glory*, 268).

proper thanatological inquest. Thanatology is, therefore, a handmaiden to soteriology. Second, the triple towers of Paul's eschatological concepts fleshed out in 1 Thessalonians 4, 1 Corinthians 15, and 2 Corinthians 5 each project their own major thrust. Individually and collectively they cast interpretative lights on the subject of the intermediate state. In the Thessalonian correspondence, Paul makes reference to the parousia in each of the five chapters.[2] Resurrection is the keynote of 1 Corinthians 15, while Christ's impending judgment bar comes to the forefront in 2 Corinthians 5.[3]

Systematically cranking these separate yet complementary themes through the exegetical turnstile with respect to the study of the intermediate state will allow the interpreter to avoid any unwarranted conclusions pertaining to the maturing of Paul's thought. According to the subject matter of these important passages, along with other more terse jolts in Paul's writings concerning eschatology, one can surmise as does F. F. Bruce: " . . . while we can trace a progression in his thought and language on this subject, his central belief and teaching do not appear to have undergone any essential change throughout his Christian career."[4]

What happens, then, to the Christian during the time between death and resurrection? The heart of this analysis is concerned with what the New Testament means by using κοιμάομαι and its synonymous semantic company to interpret death as a sleep from which there is an eschatological reanimation and subsequent transformation. Much more than euphemism must have been intended by Jesus and other New Testament authors simply because their central message of life after death would not require that kind of interpretative "softening." Jesus'

---

[2]See 1.10, 2.19, 3.13, 4.15, and 5.23. The present writer believes since so much emphasis has been placed on the Christian's final destination after death, the parousia has been unfairly minimized.

[3]A case has been made which argues that 1 Cor. 15.50-57 and 2 Cor. 5.1-5, though situated in dissimilar contexts, have a similar theme and style of argumentation. For elaboration of this view, see John Gillman, "A Thematic Comparison: 1 Cor. 15:50-57 and 2 Cor. 5:1-5," *Journal of Biblical Literature* 107 (1988): 439-54.

[4]F. F. Bruce, "Paul on Immortality," 462.

consummate victory over death and the grave drove an immovable wedge between pagan despair and Christian hope. Some do, however, maintain the innocuous use of sleep-of-death imagery in the New Testament.[5] So, by the utilization of the sleep-of-death metaphor, does the New Testament intend more than the belief that death is not final, that there is in fact an intermediate state? The following exegesis should help answer this remarkably heavy question.

Basically, the interpreter is faced with three general options for answering the question, "What happens when we die?" First, if there is an intermediate state, then a dualistic model of some kind must be presupposed. It is Cooper's opinion that most traditional Christians assert a position similar to Answer 57 of the Heidelberg Catechism:

> Not only my soul will be taken immediately after this life
> to Christ its head, but even my flesh, raised by the power
> of Christ, will be reunited with my soul and made like
> Christ's glorious body.[6]

This option indicates a discernible period of time which elapses between death and resurrection—that is, an intermediate state. Much perplexity results if the option of psychopannychism (the doctrine of "soul sleep") is chosen. Amidst a growing number who choose the intermediate state model, however, are those who opt for the "awake" texts as evidence for the intermediate state (Luke 16.19-31; 23.43; and Rev. 6.9).[7] It appears from the monist perspective that if dualism is not the case, then there can be no period of any proportion intervening personal death and

---

[5]Cf. G. E. Ladd, *A Theology of the New Testament* (Grand Rapids: Eerdmans, 1974), 554. He says: "Sleep was a common term for death both in Greek and Hebrew literature and need not carry any theological significance."

[6]*The Heidelberg Catechism*, the 1975 translation of the Christian Reformed Church; quoted in Cooper, *Body, Soul, & Life Everlasting*, 116.

[7]Gabriel Fackre, "I Believe in the Resurrection of the Body," *Interpretation* 46 (1992): 50. While not trying to ignore the probing questions of the penultimate journey between death and resurrection, Fackre interjects the reality of ontological mystery into the equation. The collective creeds and hymns Christians believe and sing have more to do with "the great 'thats' and 'whats' of the Future, not its 'whens,' 'wheres,' and 'hows'" (ibid., 51).

resurrection. Scholars who deny this eschatological interlude do so on the basis of an equal denial of the concept of an immortal soul.[8]

The remaining two alternatives are monistic and exist as rejoinders to the solutions associated with the dualistic model. The first elective is immediate resurrection based primarily on 2 Corinthians 5. Variations of this model hinge on differing definitions of resurrection, phenomenological experience of nontime, and symbolic renditions of the parousia event.[9] Secondly, John Hick's view of "Extinction—Recreation" suggests that at death the whole person dies.[10] Nothing survives death; the entire person experiences extinction until an appointed time when God will recreate the same person, only in a glorified body. The amount of time which elapses does not matter because it is phenomenologically experienced—that is, the manner in which the condition is experienced by the deceased is what matters, not the actual ontological and epistemological experience of elapsing time.[11]

Will κοιμάομαι and other sleep-of-death terminology support any of these models? While the burden of proof cannot lie solely on the grammatical shoulders of the sleep-of-death concept in the New Testament to prove the existence of an intermediate state, its very presence in key passages should prevent its hasty dismissal as euphemism and warrant its adoption as a didactic metaphor for the

---

[8] For recent elaboration, see George Carey, *I Believe in Man* (Grand Rapids: Eerdmans, 1977), 171-72, and Bruce Reichenbach, *Is Man the Phoenix? A Study of Immortality* (Washington, DC: Christian University Press, 1978), 176-88.

[9] This viewpoint has gained much contemporary popularity. For lists of advocates, see Cooper, *Body, Soul, & Life Everlasting*, 117, n. 20 and Harris, *Raised Immortal*, 98, n. 2. For a treatment of this idea by the most renowned evangelical representative in this group, see F. F. Bruce, "Paul on Immortality," 457-72.

[10] Especially see chapter fifteen, "The Resurrection of the Person", in John Hick, *Death and Eternal Life* (San Francisco: Harper & Row, Publishers, 1976).

[11] Reichenbach, *Is Man the Phoenix?*, 185. No matter how one realizes death, there must be a lapsing of time between the event of death and the reversal inacted by resurrection/re-creation because those who are alive have not witnessed the parousia of Christ. The intermediate state is still effectual as long as the parousia of Christ has not occurred.

sleep of death in the eschatological debate. In addition, it should also be noted that the intermediate state is a moot point for those who defend the annihilationist position. Although this model is directly contradictory to the evidence found in Acts 24.15, John 5.28-29, and Luke 14.7-14, there are those evangelicals who feel the plight of the unsaved is utter dissolution.[12]

Synoptic Gospels

Matthean Adoption of Ezekiel's Valley of Dry Bones

Deeply embedded in Matthew's "Passion Narrative" is a unique passage containing the sleep-of-death concept (Matt. 27.45-54 and parallels).[13] While the tearing of the temple curtain is preserved as a triple tradition, Matthew interrupts the Synoptic assonance with a unique apocalyptic echo from Ezek. 37.1-14.[14] Usually understood as a symbolic reference to the reconstitution of a new Israel, it appears not to have exerted much influence on the New Testament.[15] Such is

---

[12]For a recent discussion of this position, see Clark Pinnock and Delvin Brown, *Theological Crossfire: An Evangelical-Liberal Dialogue* (Grand Rapids: Zondervan Publishing House, 1990), 225-31. For an even more recent treatment of common eschatological ideas amidst Westerners, which incorporates the dispute about annihilationism, see Jeffrey L. Sheler, "Hell's Sober Comeback," *U.S. News & World Report* 110/11 (1991): 56-90. The consummate act of divine judgment is intricately related to the intermediate state.

[13]As is the case with other passages unique to their authors or redactors, some raise suspicions about textual reliability due to lack of corroboration in the other Synoptics. On occasion, the presence of some pericopae are attributed to church tradition. There is no good reason to support that option here.

[14]Matthew breaks the Synoptic parallel at 27.51a-53 with an Old Testament allusion. The Synoptic tracking resumes with verse 54.

[15]While W. Zimmerli rejects any notion of individual resurrection in this passage (*Ezekiel 2* Hermeneia [Philadelphia: Fortress Press, 1983], 264-66), J. W. Wevers (*Ezekiel* NCB [Grand Rapids: Eerdmans, 1969], 278) and G. A. Cooke (*The Book of Ezekiel*, International Critical Commentary [Edinburgh: T. & T. Clark, 1936], 397), leave open the possibility of individual resurrection.

the case sometimes with Old Testament Allusion, which finds its form-critical place as a sub-genre under the Traditions Material.[16]

Rabbinic tradition incorporated the recitation of this passage as a prophetic foreshadowing of the final resurrection in the messianic age.[17] Taking the Jewish character of Matthew under consideration it is likely that he is merely reflecting the language and phrase forms with which he is most familiar and in which he habitually thinks. The cataclysmic phenomena which accompanied Jesus' death is reminiscent of the account in Ezekiel.[18] In addition to the earthquake, the fissuring of the ground, and the opening of the tombs Matthew employs the perfect passive participle, κεκοιμημένων, serving as an adjective to describe the ἁγίων. One interpreter identifies these "sleeping saints" as a focal point for appraising the theology of the Matthean passion narrative.[19]

Extrabiblical evidence also bolsters the supposed connection. A mural of the so-called Ezekiel panel of the resurrection was discovered at the synagogue of Dura Europos which sharply favors Matthew's picture.[20] While the majority of

---

[16]Two excellent works on Old Testament allusion in Matthew are R. H. Gundry, *The Use of the Old Testament in St. Matthew's Gospel* (Leiden: E. J. Brill, 1967), and Krister Stendahl, *The School of St. Matthew and Its Use of the Old Testament* (Lund: C. W. K. Gleerup, 1954).

[17]For example, *Gen. Rab.* 13.6, 14.5; *Deut. Rab.* 7.7; and *Lev. Rab.* 14.9; quoted in J. Grassi, "Ezekiel XXXVII. 1-14 and the New Testament," *New Testament Studies* (1965): 162.

[18]R. H. Gundry, *Matthew: A Commentary on His Literary and Theological Art* (Grand Rapids: Eerdmans, 1982), 576. A close inspection of both passages reveals an unmistakable relationship between the two traditions. The margin in NA[27] reveals allusions to Isa. 26.19 and Dan. 12.2, passages which have already been identified as supporting the sleep-of-death idea. Cf. Amos 8.9 also in reference to the astronomical wonders which were predicted to occur at the time of Jesus' death.

[19]Delvin D. Hutton, "The Resurrection of the Holy Ones (Matt. 27:51b-53): A Study of the Theology of the Matthean Passion Narrative" (Th.D. diss., Harvard University, 1970).

[20]For amplification, see Harald Riesenfeld, *The Resurrection in Ezekiel xxxvii and in the Dura Europos Paintings* (Uppsala: Lundequistska, 1948) and R. Wischnitzer-Bernstein, "The Conception of the Resurrection in the Ezekiel Panel of the Dura Synagogue," *Journal of Biblical Literature* 60 (1941): 43-55. Recently R. M. Hals at least noted the peculiar nature of this mural while believing the major thrust of the passage is the national resurrection of Israel (*Ezekiel*, Forms of Old Testament Literature [Grand Rapids: Eerdmans, 1989], 270-71]).

interpreters rightly concede that individual resurrection is not a highly developed theme anywhere in the Old Testament, D. I. Block strongly advises not to ignore its presence in Ezek. 37.1-14 even if in embryonic form.[21] These saints are depicted as sleeping and are assumed by most commentators to be from the Old Testament era.

The central focus in this event is anything but a symbol. Although it has been explained in a purely figurative sense, the symbolism fades away as the story is sandwiched by the gloomy episode of Jesus' death (27.50) and his subsequent burial (27.57-61).[22] Some take the "holy city" in which the saints appeared as a reference to heaven.[23] If this is true, what would be the edifying purpose for this sign of manifested power to be witnessed only in heaven? There is a discernible benefit for the reader, though, if the ἁγίων are seen as living testimonies against those living persons who rejected the message of Jesus' passion.[24]

Harris points out that history and symbolism are not mutually exclusive.[25] Historical occurrences can have great symbolic significance, as in the case of this massive resuscitation. Great manifestations of this kind of death-conquering power should not be surprising because it revolves around the most significant event in salvation history—the death and resurrection of Jesus Christ. Silence

---

[21]D. I. Block, "Beyond the Grave: Ezekiel's Vision of Death and Afterlife," *Biblical Archaeologist Reader* 2 (1992): 112-41. Influenced by and in addition to Block, Lamar Cooper believes Job embraced a primitive idea of resurrection in 19.25-27 which is "a part of that seedbed of nourishment that rises to a higher revelation in Ezekiel" (*Ezekiel*, New American Commentary [Nashville: Broadman & Holman, 1994], 321).

[22]For the symbolic interpretation, see F. J. Matera, *Passion Narratives and Gospel Theologies* (New York: Paulist Press, 1986), 116-17.

[23]Notice that it is unmistakably identified as Jerusalem in Matt. 4.5.

[24]Eduard Schweizer, *The Good News according to Matthew*, trans. David E. Green (Atlanta: John Knox Press, 1975), 516. For an excellent treatment on the theology of this passage, see D. Senior, "The Death of Jesus and the Resurrection of the Holy Ones (Matt. 27:51-53)," *Catholic Biblical Quarterly* 38 (1976): 312-29.

[25]Murray J. Harris, *From Grave to Glory*, 98. For more on the historicity of this passage, see J. Wenham, "The Resurrection Narratives in Matthew's Gospel," *Tyndale Bulletin* 24 (1973): 42-46.

103

from the remainder of the New Testament corpus concerning this event does not demand its excision. The absence of this report simply suggests that it did not fit the respective theological itineraries of other authors.

Besides a word order problem associated with the tearing of the temple curtain in the first part of verse 51 and a verb tense option in verse 52, there is only one textual problem which is indirectly related to the sleep of death. This textual riddle is related to punctuation and translation. Although there is no textual problem with the saints sleeping, the question surfaces as to the time and condition related to their emergence from the tombs.[26] The pericope under consideration involves one continuous sentence in the Greek language. The key question is: "Were these ἁγίων actually raised upon the death of Jesus (verse 50) or after his resurrection (verse 53)?" Three options are available: 1) Delayed resuscitation view—three days elapsed from the opening of the tombs and the raising of the bodies;[27] 2) Delayed exit view—the saints were raised but remained in the tombs for three days;[28] and 3) Delayed appearance view—events occurred in sequence and the saints did not reveal themselves in Jerusalem until after Jesus' resurrection.[29]

---

[26] For full discussions, see J. Wenham, "When Were the Saints Raised? A Note on the Punctuation of Matthew xxvii.51-53," *Journal of Theological Studies* 32 (1981): 150-52; Harris, *From Grave to Glory*, 97-100; Walter Grundmann, *Das Evangelium nach Matthäus*, Theologischer Handkommentar zum Neuen Testament (Berlin: Evangelische Verlagsanstalt, 1971), 561-63; Joachim Gnilka, *Das Matthäusevangelium*, vol. 2, Herders Theologischer Kommentar zum Neuen Testament, (Freiburg: Herder, 1988), 476-78; and Erich Klostermann, *Das Matthäusevangelium*, Handbuch zum Neuen Testament (Tübingen: J. C. B. Mohr, 1971), 225.

[27] This position results from seeing a full stop at the end of ἀνεῴχθησαν: Wenham, "When Were the Saints Raised?," 150. Wenham believes this solution alleviates the problem of having the saints cooped up inside the tomb for three days before their exit.

[28] This view results from placing a period or semicolon at the end of ἠγέρθησαν: R. H. Gundry, *Matthew* (Grand Rapids: Eerdmans, 1982), 576. This viewpoint is the most awkward.

[29] The phrase μετὰ τὴν ἔγερσιν is understood by what ensues εἰσῆλθον not ἐξελθόντες: Grundmann, *Das Evangelium Matthäus*, 562. He believes that although αὐτοῦ is a dogmatic correction and the best reading, it opens an abundance of questions, including his puzzlement over the cooped-up saints of the second view and his question: "Wie ist ihr Verhältnis zur Auferstehung der Toten bei der Parusie?" (ibid.). Overall, the text is silent on these issues and cannot be used

Maintaining the view that Jesus is the first-born from the dead, with Matthew highlighting his resurrection, the ἁγίων must be considered strictly resuscitations, that is, they died again at a later time. After their miraculous showcase in the city of Jerusalem, they must have returned to a state described as κεκοιμημένων upon their second death just as people like Lazarus and Jairus' daughter did to await the parousia which will be the catalyst for the ultimate reinvigoration of the dead.[30]

The Raising of Jairus' Daughter

The sleep-of-death concept is conveyed with the synonym καθεύδω in the only other synoptic example of the sleep of death.[31] In the form-critical sense the account of the raising of Jairus' daughter is a miracle story.[32] This event is the only resuscitation recorded by all three Synoptic Gospels. Within each account the healing of the woman with a hemorrhage is framed by the story of Jairus' daughter.[33] Some peculiarities exist which are important for this discussion. Probably the most glaring point of debate within this episode is whether or not the girl was actually dead. Some have supposed her to be in a coma because Jesus

---

for support for the viewpoint of Jesus' descent into Hell because verse 53 is not balanced with 1 Cor. 15.20-28. They must, therefore, remain hypotheses.

[30]Four reasons given by Harris in support of this view are: 1) no reference to any spiritual translation; 2) Christ is the πρωτότοκος; 3) the complete harvest will be gathered at the parousia; and 4) the verb used here to portray the post-resurrection manifestation (ἐμφανίζω) of the ἁγίων is not the verb typically utilized (ὁράω) with reference to Jesus (*From Grave to Glory*, 99-100). While Craig Blomberg, *Matthew*, The New American Commentary (Nashville: Broadman Press, 1992), 421, mentions the hypothesis that these "holy ones" could have appeared for a short while in Jerusalem and then taken to heaven, he also says: "But the text refuses to satisfy our curiosity about these points."

[31]Matt. 9.18-19, 23-26 = Mark 5.21-24, 35-43 = Luke 8.40-42, 49-56.

[32]For more on form-critical research of this and other miracle stories, see William L. Craig, "The Problem of Miracles: A Historical and Philosophical Perspective," in *Gospel Perspectives*, vol. 6: *The Miracles of Jesus*, ed. by David Wenham and Craig Blomberg (Sheffield: JSOT Press, 1986), 9-48; C. Headlam, *The Miracles of the New Testament* (London: Murray, 1923), 26-147; and Gerd Theissen, *The Miracle Stories of the Early Christian Tradition*, 1-40.

[33]For the historical setting of this story, see Harris, *From Grave to Glory*, 85, n. 5.

replies with slight variance in all three accounts: "She is not dead, but sleeping." Notice the similarity of the three reports.

<blockquote>
Matt. 9.24: οὐ γὰρ ἀπέθανεν τὸ κοράσιον ἀλλὰ καθεύδει.
Mark 5.39: τὸ παιδίον οὐκ ἀπέθανεν ἀλλὰ καθεύδει.
Luke 8.52: οὐ γὰρ ἀπέθανεν ἀλλὰ καθεύδει.
</blockquote>

Some suppose that Jesus, with adroit medical insight, was able to detect a tinge of life which was being masked by her deathly condition and was consequently able to recover her life.[34] This explanation is unwarranted for three reasons. First, the girl is reported to have been precariously near death earlier in the story. Her death obviously occurs during Jesus' purposeful delay. Although raising someone from the dead may be a magnificent event to twentieth-century Chris-tians, one must not overlook the sizable difference that exists between temporal resuscitation and eschatological resurrection.[35]

In the second place, if the girl were not dead the mourners would not have been there causing such a commotion. From a redaction-critical perspective, Mark's Gospel is more picturesque and vivid than Matthew and Luke.[36] That Mark is describing an out-of-control, hopeless death scene is evidenced by his unique use of the onomatopoeic participle ἀλαλάζοντας in verse 38, which is translated, "wailing loudly."[37] This word is only used one other time in the New Testament. Paul employs it to portray the shrill tones of "a clashing cymbal" in 1 Cor. 13.1. Interesting is the similarity that exists between this term and another

---

[34]Vincent Taylor, *The Gospel according to St. Mark*, 2d ed. (New York: St. Martin's Press, 1966), 295.

[35]Robert A. Guelich, *Mark 1-8:26*, Word Biblical Commentary (Dallas: Word Books, 1989), 301. At the same time there is no intention to diminish the power and awe of the resuscitation performed by Jesus. The focus, however, should be on the lesson which Jesus is trying to teach. This miracle is specifically performed to address the hopelessness of those utterly stunned by the death event. The lesson is that death is not a final and formidable barrier to all action (John Nolland, *Luke 1-9:20*, Word Biblical Commentary [Dallas: Word Books, 1989], 423).

[36]Compare the accounts of "The Transfiguration" in Mk. 9.2-8 and parallels, and the "Rich Young Man" in Mk. 10.17-31 and parallels.

[37]Harris, *From Grave to Glory*, 86, describes it as a "cacophony of sounds."

word which is also onomatopoeic. The same kind of cadence can be detected in the participle ὀλολύζοντες, which is used in Jas. 5.1.[38] Mark and James couple these participles with a form of the verb κλαίω in order to paint a graphic picture of intense emotion.[39] Only death would elicit such a response. Such is the case in both passages as Mark reports the response to death, whereas James calls for this response from the merciless rich who face impending death and punitive judgment.

Thirdly, it is certain that Jairus' daughter was dead because Jesus had not seen the girl when he gave his prognosis.[40] Granted, it does appear strange for Jesus to cast sleep and death inversely (οὐκ ἀπέθανεν ἀλλὰ καθεύδει). Jesus intends, however, to convey the central idea that the girl was not *finally* dead by saying she was sleeping (καθεύδει). In this sense sleep is a qualification of death, not an antithesis of it. Another way to determine that a real death transpired is to consider the report of Luke, the physician. While all three narratives include the mourners' collective response of ridicule and mockery to Jesus' proclamation of hope, Luke embellishes the story with an explanatory note. Notice Luke's addition:

Matt. 9.24: καὶ κατεγέλων αὐτοῦ.
Mark 5.40: καὶ κατεγέλων αὐτοῦ.[41]

---

[38]In this strongly denunciatory passage, the whole phrase can be rendered "burst into weeping, howling with grief."

[39] Ολολύζω is used to express lamentation in the New Testament (see Luke 6.25; Jas. 4.9; Rev. 18.11, 15, 19; and John 16.20). Its foundation has been traced to the Hebrew הֵילִילוּ as used in Isa. 23.14. Isaiah and Jeremiah employ it the most. The repetition by Isaiah in chapter twenty-three in three verses reveals a chant-like rhythm which would not easily be forgotten by those who heard it. It is intriguing to note that for הֵילִילוּ in Ezek. 30.2, the LXX has the cry itself: ὦ ὦ, while other manuscripts retain ὀλολύζετε.

[40]Nolland, *Luke 1-9:20*, 423. He explains Jesus' pronouncement as prognosis rather than diagnosis, because the Lord is saying something important concerning the future, not the past (ibid.).

[41]Some manuscripts (W φ sa) of Mark include the addition εἰδότες ὅτι ἀπέθανεν (see Kurt Aland, *Synopsis Quattuor Evangeliorum*, 192). The reading, however, is derived from a parallel passage which must have been Luke's.

Luke 8.53: καὶ κατεγέλων αὐτοῦ εἰδότες ὅτι ἀπέθανεν.

Luke not only clears up any misunderstanding about the girl's state by recording the fuller response of the audience which explains their derision, but he also improves Mark's Greek in 8.49. When the death-watch committee informs Jairus that his "daughter is dead," Luke uses the perfect τέθνηκεν (8.49) while Mark uses the aorist ἀπέθανεν (5.35).[42] Luke intends to leave room for the abiding results of death to be interrupted by the power of Jesus which is also exercised over sickness and disease.

This Synoptic pericope is important for the present study because the reader is allowed to witness the first-century response to the sleep-of-death concept uttered by Jesus. Biblically, this event is the first example in which an audience is confronted by the sleep-of-death notion in the New Testament. Here, aided by redactional techniques, the authors cast καθεύδω as the sleep of death, albeit not understood in the sense of death by the witnesses. Why were the mourners not able to fathom the words of Jesus? It could be that their thoughts concerning death were governed by the disparaging tones of Greek philosophy rather than by Jesus, the one who would overcome death in the final sense by resurrection.

Additionally, one should not impress any Hellenistic interpretation upon the Lukan explanation of this young girl's restored life. After Jesus commands her to arise, only Luke mentions that "her spirit returned" (8.55). She was neither in a coma nor snatched back from heaven. Luke intends no more than to say that her life was restored to its former earthly existence. Correctly, Harris interprets Jesus' enunciation of the sleep of death as an "ironic hyperbole" to depict him saying, effectually: "As far as I am concerned, this young girl did not die in any final sense, but is temporarily in the sleep of death."[43]

---

[42]Joseph Fitzmyer, *The Gospel according to Luke I-IX*, The Anchor Bible (Garden City, NJ: Doubleday & Company, 1981), 748, n. 49.

[43]Harris, *From Grave to Glory*, 87.

Besides this triple tradition episode, καθεύδω is used comparably only in 1 Thess. 5.10 and arguably in Eph. 5.14. Although many commentators believe both of these passages deal with death, the minority view opts to translate καθεύδω in the sense of "spiritual deadness" or "slothfulness."[44]

Granted, the fragmented baptismal hymn in Eph. 5.14 is difficult to assess as death and resurrection if one is limited to thinking in terms of spiritual deadness, which is figuratively dispelled by the act of baptism.[45] Paul's usage of Hebrew parallelism will aid in the interpretation of this allusion from an unknown source:

ἔγειρε, ὁ καθεύδων,
καὶ ἀνάστα ἐκ τῶν νεκρῶν,
καὶ ἐπιφαύσει σοι ὁ Χριστός.[46]

As the first two lines function synonymously, there is a thematic connection between this pericope, Dan. 12.2, and Ps. 88.5 (87.6, LXX).[47] Secondly, the apocalyptic anticipation of an eschatological arousal is detected as the "sleeper" will come into the light provided by Christ himself. This antithetical imaging of light and darkness finds ample expression in the New Testament as it does in the Old Testament, Dead Sea Scrolls, and the rabbinic literature. It is employed in

---

[44]For the minority opinion, see Thomas R. Edgar, "The Meaning of 'Sleep' in 1 Thessalonians 5.10," *Journal of the Evangelical Theological Society* 22 (1979): 345-49. This view, however, has been soundly refuted by Tracy L. Howard, "The Meaning of 'Sleep' in 1 Thessalonians 5.10—A Reappraisal," *Grace Theological Journal* 6 (1985): 337-48. While Edgar strains to find a basis for Paul not changing the sense of the same word (καθεύδω) in the same context, Howard makes a case for "subconscious repetition" to explain Paul's shift of meaning based on E. Laughton, "Subconscious Repetition and Textual Criticism," *Classical Philology* 45 (1950): 75. This practice of verbal recurrence is the contrived duplication of a word or phrase which was used in its primary sense in proximity with it.

[45]See Horst Balz and Gerhard Schneider, eds. *Exegetical Dictionary of the New Testament*, 2 vols. (Grand Rapids: Eerdmans, 1991), s.v. "Καθεύδω," by M. Völkel. If this admonition is a reference to baptism, then it is related to the further admonition in verse fifteen, which is comparable to the analogous conception of light (v. 8a) and the parenesis (v. 8b) (ibid.).

[46]Consider three supposed origins of this saying in Andrew T. Lincoln, *Ephesians*, Word Biblical Commentary (Dallas, Word Books, 1990), 318-19.

[47]Bruce, *1 & 2 Thessalonians*, 115. Bruce also offers two examples of the unaugmented form εὕδειν (καθεύδω, augmented form) in Homer *Iliad* 14.482, Πρόμαχος δεδμημένος εὕδει/ἔγχει ἐμῷ ("Promachus sleeps, having been mastered by my spear") and Sophocles *Oedipus Coloneus* 621, οὑμὸς εὕδων καὶ κεκρυμμένος νέκυς/ψυχρός ("my cold corpse, asleep and concealed") (ibid.).

the dualistic models of depravity/rebirth and death/resurrection. While most commentators interpret this elusive saying as a baptismal text, B. Noack theorizes that the passage began its career as a resurrection text only later to be adopted as a baptismal hymn for the Ephesian church circle.[48] Lincoln, however, disputes the eschatological explanation on grammatical and practical grounds. Charging Noack's theory as being unwarranted and problematic, he reasons if this were a resurrection hymn ὁ καθεύδων far more likely would have been cast in the plural thus including all resurrection participants and he questions the purpose of a resurrection hymn in an early Christian worship service.[49] Is it not possible, however, for a singular term or phrase to refer to each individual in a particular group? Taking into consideration the strong possible Old Testament influence of this saying one could consider the admonition found in Mic. 6.8: "He has showed you, *O man* what is good. . ." which Paul surely knew well. *O man* is singular yet it undoubtedly refers to each individual in the clan. Similarly the admonition "Wake up, O sleeper" could simultaneously be individual and collective. As to Lincoln's second rebuttal the presence of a resurrection hymn while not necessarily more important than a baptismal hymn would certainly not have been inappropriate in the early church. The Thessalonians would have welcomed one! Thirdly, ethics and eschatology are complementary, as conversion not only initiates the trek toward ultimate immortality fully realized at the resurrection but also conversion provides a reorientation for life in the present "preintermediate state."[50] Verse 14 serves as a summary for the ethical exhortation of the preceding seven verses.[51] Similarly, Paul uses καθεύδω in thematic accord with baptism in 1 Thess. 5.6, 7. If the indicative of salvation, expressed in 5.6, 7 by καθεύδωμεν,

---

[48]B. Noack, "Das Zitat in Eph 5,14," *Studia Theologica* 5 (1952): 62-64.

[49]Lincoln, *Ephesians*, 319, 331-33.

[50]This idea can be gleaned clearly from the context.

[51]Rudolf Bultmann, *Theology of the New Testament*, vol. 1, trans. Kendrick Grobel (London: SCM Press, 1952), 174-75, sees this parenesis as Gnostic because of its dualistic fashion.

resurfaces as a Christological indicative in 5.10, also expressed by καθεύδωμεν, the term appears paradoxical. Laughton, however, has shown that the same term can have distinct meanings within the same context.⁵² In light of this conclusion, it appears best to take Paul's use of γρηγορέω and καθεύδω in 5.10 as a dynamic contrast between the living and the dead. In addition, the Pauline framing is a striking feature in the larger context. The subject of death in 4.13-18 and 5.10 sandwiches the emphasis of salvation in 5.6, 7.⁵³

Keeping in mind that eschatology always underscores Christian ethics, could not Paul be referring to the immediate emergence from spiritual death and subsequent arousal from eschatological sleep in the same passage? Rom. 13.11-14 is another paranetic section much like Eph. 5.8-14, which can be drawn into the discussion of the sleep of death. James Dunn's argument rightly emphasizes the paranetic exhortation in conjunction with eschatology.⁵⁴ He translates Rom. 13.11: "And this, knowing the time, that it is already the hour for you to wake up from sleep." The present writer believes the operative phrase, ὅτι ὥρα ἤδη ὑμᾶς ἐξ ὕπνου ἐγερθῆναι, is apocalyptic and similar to Jesus' words in John 11.11. After Jesus cryptically announces that Lazarus is dead (κεκοίμηται), he then says he is going ἵνα ἐξυπνίσω αὐτόν. With respect to the parenesis in Romans, Dunn must see some overtones of death and resurrection. In reference to the aforementioned phrase he states:

> And as linked with the metaphor of transition from sleep to waking, and so conjoint with the transition from night to day (v. 12), it is hard to avoid the sense of 'God's appointed

---

⁵²See Laughton, "Subconscious Repetition," 75.

⁵³This opinion is also shared by Markus Lautenschlager, "Εἴτε γρηγορῶμεν εἴτε καθεύδωμεν. Zum Verhältnis von Heiligung und Heil in 1 Thess 5,10," *Zeitschrift für die neutestamentliche Wissenschaft* 81 (1990): 39-59. Lautenschlager not only says that to carry the ethical meaning of καθεύδωμεν from verse 6 over to verse 10 is wholly impossible (*völlig ausgeschlossen*), it is also his belief that the majority opinion is internationally shared by the scholarly community (ibid., 39). Lautenschlager explores the relationship between sanctification and eternal salvation in 1 Thess. 5.10 in this article.

⁵⁴James D. G. Dunn, *Romans 9-16*, Word Biblical Commentary (Dallas: Word Books, 1988), 784-94.

eschatological hour,' as in Daniel 8.17 (εἰς ὥραν καιροῦ); 8.19 (εἰς ὥρας καιροῦ συντελείας); 11.35 (καιρὸς εἰς ὥρας); 11.40 (ὥρα συντελείας); John 4.23; 5.25; 1 John 2.18 (ἐσχάτη ὥρα); Rev. 3.3, 10.⁵⁵

Connecting soteriology with thanatology establishes an important point for the intermediate state. That eschatology is realized means something of the eternal has initiated a process which continues into the period between death and resurrection. Coming into the light is intended not only as an ethical imperative for the living but also as an eschatological promise to those asleep in Christ.⁵⁶ That the scenario of realized eschatology is postulated does not mean in any way that Christians have gained immortality during life on earth before death. While they are certainly locked into the total salvation process, immortality is the capstone of the process of salvation which will be fully realized at the resurrection of the believer.⁵⁷

The Lazarus Episode

The raising of Lazarus is a watershed in the Gospel of John. John 11.11-14 represents the only Johannine example of the sleep-of-death metaphor in the New Testament. It enacts, however, the second and last time Jesus attempted to address death as a sleep. While he is misunderstood by nonbelievers in the Jairus' daughter pericope, here he is misunderstood by his disciples. That the disciples fumbled Jesus' concept, however, is no cause for alarm. Thanatology, especially Jesus' own, was not grasped by the disciples from the time of their own calling to the time of Pentecost.

---

⁵⁵Ibid., 785-86.

⁵⁶For fuller treatment, see ibid., 791-94.

⁵⁷See Rudolph Bultmann's discussion of "Freedom from Death" in his, *Theology of the New Testament*, vol. 1, 345-52. Bultmann believes that the Scripture teaches the doctrine of the resurrection of the dead which is strange to Hellenistic ears. Although he feels Paul fell into disparity with the doctrine in Phil. 1.23 and 2 Corinthians 5, he says: "This contradiction betrays how little difference it makes what images are used to express the fact that 'life' has a future beyond life in the 'flesh'" (ibid., 346).

This apocalyptic blip on the Johannine screen has a binary purpose: 1) it leads the Jewish authorities to take decisive, punitive action against Jesus,[58] and 2) it is also the "sign" which discloses more clearly than any other the meaning of his death and resurrection.[59] The miraculous activity of Jesus comes to an apex in the Lazarus story. Although no miracle is ordinary, this particular one is drenched with apocalyptic overtones. By raising Lazarus, Jesus exercises power over that which he would also subject himself and decisively conquer. Jesus desires that the disciples, Mary, and Martha see that there is hope in the face of death. Rudolf Schnackenburg sees the placing of the story at this juncture as an intentional design by the author.[60] Since κοιμάομαι occurs amidst such a crucial stage in the life of Jesus and in the Gospel of John, it merits a brief discussion with regard to issues relating to form, source, redaction, and historical criticism.

Form Critical Analysis

This miracle story is unique in John's Gospel because it combines narrative and discourse elements in an inseparable whole. The difference of form and structure in John 11 from the previous portions of the Gospel is well known. In the Lazarus story the interpreter is faced with a narrative interfused with various elements of dialogue that extracts its merit, rather than a narrative followed by a

---

[58]James P. Martin, "History and Eschatology in the Lazarus Narrative: John 11.1-44," *Scottish Journal of Theology* 17 (1964): 332, believes that, in regard to the death of Jesus, the Synoptists view the cleansing of the Temple (Mk. 11.8) as the direct cause of the final plot to kill Jesus, while John attributes it to the raising of Lazarus. The problem is ultimately dispersed because there is no certainty that one episode alone directly led to Jesus' death. Mark 3.6 and John 7.32 both attest to other attempts and plots.

[59]R. V. G. Tasker, *The Gospel according to John*, Tyndale New Testament Commentaries (Grand Rapids: Eerdmans, 1975), 137. Even though the Synoptics omit the Lazarus story, the raisings of Jairus' daughter and of the widow's son of Nain are also signs that the messianic age had arrived. Perhaps prompted by this silence some have tried to engineer a connection between this Johannine miracle story and the Lukan parable of "The Rich Man and Lazarus." For an exposition of this hypothesis, see R. Dunkerley, "Lazarus," *New Testament Studies* 5 (1958-59): 321-27.

[60]Rudolf Schnackenburg, *The Gospel according to John*, vol. 2, trans. Cecily Hastings, et al, Herder's Theological Commentary (New York: Seabury Press, 1980), 316.

discourse on its meaning.⁶¹ C. H. Dodd notices the thoroughness of this apparent fusion because one cannot isolate a single parcel of unadulterated narrative. He says: "There is no story of the raising of Lazarus—or none that we can now recover—separable from the pregnant dialogues of Jesus with his disciples and with Martha."⁶²

Source and Redaction Critical Analysis

The literary complexity of this passage was first addressed by Rudolf Bultmann.⁶³ He supposes for the Lazarus story and others a foundational account derived from a σημεῖα-source.⁶⁴ The basic skeletal structure of the story is found in verses 1, 3, 5-6, 11-12, 14-15, 17-19, 33-39, and 43-44. Bultmann hypothesizes that these verses do not form an original pericope. The *Semeia-Quelle* is built on yet an older narrative which had already been edited.⁶⁵

Wilhelm Wilkens sets forth a more rigorous thesis. He delineates three levels in his source analysis: 1) a brief synoptic account which emerges from the tradition; 2) an earlier form of the present story; and 3) the final Johannine

---

⁶¹G. R. Beasley-Murray, *John*, Word Biblical Commentary (Waco: Word Books, 1987), 184. For example, compare the changing of the water to wine in John 2.1-11 and the curing of the paralytic in John 5.1-15.

⁶²C. H. Dodd, *The Interpretation of the Fourth Gospel* (Cambridge: Cambridge University Press, 1953), 363. Dodd later softened this view in *Historical Tradition of the Fourth Gospel*, 232. Heinrich Zimmermann, *Neutestamentliche Methodenlehre: Darstellung der historisch-kritischen Methode*, 7th ed. (Stuttgart: Katholisches Bibelwerk, 1982), 156, places it in his sixfold division of *Wundergeschichten* under the heading *Therapien*.

⁶³Rudolf Bultmann, *The Gospel of John*, trans. R. W. N. Hoare and J. K. Riches (Philadelphia: Westminster Press, 1971), 395.

⁶⁴On the whole question of this source-critical problem, see Robert T. Fortna, *The Gospel of Signs* (Cambridge: Cambridge University Press, 1970), and his most recent *The Fourth Gospel and Its Predecessors* (Philadelphia: Fortress Press, 1988). For another current treatment, consult Urban C. von Wahlde, *The Earliest Version of John's Gospel: Recovering the Gospel of Signs* (Wilmington, DE: Michael Glazier, 1989).

⁶⁵Fortna supposes Bultmann did not give any name to the written form the Evangelist followed when writing the Gospel. Fortna designates it the *Passions-Quelle*.

embroidering.[66] Although verses eleven through fourteen (focal for this study) are not an integral part of the original story (as are verses 3, 17, 33-34, 38-39, 41a, and 43-44), this sign marks the high point of the activity in the ministry of Jesus.[67] It directly points to his own death and resurrection as it forms a perfect culmination of the "Book of Signs." John intends to draw a parallel between the realized and imminent death of Lazarus and Jesus respectively as "Christ's word, therefore, running close to the side of Christ's deed."[68]

It must be remembered, on the one hand, that all talk of stripping away sentences to uncover the original story does not mean that what is disrobed is of no value. It stresses, on the other hand, the presence of an oral tradition which was constantly being shaped, fashioned, and improved prior to its recollection in a written form. The evolution of oral tradition was due largely to the needs of the community of faith.

Combining their results, the critical disciplines are instrumental in analyzing the miracle stories. It has been correctly stated:

---

[66]Wilhelm Wilkens, "Die Erweckung des Lazarus," *Theologische Zeitschrift* 15 (1959): 23-28. Wilkens's thesis entails not only the investigation of the biblical text but also the consideration of what lies behind the text. The preaching took place again and again in new and different situations. Thereby, one discovers traditional events, model testimonies, and a steady reconstruction of improvement.

[67]See I. T. Foretell, "I Am the Resurrection and the Life," in *Contemporary New Testament Studies*, ed. Rosalie Ryan (Collegeville, MN: The Liturgical Press, 1965), 100-101, and T. E. Pollard, "The Raising of Lazarus (John xi), in *Studia Evangelica*, vol. 6, ed. Elizabeth A. Livingstone, (Berlin: Akademie, 1973), 436-37.

[68]"Neben die Christustät tritt damit das Christuswort" (Wilkens, "Die Erweckung des Lazarus," 33). For another similar source-critical approach to this passage, see Wilhelm Stenger, "Die Auferweckung des Lazarus (John 11.1-45)," *Trierer theologische Zeitschrift* 83 (1974): 17-37. For an excellent recent historical-critical analysis of the narrative, see Gérard Rochais, *Les récits de résurrection des morts dans le Nouveau Testament*, SNTSMS 40 (Cambridge: University Press, 1981), 113-45. His conclusion is that a triple-levelled composition exists (ibid., 133). Even though the recognition of compositional tiers and a guarded unanimity among scholars pertaining to oral or primary written tradition exists, it is the opinion of Brian H. Henneberry that the Lazarus episode is wholly Johannine thus rendering futile any attempt to isolate a redacted written tradition (*The Raising of Lazarus (John 11.1-44): An Evaluation of the Hypothesis That a Written Tradition Lies behind the Narrative* [Ann Arbor, MI: University Microfilms, 1984], 64).

The postulate of a primitive narrative of the Raising of Lazarus, comparable in its brevity to other Johannine 'sign' narratives, having contacts with miracle stories in other traditions (such as the Raising of Jairus' daughter and the Epileptic Boy), developed within the Johannine circle, and finally related by the Evangelist in accordance with his profound theological insight is wholly comprehensible and by no means dismissed.[69]

Trouble arises, however, when comparisons are made with Hellenistic literature. The History of Religions School viewed Jesus as a miracle worker much like the miracle stories ascribed to the θεῖος ἀνήρ in Hellenistic literature.[70] It is unnecessary to strain the thesis of a Semeia-Source by magnifying the differences between the supposed strata. There is no bonafide evidence that the miracle stories were ever disseminated among the churches depicting Jesus as a glorified wonder worker—that is, a *divine man* as the pagans adored. Quite to the contrary, the miracle stories of Jesus were unique in content as well as in form.

The message of the miracle stories about Jesus was stitched tightly to the eschatological fabric of the kingdom of God. They were too inextricably woven into the fabric of the evangelical traditions and the church's kerygmatic program for them ever to have circulated in the manner suggested by the History of Religions School. The writer of the Gospel of John had a firm grip on the theological significance of the signs, especially the *magnum opus* sign of the raising of Lazarus from the sleep of death. Since κοιμάομαι is couched within this kind of redactional design, the author says something of the vast significance of its theological content pertaining to thanatology.

Historical Value of the Lazarus Pericope

The assessment of the sources and purpose of the Gospel will determine one's historical perspective of this episode. A strictly a priori view of the miracles

---

[69]Beasley-Murray, *John*, 186.

[70]For a full treatment of this thesis, see John M. Hull, *Hellenistic Magic and the Synoptic Tradition* (Naperville, IL: Allenson Press, 1974); Carl R. Holladay, *Theios Aner in Hellenistic Judaism* (Missoula, MT: Scholars Press, 1977); and Barry L. Blackburn, "Miracle Working 'ΘΕΙΟΙ ΑΝΔΡΕΣ' in Hellenism (and Hellenistic Judaism)," in *Gospel Perspectives*, vol. 6: *The Miracles of Jesus*, 185-218.

would necessarily exclude this event.[71] Setting this philosophical discussion aside, the leading argument against the historicity of the episode is that it has no point of contact with the synoptic tradition.[72] In addition, John's sequencing of events does not mesh with the Synoptics.[73] One attempt at solving the problem has been to propose that the occurrence of the raising of Lazarus is a fabricated story rooted in the Synoptic tradition.[74] This theory has been soundly rejected on the basis that it undermines the common understanding of Johannine tradition, namely, that the Gospel of John does not harbor independent historical tradition but is dependent on a restructuring of Synoptic minutiae.[75]

These discrepancies do not call for the historical jettison of the Lazarus pericope. As Brown warns: "We must be very cautious about the use of John in scientifically reconstructing in detail the ministry of Jesus of Nazareth, even as we must be careful in so using the other Gospels."[76] Unique features of the Gospel tradition enhance its veracity. Such is the case with the Lazarus episode and its sole usage of κοιμάομαι.

---

[71]C. K. Barrett, *The Gospel according to John* (Philadelphia: The Westminster Press, 1978), 388.

[72]For a list of the external problems, see T. E. Pollard, "The Raising of Lazarus," 434. For the historical value of John, see Raymond Brown, "The Problem of the Historicity in John," *Catholic Biblical Quarterly* 24 (1962): 1-14; A. J. B. Higgins, *The Historicity of the Fourth Gospel* (London: Lutterworth, 1960); and E. Stauffer, "Historische Elemente in Vierten Evangelium," *Homiletica en Biblica* 22 (1963): 1-7.

[73]See Raymond Brown, *The Gospel according to John I-XII*, 2d ed., The Anchor Bible (Garden City, NY: Doubleday & Company, 1966), 428.

[74]Alan Richardson, *The Gospel according to Saint John*, Torch Commentaries (London: SCM Press, 1959), 139.

[75]Brown, *The Gospel according to John I-XII*, 428-29.

[76]Ibid., l-li.

Exegesis

Greatly influenced by his fast approaching death, Jesus was able to bestow the abnormality of eternity upon the normality of the temporal sphere, that is, the didactic content of his own death and resurrection. He created the possibility by allowing Lazarus to die (John 11.4-5).[77] Verse four contains one key for the total comprehension of this event. After Jesus hears about Lazarus' illness, he says: "This illness is not unto death; it is for the glory of God, so that the Son of God may be glorified by means of it." The phrase πρὸς θάνατον in verse 4 functions as an adverbial accusative of purposive termination. Jesus, however, precludes this purpose. If the illness is not purposed for death, then why does Lazarus die? An interesting parallel has been drawn to an Old Testament story which may help one understand Jesus' design. It is the story of Hezekiah's postponement of death in 2 Kings 20 and Isaiah 38. The key differences in this story are that Hezekiah did not die before his reprieve and there was no apparent understanding of life after death. Moule draws attention to the language which describes the king's malady as terminal.[78] Unlike Hezekiah, Lazarus is allowed to die. Like Hezekiah, however, Lazarus received a fresh, undetermined lease on life.

That death is not final is revealed by the fact of Jesus' reference to Lazarus as one who κεκοίμηται (Jn. 11.11). The main thrust of this event, then, is not death but life. By raising Lazarus from the sleep of death, Jesus meant to say that one can experience death and live again. The perfect tense of the verb lends itself well to this explanation. From this usage, it has been supposed that death is a discernible state which elapses.[79] Like pagan thought, death is perpetual but only

---

[77]C. F. D. Moule, "The Meaning of 'Life' in the Gospels and Epistles of St. John: A Study in the Story of Lazarus, John 11.1-44," *Theology* 78 (1975): 115.

[78]Ibid., 116, n. 1. 2 Kgs. 20.1 has לָמוּת, πρὸς θάνατον (LXX); Isa. 38.1 has לָמוּת, ἕως θάνατον (LXX); and John 11.4 has πρὸς θάνατον.

[79]This position is expressed by Edouard Delebecque, "Lazare est mort (note sur Jean 11,11-15)," *Biblica* 67 (1986): 90, n. 6. The whole footnote runs: "La notion de repos, dans le sommeil ou bien dans la mort, est soulignée par l'emploi du *parfait* κεκοίμηται, qui signifie un *état*, soit durable, soit définitif (emphasis his)." For the same idea, see O. Merlier, "Note sur deux passages

existing until the eternal one eschatologically intervenes by means of our own resurrection prompted by his parousia. The zenith of reinstatement to life will be accomplished by the resurrection. Hezekiah and Lazarus both await this crowning event.

Jesus wants to instill faith in the disciples, Mary, and Martha by teaching them something new. Their ideas of death were incomplete until Jesus walked among them teaching the truth of His mission. Apocalyptically, Jesus sets out to remedy Lazarus' demise by announcing His intention to awaken him in verse 11.[80] From a post-resurrection viewpoint, the author was able to add a pregnant explanatory gloss in verse 13 in the spirit of interpretation for the reader. This unique double construction, περὶ τῆς κοιμήσεως τοῦ ὕπνου, betrays the uninformed thoughts of the disciples and can be translated "concerning the rest which is sleep." With this a posteriori evaluation in mind, Balz accurately summarizes John 11.11-13:

> The theological statement which relativizes the power of death by the reality of salvation moves on from the OT and apocalyptic basis beyond the assertions of Hellenistic religion, not using them to embellish the inevitable state of death, but proclaiming the basic powerlessness of death in the light of the resurrection.[81]

The atmosphere surrounding the amazing prospect of waking Lazarus was much the same as with Jairus' daughter. Jesus' intention "was as ridiculous to the

---

du quatrième Évangile," *Bulletin de Correspondance Hellénique* 54 (1930): 228-40. The verses he deals with are "Jean 11,11 et le sens de κοιμᾶσθαι," 228-35, and "Jean 11,14," 235-40. It is interesting that the disciples respond with the identical word in verse twelve, albeit minus the desired penetration of meaning. The same textual variant exists in both verses. In one of the less reliable Western texts, codex Bezae (D), κοίμαται appears.

[80]The word translated "wake" is ἐξυπνίσω. This is a *hapax legomenon* in the New Testament. Jesus used the word in contrast to κεκοίμηται. It is striking that these same two words are used in Job 14.12. The Jobian difference is apparent. "So man lies down and does not rise; till the heavens are no more, men will not awake (ἐξυπνίσω) or be roused from their sleep" (κοιμάομαι). In respect to verses 13 and 14, Marvin Pope, *Job*, 3d ed., The Anchor Bible (Garden City, NY: Doubleday & Company, 1983), 108, says: "Job gropes toward the idea of an afterlife. If only God would grant him asylum in the netherworld, safe from the wrath which now besets him, and then appoint a time for a new and sympathetic hearing, he would be willing to wait or even endure the present evil." Also consult Hartley, *The Book of Job*, 234 and Robert L. Alden, *Job*, New American Commentary (Nashville: Broadman & Holman, 1993), 167-69.

[81]Horst Balz, "Ὕπνος," 8:555.

mourners for the child as it was distant from those who mourned Lazarus (v. 33)."[82] The connotation of verse 11 should be taken seriously, especially in light of verses 25 and 26. Martha's admission that she knew Lazarus would rise on the last day (v. 24) is an apocalyptic response. In essence, Jesus boldy proclaims the substance of what Job hopelessly pondered. Notice the identical construction between the two:

Job 14.14: ἐὰν γὰρ ἀποθάνῃ ἄνθρωπος ζήσεται?
John 11.25: κἂν   ἀποθάνῃ   ζήσεται.

John's account replaces the "man" of Job with "he who believes in me."[83] The resurrection of Jesus will guarantee eternal life for those who have faith in Him. Although employed differently, the contexts of the Jobian and Johannine passages contain the term κοιμάομαι. Another Johannine peculiarity emerges in verse 24 after Jesus proclaims to the distraught sister of Lazarus that her brother would rise again. Reflecting some degree of belief in resurrection, Martha admitted that she knew of a resurrection on the last day. Jesus patiently tried to lead Martha beyond any nationalistic, anti-Saducean beliefs by elaborating upon the theological content of κοιμάομαι.

That the disciples failed to grasp Jesus' meaning of the sleep of death and Martha exhibited a spiritual paralysis of her own warranted Jesus' further exposition on thanatology. Justified is the question concerning Martha's obviously less-than-hopeful attitude. Great faith does not abound in the response to Lazarus' death. Jesus brought the dilemma sharply into focus by means of the enunciation of a new and astonishing revelation: "I am the Resurrection and the Life" (John 11.25). Jesus extends her faith by drawing attention to life, not to the disparity of death. Thanatology incorporates life by the mere fact that a spiritual resurrection had already occurred on account of faith in Christ, thus robbing physical death of its foreboding eschatological sting. The last phrase in verse 25,

---

[82]Beasley-Murray, *John*, 189.

[83]Gérard Rochais, *Les récits de résurrection*, 141.

therefore, expresses the meaning of "I am the Resurrection," while the first phrase in verse 26 is synonymous with the phrase "I am the Life."[84]

New life through salvation is the conceptual key for understanding the continuity of the salvation process pervasive during death. The believer is in mystical union with Christ upon the initiation of the salvation process through faith. Mysticism has been classically defined by Albert Schweitzer:

> We are always in the presence of mysticism when we find a human being looking upon the division between earthly and superearthly, temporal and eternal, as transcended, and feeling himself, while still externally amid the earthly and temporal, to belong to the super-earthly and eternal.[85]

This definition does not teach the immortality of the soul or any special gnosis. It is, though, a good definition of what it means to be ἐν Χριστῷ. Although not a Johannine formula, a case can be made for the assimilation of Paul's understanding of life with that taught in the Gospel of John.[86]

Κοιμάομαι is not used in this optimum sign to refer to death euphemistically but to lay the foundation for the teaching of hope in the face of physical death. Why would Jesus go to all this trouble if Lazarus were already in heaven?[87]

---

[84]Beasley-Murray, *John*, 190-91.

[85]Albert Schweitzer, *The Mysticism of Paul the Apostle*, trans. William Montgomery (New York: Seabury Press, 1968), 1.

[86]Beasley-Murray, *John*, 190-91, takes as a test case 2 Cor. 5.14-15, 17. Οἱ ζῶντες are certainly "the dead who have come to life" through the risen Christ. The present writer agrees. There must have been a temporal meaning expressed by Jesus as well as an eschatological one. Lazarus will be raised to live again along with Martha and Mary. Physical life was not consummated at that time. Yet they learned through the experience that life can be lived with a totally different perspective once one experiences life through Jesus' resurrection. Martha learned that the Kingdom of God is not only to be accomplished eschatologically but also realized in the present order. The "already-not yet" tension rushed forth with Jesus' claim. Gal. 2.20 is telling: "I have been crucified with Christ and I no longer live, but Christ lives in me. The life I live in the body, I live by faith in the Son of God, who loved me and gave himself for me."

[87]Highly convincing is the case made for Jesus being angered in John 11.33, 38 instead of the usual interpretation of deep compassion (ibid., 192-94). The difference drawn between the German and English interpretative traditions of the entry "ἐμβριμάομαι" can be seen by examining the underlying German and secondary English editions of Walter Bauer, ed., *A Greek-English Lexicon of the New Testament and Other Early Christian Literature*, 2d ed., trans. W. F. Arndt and F. W. Gingrich, F. W. Danker, rev. and aug. by F. W. Gingrich and F. W. Danker (Chicago: University of Chicago Press, 1979). The lack of faith and absence of hope displayed by the witnesses in light

Certainly, he was not snatched back to be the main course of an object lesson. Chronologically, the acquisition of heaven in relation to parousia/resurrection remains a posteriori.

Another key for understanding eternal life and the sleep of death is the Incarnation. While it is critical to evaluate the aspects of the journey from the temporal to the eternal, one must also deal with the "in-fleshing" of God. Entry into the postmortem state is the reciprocal action of Jesus' Incarnation. The Incarnation, that which was eternal became a man, quickened the distance between the two for the later patristic interpretation of "homoousion." Conversely, the intermediate state involves the passage from the temporal to the eternal. The issue of the postmortem state generated prolific debates in church history concerning Christology. In reverse, the believer is faced with the same dynamics and problems associated with interpretations of the Incarnation, that is, understanding the collision of differing spheres of ontological status. The clues available to the Christian are intricately related to the Incarnate and resurrected Christ who defines and provides the passageway between both ontic regions. Κοιμάομαι serves as an indicator that death is better than life but not as good as heaven.

The Sleep of Death in the Primitive Church
The First Christian Martyr

More has been written about the cause of Stephen's death than about the death itself.[88] With detailed information, probably supplied from the apostle Paul, Luke tersely records this death at the conclusion of a defense speech. The execution of Stephen is actually not part of this sub-genre.[89] What is instrumental for this study

---

of Lazarus' death was not pleasing to Jesus. This interpretation may challenge one's Christology.

[88]For representative bibliography, see Ernst Haenchen, *The Acts of the Apostles: A Commentary*, trans. B. Noble and G. Shinn (Philadelphia: The Westminster Press, 1971), 277-78.

[89]Form-critically speaking, the concluding part of the defense speech is known as the "preoratio," which has definite parallels to Hellenistic rhetorical forms. Its purpose was to stir the judge to act in favor with the one being accused (William Rudolf Long, "The Trial of Paul in the

is Stephen's demeanor in the face of such a horrible death. It appears that the thanatological viewpoint of the early Christians embraced the idea Jesus intended when He referred to death as a sleep.[90] Luke casts this vicious mob, which was unleashed to hunt down and kill, in an accented contrast with that of the confident Stephen.[91] Missing is any sign of hopelessness which was present at the deaths of Jairus' daughter and Lazarus. In light of this divergence, the full thrust of κοιμάομαι is unquestionably presented as to say death is totally robbed of its sting for Jesus' followers.[92]

What is the interpreter to make of Stephen's echo of Jesus' statement on the cross at the moment of death described as "giving up the spirit" (cf. Acts 7.59 and Luke 23.46)? To read a Platonic escape of the soul into the story would render the subsequent "falling asleep" a non sequitur in Stephen's case. This idea equally does not fit with Jesus' demise on account of the three days which intervened between his death and resurrection. Are both of these instances classic cases of the release of the *deus ex machina*, or is the spirit to be identified with the idea of a "life principle" much like רוּחַ in the Old Testament? The scholars who wish to avoid any kind of dualistic model opt for the latter.[93] Dualism, however, can

---

Book of Acts: Historical, Literary, and Theological Considerations" [Ph.D. diss., Brown University, 1982]). Although not an actual trial, the Stephen episode is similar. His death is not treated in the same pericope as the speech.

[90]Luke knows of two of the terms used to express the sleep of death. Κοιμάομαι is used in Acts and καθεύδω is used in the Jairus' daughter story.

[91]Such is the opinion of John B. Polhill, *Acts*, The New American Commentary (Nashville: Broadman Press, 1992), 208-9. The Mishnaic tractate, *Sanhedrin*, is extremely explicit of this manner of execution. As horrible a death as it was, Luke's intention is to characterize Stephen's executioners as a seething pack of hungry, snarling wolves eager to pounce upon their prey (A. T. Robertson, *Word Pictures in the New Testament* [Nashville: Broadman Press, 1930], 3:97).

[92]Curtis Vaughan, *Acts* (Grand Rapids: Zondervan Publishing House, 1974), 47.

[93]M. E. Isaacs, *The Concept of the Spirit: A Study of Pneuma in Hellenistic Judaism and Its Bearing on the New Testament* (London: Heythrop, 1976), 71, n. 10, holds that πνεῦμα refers to the self. In effect, Jesus and Stephen commended their lives to God.

be a viable anthropological option if it avoids the Platonic sense of the immortality of the soul. This concept aligns itself with the former model.[94]

This writer agrees with Luke's position of using the term πνεῦμα in the sense of a "discarnate person." Jesus and Stephen committed more than their "breath" or "life principle" to God. They indeed entrusted their post-mortem state to the one who inevitably controlled it, God. One huge question, however, remains: "Where was Jesus during his death?" During various crucial events in his life, Jesus offered some "incarnational" insights into the period between death and resurrection. Considering these examples will lay the foundation for answering the question pertaining to Jesus' abbreviated sojourn in the intermediate state.

At the outset of this chapter three thantological options were presented: one dualistic and two monistic models. The two monistic models—immediate resurrection and extinction recreation—can be dismissed based upon prima facie evidence in the Gospels. Jesus' timetable for the resurrection is seen in the pericope of Luke 20.35 amid a discussion about the resurrection and marriage. Although "immediate resurrectionists" will still maintain that "the age to come" is realized upon death, almost all Lukan scholars believe the age to come is properly catalogued in the scheme of *Heilsgeschichte*, as in the most remote time in the temporal future and experienced corporately by the people of God.[95] Joseph Fitzmyer points out that the traditional interpretation of this particular exchange Jesus had with the Sadducees clashes with the Greek dualistic stance of immortality.[96] E. E. Ellis holds that the former argument is erroneous

> because it would defeat the precise point of Jesus' argument. If Abraham is now personally 'living,' no resurrection would be necessary for God to be 'his God.' The premiss of the argument is the Old Testament (and Saducean) view of death. From this premiss, the nature

---

[94] Joseph Osei-Bonsu, "Anthropological Dualism in the New Testament," *Scottish Journal of Theology* 40 (1987): 586.

[95] Mattill, *Luke and the Last Things*, 130-33. In addition, see I. Howard Marshall, *Commentary on Luke*, International Greek Testament Commentary (Grand Rapids: Eerdmans, 1978), 741.

[96] Joseph Fitzmyer, *The Gospel according to Luke X-XXIV*, The Anchor Bible (Garden City, NY: Doubleday & Company, 1985), 1301.

of the 'living' God, and God's covenant with Abraham the Lord infer the necessity of a resurrection. The question between Jesus and the Sadducees is not Plato's but Job's, not 'if a man die is he still alive' but 'if a man die shall he live again.' To this question Jesus gives a firm and positive answer: the paths of glory lead *from* the grave.[97]

Also, the temporary annihilationist is damaged by the phrase that the patriarchs "are alive to God" in Luke 20.38.[98] The Transfiguration event (Matt. 17.1-13 and parallels) is equally detrimental to the idea that those who have died are temporarily extinct because two "dead" figures, Moses and Elijah, appear with Jesus and are recognized by Peter.[99]

Although the parable of the Rich man and Lazarus in Luke 16.19-31 discussed above in Chapter II is not primarily concerned with in the intermediate state and thus prevents the formulation of any firm ontological conclusions, it still yields some thanatological belief. It makes perfect sense that Jesus would appeal to the popular mind-set of the day in order to transmit his message more efficiently.

Another passage relevant to this discussion is Jesus' conversation with the thief on the cross in Luke 23.42-43. It has been utilized heavily to support the immediate resurrectionist viewpoint because Jesus said to the penitent thief: "Today, you will be with me in paradise." Granted, some have made too much or too little of the term translated "today."[100] Soteriologically, the thief began his journey to immortality upon his request to be remembered by Jesus. It would be

---

[97]E. E. Ellis, *Gospel of Luke*, (Greenwood, SC: Attic Press, 1964), 235, emphasis his. While theoretically it appears that Ellis believes in an intermediate state, functionally his model is closer to that of the immediate resurrectionist.

[98]See the discussion in Cooper, *Body, Soul, & Life Everlasting*, 134. Another revealing passage which suggests the existence of an intermediate state is found in the unique Lukan parable of "The Guest and the Host" in Luke 14.7-14. Although reference to being repaid "at the resurrection of the just" in verse 14b is couched in the context of a reward motif, this action suggests a time in the future. Ellis, however, attributes the idea to rabbinic thought (*Gospel of Luke*, 194-95).

[99]See discussion in ibid., 135. Cf. Matt. 17.1-13 and parallels.

[100]Reichenbach, *Is Man the Phoenix?*, 184-85, interprets Jesus' use of σήμερον as subjective. Similarly Hanhart, *The Intermediate State in the New Testament*, 211-13, and Fitzmyer, *The Gospel of Luke I-IX*, 1508, believe the utterance is to be seen as a chronological axiom of salvific time.

proper, therefore, to interpret σήμερον as both "already" and "not yet." Secondly, the prepositional phrase, ἐν τῷ παραδείσω, in verse 43 is extremely important. Cooper insists that in order to understand Jesus' message to the thief one should consider its employment in intertestamental Judaism and the New Testament. Both treat it similarly. Paradise is depicted as the Edenic dwelling place of the righteous, both in the intermediate and terminal sense. John saw it in an already/not yet configuration (Rev. 2.7). Paul knew of and experienced it during his lifetime (2 Cor. 12.2-4).[101]

Unlike the ethical thrust of the rich man and Lazarus parable, Jesus guaranteed the thief a continued fellowship with him even during death before the time of the resurrection.[102] There is no interruption of the sanctification process which begins upon a genuine confession of Jesus as Lord, who experienced and conquered death. Death is not the door to heaven; it is the corridor. Resurrection is the door.

If Jesus' words in Luke 23.43, therefore, are taken literally, it is safe to say that Jesus spent at least some time in paradise during his "mini-intermediate state." While no person should be too bold in this interpretation of Jesus' so-called descent into hell in 1 Pet. 3.18-20, it does at least identify another pre-parousia locale other than heaven. At best, it is an ontological subset of heaven where the dead in Christ exist until the parousia. Peter also employs an Old Testament quotation in his speech at Pentecost to make reference to the incapability of Sheol being able to circumvent the resurrection of Christ.[103] Jesus did not lounge in heaven during his death but experienced the full brunt of sin's devastating consequences in hell. Through and during his death Jesus formulated the

---

[101]Cooper, *Body, Soul, & Life Everlasting*, 140-41.

[102]The pronounced didactic thrust of Jesus' communiqué is introduced by the particle ἀμήν. Here, as in each case of divine resuscitation, Jesus demanded faith and hope in the face of death.

[103]For insightful discussions, see Polhill, *Acts*, 113-14 and Haenchen, *The Acts of the Apostles*, 181-82, 186-87.

exemplary definition of resurrection as the πρωτότοκος, "having pioneered the route which all his brothers and sisters who die before his return will follow."[104] Such is the plight of Stephen, the other martyrs in Rev. 6.9-11, and all of the κοιμωμένων to this pre-parousia day. Who is experiencing heaven in its fullness presently? Technically, it must include just the Godhead and those who are known to have escaped death by translation—Enoch and Elijah. Though one is in intimate proximity to Christ after death (cf. Rom. 8.38), salvation history is still incomplete because of the *current* pre-parousia disposition of the κοιμωμένοι (italics mine).

The Davidic Regnal Obituary Redivivus: A Key Element in a Lukan Missionary Speech

Form-critically, Acts 13.16-41 belongs to the sub-genre known as the "missionary speech."[105] Martin Dibelius exerted the greatest influence on subsequent scholarship pertaining to this genre type.[106] Dibelius's thesis was that Luke composed the speeches and fashioned their structure in his literary style. Dibelius's fourfold design in the speeches is preserved in the first half of Acts. They consistently begin with an introduction relating the situation of the speech to its subject matter. This part is followed by an account of Jesus' ministry, death, and resurrection by means of the speaker's personal testimony. It is noteworthy to see the existence of the core idea of the passion narrative in these speeches. The third element is the confirmatory evidence from the Scriptures. This trio of elements is capped by an exhortation to repentance.

---

[104]Cooper, *Body, Soul, & Life Everlasting*, 145.

[105]For a brief but excellent survey of the chief Christian speeches recorded in the book of Acts, see F. F. Bruce, *The Speeches in the Acts of the Apostles* (London: The Tyndale Press, 1942), and C. H. Dodd, *The Apostolic Preaching and Its Developments* (New York: Harper & Row, Publishers, 1964).

[106]One of the more important among many is the posthumous work, *Die Reden der Apostelgeschichte und die antike Geschichtsschreibung* (Heidelberg: Vandenhoeck & Ruprecht, 1949).

Paul includes this Old Testament reference to King David's death as an important kerygmatic element, as does Peter in the Pentecostal sermon of Acts 2.[107] This component is important because a vivid comparison is drawn between the deaths of David and Jesus with the thematic messianic promise of the Son of God fulfilled. Paul's Old Testament quotation of Ps. 16.10 in Acts 13.34 is contrasted to Peter's Old Testament allusion of the same verse in Acts 2.31. When expounding upon the term διαφθοράν, translated "corruption," the point that both apostles make is the fact that David was not referring to himself but to Christ. In its verbal form, the only time this term is used for the destruction of man as a direct result of God's judgment is in Rev. 11.18.[108] What does this corruption mean in the case of David's death, commonly known as sleep?

At this point, the reference to David sleeping in death will assist in the interpretative thrust of this significant point of the missionary sermon. While Paul refers to David's death in the same way as the LXX by using the term ἐκοιμήθη (Acts 13.36), Peter uses one of the more common words for death, ἐτελεύτησαν.[109] On the other hand, it is noteworthy that in neither of these cases nor anywhere else in the New Testament is Jesus' death described as sleep.[110] The Davidic association with Jesus is breached at the point of death because David's efficacy

---

[107]After examining Dodd's essay, this writer has extracted the following elements in a missionary speech and cast them in his own terminology: 1) Prophetic foreshadowing; 2) Lineage to David; 3) Divine Approval; 4) Betrayal and Crucifixion; 5) Resurrection; 6) Witnesses; 7) Exaltation; 8) Parousia and Judgment; and 9) Command to Repent.

[108]Günther Harder, "Φθείρω," 9:102. In its unaugmented form, Paul does employ it in 1 Cor. 3.16 as a sobering reminder of the reciprocal fate of the one who destroys God's church. The term διαφθαρτόν stands in stark contrast with terminology which belongs to the transcendant only. Paul and Peter set the stage antithetically by including terms such as ἀμίαντος, ἀμάραντος, and ἄφθαρτος (see 1 Corinthians 15 and 1 Peter 4). Immortality is the inheritance which all Christians will one day enter (ibid., 104).

[109]That Peter used κοιμάομαι similarly in 2 Pet. 3.1-7 shows that he had knowledge of the regnal obituary formula.

[110]In order for the resurrection to withstand the charge that Jesus really did not die, thus downgrading the resurrection to a mere resuscitation, all biblical authors clearly characterized his death in their kerygmatic formulas without euphemism or metaphor.

was temporally qualified. For this reason, one should accept the King James Version of verse 36: "For David, after he had served his own generation by the will of God, fell on sleep, and was laid unto his fathers, and saw corruption." The major point of contrast has been defined accurately in the following:

> For it must be borne in mind that the contrast which most aids the Apostle's argument is that, while David's services could benefit only those among whom he lived, and could not be extended to other generations, Christ by His Resurrection, never more to die and see corruption, is a Saviour for all generations, and remission of sins through Him can be promised to every one that believeth.[111]

Lastly, Peter speaks about two additional aspects of David's thanatological condition which are important for our understanding of the sleep-of-death metaphor. In Acts 2.29 Peter says: "David died and was buried, and his tomb is here to this day." In verse 34 he adds: "For David did not ascend to heaven." It is essential to notice that Paul and Peter knew of the sleep-of-death notion and that they always interpreted it in a secondary sense in comparison to the death of Jesus. Pauline and Petrine traditions both reflect an understanding of the sleep-of-death accounts within the regnal résumés found in Kings and Chronicles. Based upon the New Testament evidence reviewed thus far, this writer is convinced that only Jesus has attained the resurrection of the dead and that the κοιμωμένοι are still in the pre-parousia state.

The Pauline Witness

The Apostle Paul is responsible for the most occurrences of κοιμάομαι in the New Testament. He does, however, limit his employment of the sleep-of-death concept to the Thessalonian and Corinthian correspondences. Much has been written on the subject of Paul's view of death. Probably the chief point of contention in this discussion is determining the time of the reception of the

---

[111] J. Rawson Lumby, *The Acts of the Apostles*, Cambridge Greek Testament for Schools and Colleges (Cambridge: University Press, 1894), 248. It is probable that David knew that he was not speaking of himself as the language is too strong to pertain to his own hope of resurrection (Derek Kidner, *Psalms 1-72*, Tyndale Old Testament Commentaries [Downers Grove, IL: InterVarsity Press, 1973], 86).

resurrection body. Theologically, Paul is dealing with death from the vantage point of the Christian ontological status of ἐν Χριστῷ. 1 Thessalonians 4 and 1 Corinthians 15 will be treated as primary because they contain the terminology and concept of the sleep of death. 2 Corinthians 5 and Philippians 3 are secondary because they offer clues to Paul's thanatology which are delicately intertwined with his thoughts on the resurrection, parousia, and judgment.

Although this writer does not believe that Paul's eschatology developed in a way suggesting correction of a previous error, his writings, in the primary sense, will be considered chronologically and contextually. The reader will remember that diachronic analysis is not as important as the synchronic analysis that takes place within. It is thematically logical to treat death before the resurrection. Saying that Paul's eschatological stances were more mature in 2 Corinthians 5 than they were in 1 Thessalonians 4 may call into question the latter's scriptural integrity. Additionally, even if it were true that Paul's early epistles were eschatologically juvenile, where does the interpreter discontinue his scrutiny? Does this apparent Hegelian method hold true for all Pauline themes? A contextual, synchronic appraisal should provide answers for these questions and prove fruitful for understanding Paul's thanatology.

The Thessalonian Correspondence

1 Thess. 4.13-18[112] represents the earliest Pauline passage to deal with the postmortem state. A display of unnatural grief prompted Paul to give comfort to living Christians concerning τῶν κοιμωμένων (4.13). He intends to teach something new in that he employs the phrase "we do not want you to be

---

[112]The greatest problem in this passage is the nature of the parousia as is proposed by N. Hyldahl, "Auferstehung Christi—Auferstehung der Toten (1 Thess. 4:13-18)," in S. Pedersen, ed., *Die Paulinische Literatur und Theologie* (Göttingen: Vandenhoeck & Ruprecht, 1980), 119-35.

ignorant."[113] Especially in this passage, it appears that the time of the resurrection is unmistakable. It is at the parousia. Those who hold to the immediate resurrection view must see that this pericope is totally wrong. More clearly than any other passage, however, this small section indicates the reality of an intermediate state.[114] Grammatically, the present active participle, κοιμωμένων,[115] is significant in that it represents something of a durative nature and lends itself better to the idea of a future arousal than would even the perfect tense.[116]

Another important grammatical issue related to the intermediate state needs to be addressed in verse 14. A problem arises concerning the syntactical function of the prepositional phrases διὰ τοῦ Ἰησοῦ and σὺν αὐτῷ in relation to the aorist passive participle κοιμηθέντας and the future active indicative verb ἄξει. To which term should the prepositional phrases be affixed? One solution, represented by the Revised Standard Version, suggests that both phrases be connected with ἄξει. This option renders the translation: "Even so, through Jesus, God will bring with him those who have fallen asleep." The problem with this view is that ἄξει is too overweighted by both prepositional phrases.[117]

A better solution, as is reflected in the New English Bible, is to relate διὰ Ἰησοῦ with κοιμηθέντας and σὺν αὐτῷ with ἄξει. Then the translation becomes: "So also God will bring with him those who have fallen asleep through Jesus."[118] Opting for this syntactical structure a beautiful picture of Christian death is

---

[113]Leon Morris, *The First and Second Epistles to the Thessalonians*, rev. ed., The New International Commentary on the New Testament (Grand Rapids: Eerdmans, 1991), 135. For other instances of this usage, see Rom. 1.13, 11.25; 1 Cor. 10.1, 12.1; and 2 Cor. 1.8.

[114]Cooper, *Body, Soul, & Life Everlasting*, 151.

[115]J. E. Frame, *The Epistles of St. Paul to the Thessalonians*, International Critical Commentary (Edinburgh: T. & T. Clark, 1912), 166-67.

[116]George Milligan, *St. Paul's Epistles to the Thessalonians* (Grand Rapids: Eerdmans, 1953), 55.

[117]Bruce, *1 & 2 Thessalonians*, 97.

[118]Ibid., and Morris, *The First and Second Epistles to the Thessalonians*, 139.

presented, one which I. Howard Marshall depicts as "a new and unparalleled conception of Christian dying in which Jesus brings believers into a state of death."[119] While the present participle κοιμωμένων refers to the durative nature of pre-parousia death in verse 13, the instant of death is portrayed by the aorist passive participle κοιμηθέντας in verse 14. If κοιμηθέντας is a true passive, then it can be translated: "They were put to sleep."[120] Christians who have died, therefore, are presently in a new realm of the eschatological scheme of events which is the intermediate state. The resurrection of all believers is the next eschatological event slated to occur on the heels of the parousia. Ernest Best, however, rejects this and all other views as he maintains the critical point is related directly to the preposition σύν—that is, the Christian dead are "with Christ" and Paul's task was to deal effectively with their grief.[121]

Extinctionists demand, however, that Paul is speaking euphemistically, not ontologically.[122] Similarly, is it cogent to say that all accounts of the sleep of death in the New Testament are merely euphemistic and collectively mean that the deceased are extinct until a general eschatological recreation? If one cannot disprove this theory by the distinct evidence of 1 Thess. 4.13-18, then proof from

---

[119]I. Howard Marshall, *1 and 2 Thessalonians*, The New Century Bible Commentary (Grand Rapids: Eerdmans, 1983), 124.

[120]J. H. Moulton, *Prolegomena*, vol. 1 in *A Grammar of New Testament Greek*, ed. J. H. Moulton (Edinburgh: T. & T. Clark, 1906), 162; quoted in Morris, *The First and Second Epistles to the Thessalonians*, 139. Also see G. Milligan, *St. Paul's Epistles to the Thessalonians* (Grand Rapids: Eerdmans, 1953). He speaks of διά as "pointing to Jesus as the mediating link between his people's sleep and their resurrection at the hands of God" (57). C. F. D. Moule and the New English Bible take the expression to mean, "those who have fallen asleep (i.e. died) as Christian (perhaps in contact with Jesus)" (*Idiom Book of New Testament Greek* [Cambridge: Cambridge University Press, 1953], 57). In addition, E. H. Askwith, "The Eschatological Section of 1 Thessalonians," *Expositor* 8,1 (1911): 62-63, considers the διά in the function of attendant circumstances: "They were in a certain relationship with the risen Jesus when they died." Askwith's position is equally shared by E. von Dobschütz in *Die Thessalonicherbriefe*, reprint ed., Kritisch-Exegetischer Kommentar (Göttingen: Vandenhoeck & Ruprecht, 1974), 191.

[121]Ernest Best, *The First and Second Epistles to the Thessalonians*, reprint ed., Black's New Testament Commentary (Peabody, MA: Hendrickson Publishers, 1986), 189.

[122]Reichenbach, *Is Man the Phoenix?*, 185.

the intertestamental period and from the Old Testament discussed above can be reexamined and entered as exhibits. For the annihilationist view to be correct, God would be required to recreate persons at the end of the temporal order to fit them for heaven. A phenomenal occurrence, such as the Transfiguration, should discourage the adoption of extinctionism, unless one believes that, in performing this act, God had recreated Moses and Elijah as a couple of "ontic moments" and then dissolved then back into nothingness when their mission was accomplished. This is the monistic requirement for such a view. Also, the extinctionist model is damaged by Paul's statement in 1 Thess. 5.10: "He died for us so that, whether we are awake or asleep (καθεύδωμεν), we may live together with him." To be with Christ during death is not to be extinct. This explicit guarantee of the continuity between life and death "constitutes no unbridgeable gulf: both alike, those still alive and those fallen asleep, will soon be forever united with the Lord."[123]

The Corinthian Correspondence

Paul's association with the church in Corinth was both very complex and very likely his most personal; because this church probably generated more agitation than any other. Paul addressed a variety of difficult problems which included, at best, a misunderstanding about the resurrection, or, at worst and most likely, a notorious denial of it.[124]

---

[123]Günther Bornkamm, *Paul*, trans. D. M. G. Stalker (New York: Harper & Row, 1971), 222; quoted in Bruce, *1 & 2 Thessalonians*, 114.

[124]When reference is made to 1 and 2 Corinthians, the reader should be aware that this pertains to the extant letters. One of the stickiest problems which faces students of the Corinthian correspondence is the determination of the actual number of letters Paul wrote. This writer believes there were five possible letters. For support of this view, extensive bibliography, and history of interpretation, see Ralph P. Martin, *2 Corinthians*, Word Biblical Commentary (Waco: Word Books, 1986), xxxiv-lii and Victor Furnish, *II Corinthians*, The Anchor Bible (Garden City, NY: Doubleday & Company, 1984), 26-48.

1 Corinthians 15 is the most extensive chapter on the topic of the resurrection in the New Testament.[125] Paul uses a form of the word κοιμάομαι four times in this chapter.[126] This whole discourse is tempered by the manner in which Paul began his strategy. 1 Cor. 15.1-2 reveals that for the Christians at Corinth the preached content of the gospel was something they received (παρελάβετε), in which they stood (ἑστήκατε), and by which they were being saved (σῴζεσθε). Within the context of the kerygma, Paul couches his thanatological plan which clearly allows for the existence of an intermediate state.[127]

The most revealing of the four references is found in verses 51 and 52:

> Listen, I tell you a mystery: We will not all sleep (κοιμηθησόμεθα), but we will all be changed—in a flash, in the twinkling of an eye, at the last trumpet. For the trumpet will sound, the dead will be raised imperishable, and we will be changed.

Obviously, the resurrection is futuristic, corporate, and culminative. Here, the parousia is the key event which will provoke the general resurrection from the intermediate state. It was not Paul's intention to settle the monist/dualist debate in this chapter. It is plain in light of the contents of this chapter, however, that the immediate resurrectionist model is unsupportable, and the Hickite model of extinctionism must depend upon an argument from silence in order to prove its case.[128] The phrase, therefore, dedicated to the deceased, οἱ κοιμηθέντες ἐν Χριστῷ, refers to a provisional state of death from which the faithful will be eschatologically aroused.

---

[125]Κοιμάομαι as the sleep of death also occurs in 1 Cor. 7.39 in relation to the question about remarriage after the death (κοιμηθῇ) of a spouse and in 1 Cor. 11.30 in reference to those Corinthian Christians who had died (κοιμῶνται) due to abusive treatment of the Lord's Supper. The topics are important but will be omitted in order to treat the passages more closely related to the resurrection.

[126]1 Cor. 15.6, 18, 20 and 51.

[127]Ronald Berry, "Death and Life in Christ: The Meaning of 2 Corinthians 5.1-10," *Scottish Journal of Theology* 14 (1961): 60.

[128]Cooper, *Body, Soul, & Life Everlasting*, 152-53.

1 Cor. 15.20 is also interesting. Paul emphasizes the distinctive characteristic of Jesus' resurrection by saying: Νυνὶ δὲ Χριστὸς ἐγήγερται ἐκ νεκρῶν ἀπαρχὴ τῶν κεκοιμημένων. The prepositional phrase, ἐκ νεκρῶν, should not be seen as ablative of separation but as ablative of source. It has been pointed out that by referring to Jesus as ἀπαρχή, Paul does not relate this mode to those who have been raised but to those who have fallen asleep (κεκοιμημένων).[129]

Different kinds of problems are encountered, however, when 2 Cor. 5.1-10 is considered. Some scholars believe that Paul edited his former view of what happened to the believer at the time of death.[130] The emphasis does shift from the main theme of the general resurrection in 1 Corinthians 15 to that of his personal death and subsequent judgment in 2 Corinthians 5. Although κοιμάομαι, or any other sleep-of-death metaphor, is not employed, this text is thanatological in tone and relevant to the discussion concerning the sleep of death. The pericope has evoked no consensus among scholars regarding answers to the following questions. These questions concern the subject matter of verses 2, 3, and 4. Does the Christian receive the spiritual body at death or at the parousia? Paul speaks of donning (ἐπενδύσασθαι) the heavenly body over the earthly tent in verse 2. Paul also introduces the idea of nakedness (γυμνός) into the discussion in verse 4. Is this spiritual body something, therefore, that the Christian already has? Does the idea of nakedness suggest that there is an ontological region which Paul desperately wants to avoid? Or is this nakedness to be equivocated with an Old Testament concept of judgment?[131]

The interpretations pertaining to whether or not a major shift occurred in Paul's thanatology between 1 Corinthians 15 and 2 Corinthians 5 is heavily debated. There are three major classes of interpretations to consider. One view involves

---

[129]Hans Conzelmann, *1 Corinthians*, trans. James W. Leitch, Hermeneia (Philadelphia: Fortress Press, 1975), 268-69.

[130]Harris, *Raised Immortal*, 100-101, 225-26, n. 5.

[131]For elaboration on this view, see E. E. Ellis, "II Cor. v. 1-10," 211-24.

those thinkers who see a significant shift in Paul's eschatological thinking in the midst of the complex Corinthian correspondence. Scholarship provides three different options within this view. The most popular of the three is that by the time Paul wrote 2 Corinthians 5, as opposed to earlier writings, he no longer expected to be alive at the parousia.[132] A related theme with this view is the shift in the time of the resurrection from the event of the parousia in 1 Corinthians 15 to the event of death in 2 Corinthians 5.[133] The second view which involves some kind of shift is represented by those scholars who retain the idea of the resurrection being precipitated by the parousia as consistent in Paul's theology, but their shift involves the nature of the intermediate state. Basically, the interim period becomes more attractive in 2 Corinthians 5, having been upgraded from the more shadowy, Sheol-like existence in 1 Corinthians 15, to a more intimate involvement with Christ.[134]

The third strand of "shift interpretation" focuses on the ontological aspect of matter. Paul somehow was infected by Hellenistic dualism between the writing of both Corinthian pericopae. Simply stated, Paul exchanged the idea of the "transformation" of the physical body at death in 1 Corinthians 15 for the

---

[132]C. E. Faw, "Death and Resurrection in Paul's Letters," *Journal of Bible and Religion* 27 (1959): 297. For more examples of this view, see Gillman, "A Thematic Comparison," 439, n. 2.

[133]For a good example of this view, see M. J. Harris, "2 Corinthians 5:1-10," 32-57. For a list of other examples, see F. C. Lang, "Auferstehung im Tod und Änderung der Eschatologie," chap. in *2 Korinther 5, 1-10*, 64-92.

[134]Although Hoffmann believes there is no shift in Paul's idea of the intermediate state, he enumerates many who do (*Die Toten in Christus*, 4-20).

"replacement" model in 2 Corinthians 5.[135] All three of these views argue for some kind of shift relating to some aspect of Paul's thanatology.

The second major vein of interpretation holds that both Corinthian passages teach that the deceased believer experiences the resurrection at the parousia. A thematic consistency based on the clothing metaphor and Old Testament allusion and citation are evident.[136]

In support of this view, Ronald Berry offers four good reasons why change is not acceptable in 2 Corinthians 5: 1) it is in direct contradiction with the more detailed assessment found in 1 Corinthians 15; 2) even in light of Paul's numerous afflictions and imminent death, would Paul now soften his earlier view in order to accommodate himself?; 3) there is no hint of an earlier preparation for this change; and 4) the presence of the introductory phrase οἴδαμεν γάρ does not indicate fresh teaching.[137] One does not encounter a whimsical Paul at this juncture but a man with two minds about death.[138]

This leads to the third major strain of interpretation which contends for a distinction in subject matter between the passages while maintaining the coherence of Paul's eschatology. This view is not a shift; rather it represents an

---

[135]For this view, see W. L. Knox, *St. Paul and the Church of the Gentiles* (Cambridge: University Press, 1939; repr. 1961), 127, n. 1. According to Knox, there appears to be a drastic positional change here in comparison to 1 Cor. 15.51-58, 1 Thess. 4.13-18, and Phil. 3.20-21 with respect to death. Another reason offered for the shift is that Paul, exhibiting "an unconscious ambiguity of thought," was thinking individually not corporately about death (see W. D. Davies, *Paul and Rabbinic Judaism*, 317-18, and R. F. Hettlinger, "2 Corinthians 5.1-10," *Scottish Journal of Theology* 10 (1957): 174-94.

[136]This is the viewpoint of Jacques Dupont, ΣΥΝ ΧΡΙΣΤΩ, 139. The present writer agrees with this model, which is also consistent with Cooper's model of wholistic dualism.

[137]Ronald Berry, "Death and Life in Christ," 61-62. In addition, the employment of εἰδότες at the beginning of the section in 5.11-21 displays the same confidence in matters related to the ministry of reconciliation that Paul expressed in matters relating to death. Harris also numbers some additional objections to his view of immediate resurrection: 1) too little time expired between the writing of 1 and 2 Corinthians; 2) defamation of parousia and already/not yet tension; and 3) the lack of non-Pauline texts to corroborate the notion of transformation at death (*Raised Immortal*, 255, n. 4).

[138]Ronald Berry, "Death and Life in Christ," 67.

embellishment of Pauline thanatological conception. Paul emphasizes individual resurrection in 1 Corinthians 15, whereas he stresses corporate resurrection in 2 Corinthians 5.[139] In fact, the second and third major concepts are not that much different because whether the resurrection is individual or corporate, individuality is retained in the corporate experience, which is also compatible with Pauline ecclesiology. This emphasis is important because it moves the interpreter to a crucial key for establishing the thematic cohesion of both passages and, therefore, the strong plausibility of Paul's progressive teaching about the intermediate state.

What should the interpreter make of Paul's reference to the groaning (στενάζομεν) in verse 2 and the burden (βαρούμενοι) in verse 4? It is immediately crucial to dismiss completely any thought that Paul had in mind any Platonic idea of escape from the body. Paul did not consider the body evil; it was simply the playground for sin. Hamartiology, therefore, in addition to soteriology, has much to do with Paul's thanatology. The two tracks at this point are the escape from moral frustration and the fear of the unknown.[140] The escape, therefore, is from the jaws of sin's continued pressure, not from the body. The body just happens to be the context in which sin finds expression.

Paul can still say "we have this building" in verse 1 and not be speaking about the immediate acquisition of the resurrection body. The term ἔχομεν should be seen as a futuristic present which indicates the certainty, not the time of the resurrection body's appropriation. The "down payment" of the spirit referred to in verse 5 summarizes the confidence of verses 1-4; it provides the basis for the hope expressed in verses 6-10. That Paul was acutely aware of his own mortality

---

[139]For this view, see Victor Furnish, *II Corinthians*, 294.

[140]Although hotly disputed, a good case can be made for the postconversion nature of Paul's thoughts on Rom. 7.14-25 in which Paul admits of a daily jousting with sin. For an excellent treatment on Romans 7, see James D. G. Dunn, *Romans 1-8*, Word Biblical Commentary (Dallas: Word Books, 1988), 374-412. The already/not yet tension is operative in relation to indwelling sin. There is an overlap of the ages which can be identified as the sanctification period of a Christian's life. During this time an awful struggle takes place. This battle is over at the time of death, not conversion. Dunn says, "It is precisely in the overlap of the ages that the law and 'I' dance our frustrated fandango, and sin can play cat and mouse with both" (ibid., 406).

at this point in his career demonstrates a man whose thinking about death was intensified, not corrected. In a related sense, Christians would do well to remember the agony that Jesus displayed before his death. Being the Son of God afforded Jesus no escape from the mental and physical pain associated with the prospect and actual event of death. Compounding Jesus' pain, however, was the lonely burden of accomplishing the atonement. With the huge exception of that atonement, Paul's experience of death was to be no different. Paul was disturbed because he believed that the only way to attain heaven was at the time of the parousia, either by resurrection of his dead body or the transformation of his living person. Paul lamented, therefore, either about the war sin would continue to wage in his members if he remained alive until the parousia or about the incompleteness of the intermediate state if he died before the parousia.[141]

Late Pauline Texts Related to the Intermediate State

Those who demand the reader to see a shift in Paul's theology of death in 2 Corinthians 5 are equally required to see a shift back to his original eschatological position in late Pauline materials. If Paul did return later to his early eschatology of 1 Thessalonians 4 and 1 Corinthians 15, then a second shift would be required. In the first of these passages, 2 Cor. 12.1-4, Paul tells of a mystical experience in which he was caught up into the third heaven (12.2). Even though Paul experienced something which he did not fully grasp, this ecstatic state incorporated some sort of incursion into a sphere made possible by being ἐν Χριστῷ. By this experience Paul is saying that the self can resonate from the σῶμα.[142] This σῶμα is identified as the physical body even before the resurrection.

---

[141]Also see Lorin L. Cranford, "A Study of II Corinthians 5:1-10 in the Light of Various Interpretations of Pauline Eschatology" (Th.D. diss., Southwestern Baptist Theological Seminary, 1975), 73-168, 257-59. Cranford confirms: "This religious-oriented concept of the intermediate state is maintained by Paul within the framework of a parousia dominated eschatology" (ibid., 259). .

[142]Bultmann, *Theology of the New Testament*, 202.

139

For Paul, temporary entrance into this heavenly locale was possible. Following Cooper's assessment, therefore, this writer believes it is easier to maintain a case for dualism than a case for monism.[143]

There are two additional late texts, both in Philippians, which demand attention because of their obvious association with the themes of death, the intermediate state, and the resurrection. If there is an intermediate state, what does Paul mean by Phil. 1.21-24?

> For to me, to live is Christ and to die is gain. If I am to go on living in the body, this will mean fruitful labor for me. Yet what shall I choose? I do not know! I am torn between the two: I desire to depart and be with Christ, which is better by far; but it is more necessary for you that I remain in the body.

What is the source of his alarm? Having struggled with the rigors of Christian servanthood, the challenging problems associated with his opponents and the churches he founded and tried to maintain as well as the hardships of an extended incarceration, Paul keenly realized the tenuous line which separated life and death.[144] His spiritual exasperation expressed here is akin to that found in 2 Cor. 5.1-10.[145] Does Paul's statement leap over an intermediate state? No! Being with Christ would be no different than the fellowship the penitent thief on the cross shared with Jesus in paradise. The text does not support the idea of an unconscious "soul sleep."[146] If Paul felt that death would be far better than life, then any postmortem picture less than that would be erroneous. Paul desires to

---

[143]Cooper, *Body, Soul, & Life Everlasting*, 165. This particular type of dualism is termed wholistic.

[144]So Moisés Silva, *Philippians*, Baker Exegetical Commentary on the New Testament (Grand Rapids: Baker Book House, 1992), 81-82. See also Peter T. O'Brien, *The Epistle to the Philippians*, New International Greek Testament Commentary (Grand Rapids: Eerdmans, 1991), 118-23.

[145]Gerald Hawthorne, *Philippians*, Word Biblical Commentary (Waco: Word Books, 1983), 44. Hawthorne points out the emphatic position of ἐμοί in verse 21. Paul was able to speak to issues with effective insight because he was an active participant in the Christian life. Ontologically speaking, being related to Christ brings suffering. The modern day "health and wealth" gospel cannot be supported correctly by any Pauline text.

[146]See R. P. Martin, *Philippians*, rev. repr. ed., Tyndale New Testament Commentaries (Grand Rapids: Eerdmans, 1987), 81-82.

upgrade the ἐν Χριστῷ to the σὺν Χριστῷ. Being with Christ at death enhances the relationship which at that time will be a "more intimate, open, and total relationship with Christ himself."[147] It will, however, still be pre-parousia.

This thought leads into the next passage for consideration. Phil. 3.10-11 reminds the reader that the only available model that fully defines resurrection is that of Christ.[148] This passage provides the evidence needed to counteract the notion of an eschatological shift in 2 Corinthians 5. Here again Paul's agitation surfaces because he realizes that the mechanism of salvation will not be completed until the parousia. A spiritual resurrection was indeed inaugurated at conversion, but the physical resurrection will constitute the full transition from sanctification to glorification. Paul craved for this complete resurrection at the parousia.[149]

Albert Schweitzer portrays the general resurrection in a unique fashion. He utilizes a magnificent metaphorical figure to liken Paul's conception of the resurrection of Christ, of the elect, of nature, and finally all mankind, to a series of volcanic disturbances:

> Paul knows that the immortal world is about to rise by succesive volcanic upheavals out of the ocean of the temporal. In the Resurrection of Jesus (the firstfruits of them that have fallen asleep) one island peak has already become visible. But this is only part of a larger island which, still beneath the waves, is actually in the process of rising, and is only so far covered as to be just invisible.[150]

---

[147]Richard R. Melick, Jr., *Philippians, Colossians, Philemon*, The New American Commentary (Nashville: Broadman Press, 1991), 85-86. One should also remember that Rom. 8.35-39 must always be a part of any discussion concerning Paul's view of death and the afterlife. "An eternal life that begins in this world, by grace through faith, will not be severed at death" (Gabriel Fackre, "I Believe in the Resurrection of the Body," 51).

[148]Melick, *Philippians, Colossians, Philemon*, 135.

[149]"This is the burden of 2 Cor. 5:1-10. He longed there to be clothed with the new body, at which time the work of salvation will be complete. In that text, he also implied that he expected a time when he would be in heaven without his body—that is, a 'naked state.' Since the body is both the vehicle through which we communicate and receive communication and the 'housing' which shapes our self-identity, we cannot conceive of existence without it. The dead in Christ will have an intermediate state of existence, but Paul looked forward to the completion of salvation" (ibid., 136, n. 37). See the excellent discussions in Silva, *Philippians*, 191-93 and O'Brien, *Philippians*, 411-15.

[150]Schweitzer, *The Mysticism of Paul the Apostle*, 112.

By the consideration of these texts in which κοιμάομαι was put into service, and by associative death texts, this writer believes that Paul believed in an ontological intermediate state which intervened death and resurrection. During this interval, he also believed that the deceased exist in sweet communion with Christ until the time the Father initiates the parousia. At that time the resurrection which Schweitzer describes will complete its process.

It has been pointed out that as the Old Testament never uses נֶפֶשׁ or רוּחַ to refer to people in the afterlife, neither does Paul use ψυχή or πνεῦμα for those in the postmortem state.[151] This does not prove monism, nevertheless because Paul sets up a dualism between "self" and "body." What continues after death is the self, so both the immediate resurrectionist and extinctionist models are unnecessary. Correctly stated: "If Paul is a dualist, he is strictly speaking a self-body, person-body, or ego-body dualist, not a soul-body dualist."[152] Paul is now a participant in the intermediate state.

The Scoffers' Old Testament Allusion in 2 Pet. 3.1-7

In a section devoted to the promise of the parousia, the last example of κοιμάομαι appears. Similar to Paul's usage in Acts 13 the reference is to the ancient fathers sleeping.[153] The major difference, however, is that instead of κοιμάομαι proceeding out of the mouth of an apostle, the word is a part of a query issued by heretics concerning the delay of the parousia.[154] Their contention runs: "Where is the promise of his coming? For ever since the fathers fell asleep

---

[151]Cooper, *Body, Soul, & Life Everlasting*, 171.

[152]Ibid.

[153]The only technical difference is that Paul referred specifically to King David in his missionary speech.

[154]William Barclay, *The Letters of James and Peter*, The Daily Study Bible (Philadelphia: The Westminster Press, 1976), 338. In addition, see Julius Schniewind, "'Επαγγέλλω," 2:585. Compare their complaint with Mk. 13.30 and par., and Mt. 10.23.

(ἐκοιμήθησαν), all things have continued as they were from the beginning of creation" (2 Pet. 3.4). Probably stemming from the missionary preaching itself, these doubters pick up on one of its key elements, the parousia. The charge levelled is that this resurrection-initiating event is a falsehood. They go beyond the anxiousness of the Thessalonians to say that nothing actually awaits the fathers who have been asleep a long time.

Peter uses the accusation to give a lesson pertaining to ontology in its widest scope, that is, existence from creation to the time of total recreation. Each person lives between the time of two destructions as well, the first accomplished by water in the Noanic flood followed by the eschatological judgment of fire (verses 5-7). Time is a moot point with the Lord, thus enhancing the urgency of repentance (verse 9). Echoing the sentiments of Jesus and Paul, Peter reminds them that this culminating day of judgment will accompany the parousia which will dawn on them unexpectedly (verse 10). Verses 11-13 provide information concerning the ultimate transformation from the cataclysmic dissolution of the temporal order to the new heavens and the new earth. In light of these looming eschatological events, Peter calls the people to moral uprightness. Moving toward the end of the letter, Peter encourages the readers to be found unblemished from the twisting of difficult doctrines, some of which Paul wrote (verses 14-18).

Peter is careful to note throughout his treatment that these future incidents were going to emerge according to the promise of God. While Peter does not establish the idea of an intermediate state, he certainly said that the final transformation had not taken place at that time. The major point he belabors is the harsh retribution which will accompany the suddenness of the parousia for those who deny Christ and his promises. Spurred by the voice of dissension, Peter is able to produce some eschatological claims which indirectly point to the existence of an interval between death and life because God has not completed the process of salvation with his people, living or dead.

Conclusion

Basically, the entire New Testament teaches the same eschatology. Death is not pictured as horrific or as a terminus. While there is normal human trepidation about experiences which are a posteriori, especially death, there exists a strongly accented measure of hope in the resurrection of the dead. It is true that the New Testament does not elab-orate on the actual ontological condition of the intermediate state, which for the most part remains what Cooper calls "*terra incognito*—unknown territory."[155] Because the communicators of God's truth realized this fact, they collectively placed the accent on that which they observed, the death and resurrection of Jesus Christ, still the crux of the gospel message. Upon death, Christians can expect a more passionate fellowship with Christ, persisting to the time of glorification in a resurrected body. This eschatological configuration is expressed by the use of κοιμάομαι as the sleep of death.

The majority of the appearances of κοιμάομαι in the New Testament are intended to express Christian death. Although previously used by pagans in an attempt to extinguish the pain of death, the important and indispensable detail of the hope of an eschatological resurrection was noticeably missing. New Testament spokesmen did not steer away from the term nor other synonyms because they desired to inject a strong optimism into the universal experience of death. They accomplished this goal, at least in part, by the theological rendering of κοιμάομαι.

Since it is fairly certain that many, if not all, New Testament authors were aware of ancient sources and concepts (e.g., Paul in Acts 17.16-34), this field of knowledge would no doubt include the pagan notion of the sleep of death. It appears, therefore, to be a logical conclusion that if the writers of the New Testament wanted to convey the idea of the immediate posthumous transportation of believers to heaven, they would have categorically avoided all semantic contact with the pagan sleep-of-death terminology. They did not avoid it; they pointedly

---

[155] Cooper, *Body, Soul, & Life Everlasting*, 172.

engaged it. The ancient Greeks had the proper skeletal terminology, although without the matching exposition. New Testament κοιμάομαι holds the Christian in a pre-parousia pattern, which includes an eschatological interest in a resurrected, transformed body, while Platonic κοιμάομαι envisions a radical break of an imprisoned immortal soul from an evil, temporal body.

Chronologically and ontologically, the New Testament teaches that there is a boundary which can be fully crossed only after the resurrection. During death the Christian is on the line of that boundary in the pre-parousia state. The already/not yet tension of salvation and eternal life continues even during death. This state is not to be equated with any Catholic purgatory or limbo, eschatological pauses of punishment. Neither is it to be seen as unconscious sleep.[156] Immortality, therefore, is a consequence of the resurrection not death. It is not a Hellenistic investment of a preexistent soul enacted upon physical birth. Millard J. Erickson expresses succinctly what this writer conceives the intermediate state to be:

> I can tell you something else that will definitely happen. After death you will be in a state of conscious existence, whether of blessedness or of misery. . . . Our condition will be incomplete, since the resurrection will not yet have taken place; we will not yet have our resurrection bodies. Since Jesus said, 'Today you will be with me . . . ,' it appears that believers will experience the actual presence of the Lord, in other words, heaven, but not as fully as will be the case after the resurrection.[157]

It could be that the intermediate state is a part of heaven. This spatial location at the time of death, however, still appears anachronistic. As has been pointed out above, Paradise was also used to refer to Sheol, or the intermediate state. This "incompleteness" to which Erickson refers, is the intermediate state and not the final state.

---

[156]The misconception of taking the sleep of death to mean "soul sleep" is cited in Johannes P. Louw and Eugene A. Nida, eds., *Greek-English Lexicon of the New Testament Based on Semantic Domains*, 2d ed. 2 vols. (New York: United Bible Societies, 1989), 1:265.

[157]Millard J. Erickson, *Does It Matter What I Believe? What the Bible Teaches and Why We Should Believe It* (Grand Rapids: Baker Book House, 1992), 154-55. The order in which Erickson treats the eschatological themes is interesting: death, the intermediate state, the second coming, the final judgment, then heaven and hell.

CHAPTER V
POST-BIBLICAL REFLECTION

This chapter is not intended to be an exhaustive treatment of all post-biblical response to the New Testament tradition of the sleep of death. Early apostolic witness will be accompanied by the earliest patristic writers. Reference will be made to the use of κοιμάομαι as the sleep of death through the fourth and fifth centuries of the Christian era. This study did not end diachronically with the New Testament because the present writer feels it is important to explore early Christian eschatological exegesis. More research and analysis can be accomplished in relationship to the eschatological beliefs in this era than will be done here. There are three goals of this chapter. First, the reader will be furnished enough information to understand the eschatological tendencies which were crucial for early Christian exegesis. Second, contemporary Christians will reevaluate their own eschatological notions in light of this evidence in order to know whether one is primarily biblical or Hellenistic in relation to postmortem issues. Third, the reader will see the legitimacy to conclude that, for the majority, the early Christian church believed in an intermediate state and chose to express it best by employing the sleep of death concept, particularly with the term κοιμάομαι.

The Apostolic Witness and the Early Church

The writings considered in this section are those which are contemporary with the later books of the New Testament.¹ One qualification for this category was that the author generally was regarded to have been associated either with the apostles or with their immediate disciples.² Important for this work, therefore, is the investigation of how these writers responded to the New Testament use of κοιμάομαι as the sleep of death by incorporating it into their own writings. With respect to these and later works, was there a gradual softening or hardening of eschatological viewpoints? At least in the field of ethical studies, some have shown these parallel forces at work the further one moves away from the time of Jesus and the rest of the New Testament witness.³

Due to the proximity of the early church experience in relation to the decisive New Testament witness, should the contemporary interpreter pay closer attention to apostolic and patristic exegesis for biblical understanding? By far, κοιμάομαι was used more in the patristic period than any other.⁴ In respect to thantology, to what can this semantic escalation be attributed? No doubt fueled in part by ever worsening persecution, the Christians' sensitivity to death was at its apex. In addition, the postresurrection missionary zeal was gaining power as time

---

¹J. B. Cotelier was the first editor of the collection which included the pseudo-Epistle of Barnabas; the two epistles associated with Clement of Rome; the epistles of Ignatius of Antioch; the single epistle and martyrdom of Polycarp, bishop of Smyrna; and the Shepherd of Hermas, a prophet of the Roman church. Lesser known works routinely added to these are the Didache; fragments of Papias of Hierapolis; a fragment of the Quadratus Apology; and a mysterious anonymous apologetic work, the Epistle to Diognetus.

²For further discussion concerning the integrity, quasi-canonical authority, and bibliography pertaining to these writings, see M. H. Shepherd, Jr., *IDB*, s.v. "Apostolic Fathers," 174.

³See Cecil J. Cadoux, *The Early Church and the World* (Edinburgh: T. & T. Clark, 1925). By comparative analysis, Cadoux examined the ethical and doctrinal positions present from the time of Jesus to the implementation of the Constantinian Church. While this period boasted of an unparalleled reformative movement in regard to some issues, it also exhibited a tendency to regress in some matters the farther the church was temporally removed from the New Testament.

⁴Oepke points out that καθεύδω does not appear in the immediate post-New Testament writings ("Καθεύδω," 3:437).

progressed. That κοιμάομαι was used so prolifically reveals a thanatology which was firmly rooted in the hope of the resurrection. It was in this period also that the cognate term, κοιμητήριον, was adopted and used to designate what is known to Christians as a "cemetery."[5]

Clement of Rome and Ignatius

Several apostolic fathers used κοιμάομαι as the sleep of death in the first two centuries of the Christian era. Clement of Rome and Ignatius of Antioch were both born in A.D. 30. Important is the strongly held belief that Clement knew the Apostle Paul and was looked upon as his representative.[6] Because of this association one would expect Clement at the very least to set forth a knowledgeable apostolic reflection and at best an intentional propagation of Pauline thought. But this concept is not the case. To the contrary, Clement presented a Christianity which had a stronger Old Testament flavor.[7]

His usage of κοιμάομαι is limited. The term appears in his letter to the Corinthians three times. Resurrection is the theme of his first entry. Well rounded in the language of the LXX, Clement refers to Ps. 3.6 and Job 19.25, 26 as support for promise of the resurrection.[8] The second occurrence of κοιμάομαι

---

[5]For an example of the "semantic flooding" of κοιμάομαι and κοιμητήριον, John Chrysostom, who lived in the fourth and fifth century A.D., used κοιμάομαι at least 247 times in his works.

[6]A. Roberts and J. Donaldson, eds., *The Ante-Nicene Fathers*, vol. 1 (Grand Rapids: Eerdmans, 1979), 1.

[7]Ogle, "The Sleep of Death," 96. Throughout his works, Clement quoted the Old Testament over a hundred times, while only quoting the Jesus tradition and Pauline material a few times. Clement died in A.D. 100, so it is not surprising that he quoted more from the "Scripture" he knew. Although the letters of Paul were being circulated, Clement wrote some 250 years before an established canon. Besides dependence on the Old Testament, Clement also depended on Stoic doctrine to some extent.

[8]*1 Clem*. 26.2.1-2. Of these two quotations, κοιμάομαι only appears in Ps. 3.6. While Clement viewed this verse as the sleep of death, this writer has rejected that viewpoint (see above, page 98, n. 85). Clement was the first to refer to the legend of the Phoenix as an emblem of the believer's resurrection (ibid., 25). This argument is used by Tertullian in *De Resurrectione Carnis* and by a host of other church Fathers.

in this letter involves a discussion concerning the posthumous plans made by the Apostles for the assignment of successors, so that no contentions regarding the priestly office would arise:

> For this reason, therefore, inasmuch as they had obtained a perfect foreknowledge of this, they appointed those [ministers] already mentioned, and afterwards gave instructions, that when these should 'fall asleep' (κοιμηθῶσιν), other approved men should succeed them in their ministry.[9]

Clement's third example surfaces in a chapter which deals with the revelatory evidence God continually provides his people through nature concerning the promise of the resurrection.[10] He takes as a paradigm the repetition of night and day. Night sinks to sleep, and the day arises (κοιμᾶται ἡ νύξ, ἀνίσταται ἡ ἡμέρα). This incessant process anticipates the resurrection.

Ignatius of Antioch also provided only a few sleep-of-death endorsements. Out of six examples of κοιμάομαι, only four refer to death, three of which are in spurious writings.[11] The most popular citation is the martyr's "death-wish" in his letter to the Romans:

> I am the wheat of God, and let me be ground by the teeth of the wild beasts, that they may become my tomb, and may leave nothing of my body; so that when I have fallen asleep (κοιμηθείς), I may be no trouble to any one.[12]

---

[9] *1 Clem.* 44.2.2-3. Although disputed, this instruction may indicate that a list of approved persons was ready in case of death. This direction is reminiscent of the Pauline admonition in 1 Cor. 7.39. Justo González, *A History of Christian Thought*, vol. 1 (Nashville: Abingdon Press, 1970), 64, points out that in this section of this epistle the first claim for authority based on apostolic succession is found.

[10] *1 Clem.* 24.2.2.

[11] The two nondeath usages clearly echo the Philonic practice of negating κοιμάομαι in order to express the idea of an "unsleeping" spirit in an individual (see above, p. 105, n. 99). One of these examples is found in Ign. *Pol.* 7.1.3.1-2, and the second is in *Epistulae spuriae* 8.1.3.1-2. For an explanation of how these spurious writings may have arisen, see González, *A History of Christian Thought*, 72, n. 37.

[12] Ign. *Pol.* 4.4.2.2-3. This desire is repeated in the spurious third letter to the Ephesians (*Epistulae spuriae* 12.4.2.1-2).

Justin Martyr

Although not considered an Apostolic Father, Justin Martyr will be considered here because of the time he lived and wrote in relation to Clement and Ignatius.[13] Like Clement, also of Rome, he used Ps. 3.6 twice for support of the future resurrection of the Christian.[14] A third example comes from an unknown source, although Justin attributed it to Jeremiah:

> And the Lord God remembered his dead ones (τῶν νεκρῶν) from Israel, the ones lying (sleeping?, κεκοιμημένων) in their own graves, and he descended to them to preach to them his salvation.[15]

Some have detected Justin's tactic of using Hellenistic philosophy to demonstrate the Christian faith. With reference to eschatology, though, was he able to differentiate between the two? Because of pagan derision, Justin, along with other defenders of the faith, looked for assistance from the Platonic doctrine of the immortality of the soul.[16] This methodology backfired as it caused the line separating the Greek concept of the immortality of the soul and the Christian doctrine of the resurrection of the dead to be blurred. One study of Justin's works reveals that he was not deceived by Hellenism because he does advocate that the soul is mortal and he believes in the hope of the resurrection keyed by the glorious return of Christ.[17]

---

[13]He is normally dated A.D. 110-165 and technically categorized as the most important Greek Apologist of the second century (González, *A History of Christian Thought*, 102).

[14]Justin Martyr *Apologia* 38.4.3, and idem, *Dialogus cum Tryphone* 97.1.6-7.

[15]Justin Martyr *Dialogus cum Tryphone* 72.4.3-4.

[16]González, *A History of Christian Thought*, 110.

[17]See L. W. Barnard, "Justin Martyr's Eschatology," *Vigiliae Christianae* 19 (1965): 86-98. It is important to note that in the 3d or 5th century some writings circulated which are known under the name Pseudo-Justin Martyr. All of the occurrences of κοιμάομαι except one appear in one writing entitled, *Quaestiones et responsiones ad orthodoxos*, and make definite comments on Matt. 27.52 (443.A.8-B.1 and 443.D.8-9); 1 Cor. 15.20 (444.B.4-5); and 1 Thess. 4.13-18 (464.C.3-4). For comments on this writer's theology of the afterlife, see Walter Delius, "Ps.-Justin: 'Über die Auferstehung,'" *Theologia Viatorum* 14 (1952): 181-204.

Contemporary Christians must realize that the ones who are deceived are those who see no distinction between the two concepts. Locating these unfortunate detours in church history is crucial for finding one's way back to the proper path of thanatological understanding.

To understand fully what happened in this period with respect to thanatology, one must recognize the operative tension in eschatology. Of a twofold emphasis, first, early Christianity attached itself to the reality and completeness of present salvation. In the second place, it also looked forward to certain eschatological events of the future. As a rule these included the parousia, the resurrection, the judgment, and the calamitous end of the temporal sphere. The Incarnation coupled with the death and resurrection of Jesus Christ established an important beachhead for the theological rubrics of the early church experience. According to Jesus' teaching spiritual resurrection at conversion and the subsequent indwelling of the Holy Spirit granted each Christian a powerful taste of the consummative age which had already been set in motion.[18]

A radical transformation occurred within early Christianity. Conceptually, God's kingdom was considered a spatial, futuristically located sphere, which was the ultimate prize for arduous perseverance and good works. Clement and Ignatius believed that Peter, Paul, and a sacred host of martyrs had already reached the celestial shores of heaven. What is more and worse, some believed they had earned heaven. Justin Martyr, however, taught the existence of an intermediate state substantiated in part by his employment of κοιμάομαι. His belief in the literal thousand-year reign of Christ on earth also fit into the concept of an interim

---

[18]For an informative work on this subject, see C. H. Dodd, *The Parables of the Kingdom* (London: Nisbet, 1935), 34-80. A major theme among the fathers was that a "realized eschatology" was continuously available by participation in the sacraments. Baptism and the eucharist were referred to by Ignatius as the φάρμακον άθανασίας, "the medicine of immortality." It could be that this concept of experiencing the eternal during the present age led them to minimize the future events which would precede the acquisition of the resurrection body.

state.[19] On the other hand, where eschatological anachronisms can be uncovered, one can surmise that they were caused, at least in part, by the message of New Testament Christianity being filtered through various Platonic and Stoic philosophies.

The Apocryphal Gospels

One example from this literature will shed light on the sleep-of-death motif in the apocryphal material. The *Gospel of Peter*,[20] written in Syria in the second century A.D., contains a saying which may have some affinity with the descent of Jesus into Hell recorded in 1 Pet. 3.19. The saying runs: Φωνῆς ἤκουσον ἐκ τῶν οὐρανῶν λεγούσης. ἐκήρυξας τοῖς κοιμωμένοις;[21] This verse can be translated: "He heard a voice from heaven saying, 'Have you preached to those who are asleep?'"[22] The words were evidently spoken to Jesus after two figures, who had descended from heaven, brought him out of the tomb. Jesus responded that he did in fact preach to those who were asleep.

---

[19]See González, *A History of Christian Thought*, 110 and J. N. D. Kelly, *Early Christian Doctrines*, rev. ed. (New York: Harper & Row, 1978), 465. Justin has been designated a premillenialist. The millenarian doctrine was popular during this time in church history. His rejection of Plato's doctrine of the immortality of the soul can be found in *Dialogus cum Tryphone* 5, entitled "The Soul Is Not in Its Own Nature Immortal."

[20]This writing is a passion gospel, allegedly written by Peter and displaying a clear Docetic view of the divine Christ and the human Jesus (M. S. Enslin, *IDB*, s.v. "Peter, Gospel of."). Only a fragment remains of this work. Although E. Hennecke and W. Schneemelcher, eds., *New Testament Apocrypha*, has long been regarded as the best text of New Testament Apocrypha because of valuable introductions and bibliographies, it does not contain the original texts. For the original text of the *Gos. Pet.*, see A de Santos Otero, ed., *Los evangelios apócrifos: Colección de textos griegos y latinos, versión crítica, estudios introductorios, comentarios e ilustraciones*, 3d ed., BAC 148 (Madrid: Edica, 1975), 380-93. In relationship to *Gos. Pet.* 41, the verse under consideration in this section, A de Santos refers to Eph. 4.9, 1 Pet. 3.19; 4.6, Ign. *Magn.* 9.3, and *Herm. Sim.* 9.16.5 to establish biblical and patristic touchstones for this apocryphal citation.

[21]*Gos. Pet.* 41; quoted in Ogle, "The Sleep of Death," 95.

[22]Translation mine.

The Church Fathers

By the fourth and fifth centuries A.D. a verbal explosion of the usage of κοιμάομαι for the sleep of death had occurred. "Falling asleep" was absolutely synonymous with "dying." Many of the early church fathers adopted the word as a technical term for the cessation of earthly life. Church spokesmen from the Greek and Latin fathers are well represented. Consideration will be given mainly to writers in the first centuries of the early church to provide a window through which the thanatological perspectives of early Christianity can be evaluated. The trifocal eschatological themes of parousia, resurrection, and judgment were discussed among them as much if not more than any other doctrinal issue. Each father's particular stance on the intermediate state is tightly related to these three inseparable prongs of eschatology.

Perhaps this sudden eruption of the appearance of κοιμάομαι in the fourth century coincided with the canonization of the New Testament in A.D. 367.[23] It is certain, though, that the canonization process was gradual as Irenaeus (A.D. 120-202) was the first Christian writer to refer to a New Testament as a body of writing.[24] Whether by means of oral tradition or written document, the fathers exhibited a knowledge of at least part of what came to be known as the New Testament.

Not all of the occurrences of κοιμάομαι or all of the fathers will be discussed in the final chapter of this study because they are too numerous. Key advocates from this early Christian period, however, will be investigated so that a clear picture of patristic thanatology can be painted.[25]

---

[23]The first official document which established the canonicity of the twenty-seven books of the New Testament was Athanasius's 39th Festal Letter.

[24]For a brief but excellent treatment of this subject, see J. N. D. Kelly, *Early Christian Doctrines*, 1978), 56-60.

[25]See Appendix G for a compilation of patristic "κοιμάομαι" references to Old and New Testament sleep-of-death passages.

The Alexandrians

If one were looking for a major factor in the apparent fusion of Christianity with foreign elements, it can be found primarily in the works of Clement and Origen. In trying to explain the Gospel in terms that their contemporaries might comprehend, Clement and Origen blended Neoplatonistic elements with Christianity.[26] This method severely affected their eschatological viewpoints as well as their entire theologies. Clement was a dualist *par excellence*. He believed in a spiritual doctrine of the resurrection, the ethereal nature of the spiritual body, no earthly paradise (nonmillenarianism), no intermediate state, and the doctrine of final restoration (ἀποκατάστασις).[27]

Clement uses κοιμάομαι for the sleep of death for the most part in the *Stromata*. His idea of the spiritual resurrection is advanced as comments on various aspects of the salvation of Gentiles set forth by Paul in Romans 11 are combined with an allusion to Christ's descent into Hades in 1 Peter 3. This salvation was also effected through the postmortem preaching of the apostles and teachers who had fallen asleep (κοιμηθέντας) and preached to those who had previously fallen asleep (προκεκοιμημένοις).[28]

As was typical of many church fathers, they referred to David's sleep of security in Ps. 3.6. In this context, however, Clement alludes to the Platonic

---

[26]It should be remembered that from a very early date the Christian church had to propagate its message amidst some lethal heresies. These threats included: 1) the Judaizing of Christianity which was characterized chiefly by dualistic-based Ebionism; 2) syncretistic Gnosticism whose chief advocates were Cerinthus, Saturninus, Carpocrates, Basilides, and Valentinus; 3) anti-Semitic Marcionism (who technically was not a Gnostic); 4) Montanism; and 5) Monarchianism (for a detailed discussion on these factors, see González, *A History of Christian Thought*, 123-59).

[27]As with his successor Origen, he believed that all things would eventually be restored to their primeval order. For both thinkers, this event will be the culmination of eschatology. The intermediate state for the Alexandrians was a non sequitur.

[28]Clement *Stromata* 2.9.43.4.2-44.3.3.

doctrine of the "descent of the soul into the body, sleep and death, similarly with Heraclitus."²⁹ Proof of this truth is seen by Clement through the Platonic David:

> And was this not proclaimed, verbally, of the Saviour, by means of the Spirit, saying by David, 'I slept (ἐκοιμήθην) and slumbered; I awoke: for the Lord sustained me?' For he not only figuratively calls the resurrection of Christ rising from sleep; but to the descent of the Lord into the flesh he also applies the figurative term sleep.³⁰

The impressive mass resuscitation of the ἁγίων in Matt. 27.52 is also given a Platonic twist by Clement as he says, "many of the bodies of those that slept (κεκοιμημένων) arose, clearly as having been translated to a better state."³¹ Clement communicates his idea of spiritual resurrection by repeating the "descending dead, ascending alive" equation. Although he does not believe in an intermediate state, this event constitutes a noble mystery which is reminiscent of the eschatological opening of the graves predicted in John 5.25.

In the same manner but with much greater frequency, Origen also used κοιμάομαι for the sleep of death. Like Clement, he also baptized Neoplatonism into his theology.³² Although a spirited allegorist, he was the most outstanding theologian of the ante-Nicene period, a prolific writer, and the first great exegete of the Bible. His reflections on eschatology are far reaching. His doctrine of ἀποκατάστασις governs his thinking on creation and eschatology. The pre-existence of the world, evil, souls, and fall of mankind dominate his works on creation and its counterpart, eschatology. For Origen, the world was created so that pre-existent souls could have an incarnate state.³³ As for eschatology, there is a temporary division of the end state between Hades and Paradise lasting from the time of death until the end of the age. This intermediate state is a

---

²⁹Ibid., 5.14.105.2.2-3.1.

³⁰Ibid., 3.1-4.2.

³¹Ibid., 6.6.46.5.4-47.1.1.

³²González, *A History of Christian Thought*, 210-33.

³³Kelly, *Early Christian Doctrines*, 472.

"probationary school" whose end is signalled by the parousia.[34] The Platonic influences that characterized his doctrine of creation also color his eschatology. His idea of restoration is not final after the judgment because his eschatological universalism included the possibility of many subsequent worlds to follow endlessly.[35] Judgment, however, is more important than the parousia. Like Clement, there is no millenarianism.

That Origen uses some form of κοιμάομαι (usually in the perfect active or aorist passive tense) over seventy times, the noun κοίμησις[36] (interpreted "death") ten times, and refers only once to the κοιμητήριον (resting place) of deceased Christians, displays his belief in some kind of an intermediate state. In addition, Origen perpetuates the term προκεκοιμημένοι, a neologism of Clement's, which is translated, "those who have been asleep before."[37] Interesting is the repetition of other phrases throughout the liturgies of the early church which reflect a belief in the intermediate state. Key phrases include: 1) κοιμηθέντες ἐν δυνάμει καὶ πίστει τοῦ υἱοῦ τοῦ θεου, 2) οἱ προκεκοιμημένοι νεκροὶ κατέβησαν, ζῶντες δὲ ἀνέβησαν, and 3) ἐν δικαιοσύνῃ γὰρ ἐκοιμήθησαν καὶ ἐν μεγάλῃ ἁγνείᾳ.[38] Although Clement

---

[34]Ibid.

[35]González, *A History of Christian Thought*, 230-31. For a more detailed discussion on Origen's doctrine of ἀποκατάστασις, see A. Méhat, "Apocatastase," *Vigiliae Christianae* 10 (1956): 196-214; and G. Müller, "Origenes und die Apokatastasis," *Theologische Zeitschrift* 14 (1958): 174-90.

[36]Origen makes the statement that, "'Η δὲ κοίμησίς ἐστιν ὁ θάνατος" (*Selecta in Psalmos* 12.1413.41-2), demonstrating the Christian understanding of the phrase. See Appendix G for tabulations.

[37]The participle is used four times in *De oratione* 11.1.3-31.5.5, and twice in *Commentarii in evangelium Joannis* 13.59.405.8 and 28.21.183.5. The participles κεκοιμωμένων (Matt. 27.52; John 11.11, 12; 1 Cor. 15.20) and κοιμηθέντας (1 Cor. 15.18; 1 Thess. 4.14) are expected and are picturesque renditions of the dead as they suggest both a mode or an agent in relationship to death. These descriptions are reminiscent of previous employment by the LXX and Paul. The patristic term προκεκοιμημένοι, however, is nonbiblical but represents a further explanation of the sleep of death.

[38]Ogle, "The Sleep of Death," 99. A careful probing through the documents provided by the *TLG* search will uncover these patterns.

and Origen were concerned with opposing the heresies of their day, they adulterated the Christian message. Many of the eschatological viewpoints of contemporary Christianity, which are more similar to Hellenistic influences than to the biblical record, can find their origin in the first centuries after the time of Christ. Granted, some thinkers will hold to the existence of an intermediate state. Origen, though, propogates so much other wild-eyed theology that his thanatology regresses to a hybrid form of Christianity far removed from biblical truth. Surely, the notions of the eternity of the world, the preexistence and reincarnation of the soul, the actuality of future worlds, and the ultimate salvation of Satan are categorically unacceptable.

Latin Representatives

Latin Christianity was a parallel movement centered in North Africa. Although Clement of Rome wrote his first epistle to the Corinthians from Italy, it was written in Greek. As has been seen in Chapter I, some Latin texts which portrayed the sleep of death were examined. Briefly, the eschatological perspective of Tertullian will be considered as a representative of Latin sleep-of-death terminology in the patristic period.

The occurrence of the verb *dormire*, in correspondence with κοιμάομαι, is scarce in the early Latin Fathers, excluding citations from various biblical sources.[39] Tertullian does use the term to refer to an intermediate state. In *De anima* 51, *dormire* is used in the context of a discussion on the separation of the body and soul at death.[40] "I am acquainted with the case of a woman . . . who in the very flower of her age and beauty slept (*dormuisset*) peacefully."[41] Possibly

---

[39]Ibid., 100.

[40]Tertullian lambasts Democritus for attributing the lingering presence of the soul after death in the grave due to the brief postmortem growth of human hair and nails (ibid.).

[41]Ibid. For the text used in this translation, see Roy Joseph Defarrari, gen. ed., *The Fathers of the Church*, vol. 10: *Tertullian: Apologetical Works and Marcus Felix Octavius*, trans. Rudolph Arbesmann, Emily Joseph Daly, and Edwin A. Quain (Washington, DC: The Catholic University

echoing the Davidic cry for help in the Ps. 13.3 sleep-of-death passage, Tertullian draws a parallel to the deep sleep God caused to overcome Adam in Gen. 2.21 to the future death and resurrection of Christ:

> From this primary instance also we are led to trace the image of death in sleep. For as Adam was a figure of Christ, Adam's sleep (*somnus*) shadowed out the death of Christ, who was to sleep a mortal slumber.[42]

The previous example leads to some broader considerations of Tertullian's theology. Although the New Testament never describes Jesus' death as a sleep, Tertullian at least hints at that possibility. For Tertullian, the interim state was established by Jesus' descent into hell described in 1 Pet. 3.19.[43] Ignatius, Polycarp, and Irenaeus also mention the descent and even one vein of patristic exegesis sees it prophesied by Jesus in Matt. 12.38-42 and alluded to by Paul in Rom. 10.7 and Col. 1.18, and an element in Peter's Pentecostal speech in Acts 2.27-31.[44] Kelly substantiates Tertullian's belief in an interim state as he says:

> It was no more than the natural corollary of Judaeo-Christian ideas about the condition of the soul after death. To say that Jesus Christ had died, or that he had been buried, was equivalent to saying that He passed to Sheol. The unquestioned premiss, for example, of the lengthy passage in Tertullian's *De anima* 50ff. is that all souls descend to Hades immediately after death.[45]

---

of America Press, 1950), 175-309.

[42]Ibid. It is noteworthy that Tertullian discusses the topic "Sleep, the Mirror of Death, As Introductory to the Consideration of Death" in Chapter 42. The Greek-Hebrew semantic pair for sleep in Gen. 2.21 is ὑπνόω-יָשֵׁן. This example was not treated as a sleep-of-death passage in Chapter II or III. The whole phrase in Latin attributes sleep and death to both Adam and Christ: *Somnus Adae mors erat Christi dormituri in mortem.* Even though the early fathers were inclined toward allegorism and typology, they must have thought highly of Paul's depiction of Christ as the second Adam (e.g., Rom. 5.12-21).

[43]For an excellent discussion on this crucial element (*descendit ad inferna*) of the Apostle's creed in the early church, see J. N. D. Kelly, *Early Christians Creeds*, 3d ed. (Essex, UK: Longman Group, 1972), 378-83.

[44]Ibid., 379.

[45]Ibid., 380. Although Christ is never referred to as sleeping, his resurrection is depicted frequently as emerging ἐκ νεκρῶν, "from the dead" (ablative of source). The Syriac translation of this prepositional phrase can be rendered "from the place, or house, of the dead." Also, in the Peshitta version of Rom. 10.6-7, there is introduced a precise reference to Sheol.

It was the mission of Tertullian, as it was with Irenaeus and Hippolytus, to be on their guard against Gnosticism.[46] In order to sidestep the Platonic belief of the denigration of the body, they believed that the body must also participate in the resurrection.[47] For Tertullian, just as Jesus had to descend into the bowels of the earth during his death before he was resurrected and taken to heaven, so must the Christian complete the entire postmortem process. By the time of Tertullian, the verb *dormire* and the noun *dormitio* were already established as figurative expressions for death.[48]

Subsequent Patristic Thought

A vast number of other church fathers could be referred to in an investigation of the use of κοιμάομαι as the sleep of death. From the later Alexandrian and Egyptian period stand Athanasius and Macarius the Egyptian. The region of Asia Minor includes the works of Marcellus of Ancyra, Amphilochius of Iconium, Asterius of Amasea and the great Cappodocian Fathers, Basil of Caeserea, Gregory of Nazianzus, and Gregory of Nyssa. Eustathius of Antioch, Eusebius of Caeserea, Cyril of Jerusalem, Epiphanius of Salamis and John Chrysostom[49] represent the region of Antioch and Syria. Also a study of the greatest of all patristic theologians, Augustine, will be profitable to see how eschatological

---

[46]Kelly, *Early Christian Doctrines*, 467.

[47]Ibid., 468. Tertullian refers to Isa. 40.5; Joel 2.28; 1 Cor. 3.17; and Gal. 6.17 as proof of God's approval of the physical body (*De resurrectione carne* 5-11).

[48]Ogle, "The Sleep of Death," 101. For more on the eschatology of Tertullian, see Robert E. Roberts, *The Theology of Tertullian* (London: Epworth Press, 1924), 203-18 and H. Finé, *Die Terminologie der Jenseitsvorstellungen bei Tertullian* (Bonn: P. Hanstein, 1958).

[49]John Chrysostom represents the most prolific employer of all time of κοιμάομαι as the sleep of death. This gifted speaker and voluminous writer is famous in this context for his work entitled *De coemeterio et de cruce* in which κοιμητήριον (= *coemeterio*), "sleeping place, cemetery" is discussed. The title is "ΕΙΣ ΤΟ ΟΝΟΜΑ ΤΟΥ ΚΟΙΜΗΤΗΡΙΟΝ" and runs from 49.393.1t-394.34. His use of κοιμάομαι is the greatest in his commentaries on Genesis, 1 Corinthians, and 1 Thessalonians. The remainder of the occurrences are sprinkled through hundreds of other works.

thinking progressed through this pivotal character in church history.⁵⁰ Probing into the eschatological frameworks of all these thinkers, however, is beyond the scope of this work.

The writings of the fathers are replete with references to the sleep of death using many different forms of κοιμάομαι. That κοιμάομαι became the "term of choice" among the fathers to refer to death illustrates a conscious effort on their behalf to adopt predominantly one word and attach a Christian meaning to it. Their continual belief in the resurrection of the dead and their desire to strip away the disparaging connotations Homer and Sophocles had given κοιμάομαι enabled them to fashion eschatological thinking containing hope instead of despair. Grammatically, the fathers employ the perfect active participle and various aorist passive forms of κοιμάομαι almost exclusively in sleep-of-death passages.⁵¹ The following table will illustrate this inclination.

---

⁵⁰While Tertullian utilized the verb *dormire* in his quotation of 1 Thess. 4.13, Augustine chose to use the phrase *dormitionem accipere* (*De civitate Dei* 20.20), which he may also have read in a Latin version of 2 Macc. 12.45 (Ogle, "The Sleep of Death," 102). As far as eschatology is concerned, he retained the Platonic view of eternity (changelessness rather than endless duration). In addition, two viewpoints which he never reconciled were the objective interpretation of time and eternity found in the *City of God* and the subjective viewpoint of the same espoused in his *Confessions*. His theology of history included a persistent conflict between the earthly city and the City of God. He rejected the chiliastic view of the literal thousand-year reign of Christ on earth; thus some have dubbed him the Father of amillennialism.

⁵¹Although the teaching of the interim state in the New Testament cannot be proven on grammatical grounds alone, much can be said about the fathers' collective belief about the intermediate state based on their interpretative grammatical renditions of κοιμάομαι. A grammatically strong way to say something in fact "exists" is to render the verb in a perfect active, perfect passive, or aorist passive tense.

Table 5.--Grammatical Usages of Κοιμάομαι That Reflect Patristic Belief in the Intermediate State

Form of Κοιμάομαι	Tense Designation
κεκοιμημένοι	perfect deponent participle
κεκοίμηται	perfect deponent indicative
κεκοίμηνται	perfect passive indicative
κεκοιμῆσθαι	perfect passive infinitive
κοιμηθείς	aorist passive participle
ἐκοιμήθην	aorist passive indicative
κοιμηθῆναι	aorist passive infinitive
κοιμηθήσομαι	future passive indicative
κοιμᾶσθαι	present passive indicative

It is not surprising that κοιμάομαι appears so regularly in early church literature.[52] Scanning through the κοιμάομαι documents reveals that most of these writers at least made allusions to the bulk of the sleep-of-death passages in the New Testament. One of their favorite passages to quote from the Gospels was the great resuscitation of the holy ones in Matt. 27.52. The story of the raising of Lazarus in John 11 was also a prime patristic target. Pauline sleep-of-death passages received marked attention with 1 Corinthians 15 and 1 Thessalonians 4 being the key texts. As part of their defense of the belief in the resurrection, the fathers who chose to do so, easily brought in the idea of death being a sleep from which there would be an eschatological arousal. They chose κοιμάομαι as a primary word to describe this pre-parousia event. Not only did they continue to battle the deception that Platonism had sprinkled over κοιμάομαι, but they also

---

[52]The forms which appear the most are ἐκοιμήθη, 229 times; κοιμᾶσθαι, 130 times; and κεκοιμημένων, 109 times. The passive voice was probably used so often in order to express divine agency, and the present and perfect tenses were used to reflect the durative and abiding kind of action related to the sleep of death.

carried on the reinterpretation process of κοιμάομαι as the sleep of death, which was initiated in the Old Testament in embryonic form and brought to full fruition in the New Testament, it became a sign of hope, not disparity.

It is a sound judgment, therefore, that through the translational efforts of the Greek and Latin fathers in regard to the Hebrew writings, both apocryphal and canonical, the Hebrew metaphor for the sleep of death, particularly the noun מִשְׁכָּב and the verb שָׁכַב, found correspondence among the Greek and Latin writers with the terms, κοιμάομαι, κοίμησις, *dormire*, and *dormitio*. Just as it was in the New Testament, κοιμάομαι retained its leading position as the chief Christian metaphor depicting the sleep of death.

This early exegetical effort, however, was not without its flaws. An unfortunate result of the syncretistic efforts of Clement of Alexandria and Origen is that while some reacted vehemently against Origen's theology chiefly (although he believed in an intermediate state), the conditions of the postmortem state were skewed by their "overboard" exegesis. Specifically, the idea that the Christian goes to heaven immediately upon death is not biblical. It is a conclusion based upon the dualistic-flavored eschatology of Clement. While this belief was not taught *in toto*, it nevertheless is a mainstay of many eschatologies. It is a strange reality that while the intermediate state was taught by many of the church fathers, it is still the case that many Christians are more comfortable with the idea of the immediate attainment of heavenly bliss upon physical death than with the concept of an interim state. But as has been the case throughout this study, substantial evidence has been provided which should suggest strongly that the idea of the immediate acquisition of heaven upon death is biblically unsupportable because it is eschatologically anachronistic.

Memorial Epitaphs and Inscriptions

Ogle reports that the oldest parts of the Roman catacombs have not given up any inscriptional examples of either κοιμᾶσθαι or *dormire* dating before the second century.⁵³ The forms which do appear, however, have the phrases εἰρήνη σοι, ἐν εἰρήνῃ, *pax tibi*, and *in pace* in combination with the name of the deceased.⁵⁴

An inscriptional example which relects the parable of the "Rich Man and Lazarus" (Luke 16.19-31), in addition to the one reported above (Chap. II, 73-74), reflects the noun form κοιμήσις in synonymous tandem with ἀναπαύσεως in a sleep-of-death epitaph.⁵⁵ Consider G. Lefebvre's translation:

> God almighty, the one who is, who was and who is to come, Jesus Christ, son of the living God, remember the sleeping (κοιμήσεως and repose (ἀναπαύσεως) of your slave Zoneene, who was most pious and loved the law. And deem her worthy to dwell, through the agency of your holy and light-bringing archangel Michael, in the bosoms of the holy fathers Abraham, Isaac and Jacob. Because yours is the glory and the power to the ages of ages, amen. She lived in blessedness 77 years and this is her tomb. Phamenoth 23rd, after the consulship of Bassos and Philip.⁵⁶

It appears that the phrase "bosom of Abraham" was a technical designation for the locale of deceased Christians who were not martyrs. An important study on the eschatological ideas found in Christian epitaphs reveals that in the first couple of centuries a clear demarcation was retained between the pre-parousia state of the Christian dead and the immediate acquisition of heaven by martyrs based on Rev. 6.9-11.⁵⁷ In time, the state possessed by this distinct class was thought to be inhabited by the faithful dead as well. Kajanto believes that this was done in the

---

⁵³Ogle, "The Sleep of Death," 108. This section will be in no way exhaustive. The field of epigraphy is ever widening with new discoveries and translations emerging rapidly. Several representative examples will be offered.

⁵⁴The first dated example is A.D. 369 (ibid.). For the semantic evolution of the appearance of κοιμήσις and κοιμητήριον, consult Ogle's work which contains many technical references in the appropriate footnotes. This section will contain only a few examples of the sleep-of-death formula found on epitaphs and inscriptions representing death in early Christianity.

⁵⁵For the citation of this inscription, see Horsley, *New Documents*, 3:105 or its full reproduction in Appendix H.

⁵⁶G. Lefebvre, *Inscriptiones Graecae Aegypti*, vol. 5: *Inscriptiones Christianae Aegypti*, repr. ed. (Chicago: University of Chicago Press, 1978), 48. For more discussion of the "bosom of Abraham" formula, see Horsley, *New Documents*, 3:106.

⁵⁷I. Kajanto, "In gremio Abraham," *Arctos* 12 (1978): 27-53.

preeminent concern of extending consolation.⁵⁸ Though it is not clear whether the reference to the bosom of Abraham indicates the Christian's proximity to either heaven or Hades, it is Kajanto's conclusion that the "rest" is happening in heaven.⁵⁹ It appears, therefore, that no theological basis supports this shift of emphasis; rather it was done so the mourners would "feel" better. Taking into consideration the awful persecution that persisted through much of the early Christian era, it is not surprising that there was a special affection for those who were martyred. Although this inclination was based in part on Rev. 6.9-11, there is no guarantee that these verses refer to a scene in heaven.

Reflecting biblical origins, there are many more inscriptions which have been uncovered reflecting the Christian usage of κοίμησις and κοιμάομαι. Basically, a peculiar Christian stamp was placed upon the formula κοιμάομαι ἐν κυρίῳ/ἐν Χριστῷ based on sleep-of-death phrases found in 1 Cor. 15.18 and 1 Thess. 4.14.⁶⁰ An additional epigraphical formula also reflecting the Corinthian passage is κοιμητήριον ἐν Χριστῷ and κοιμητήριον ἕως ἀναστάσεως.⁶¹ Κοιμητήριον, which can be translated "sleeping-place," was adopted by Christians to refer to the graveyard or tomb. Its Christian distinctiveness is seen in its replacing the more normal term for tomb, ἡρῷον. It was also used in the sense of the "family grave," which may at least be an allusion to the Old Testament picture of the Hebrew

---

⁵⁸Ibid., 33. This tendency is reflected on Christian gravestones and *consolatio* poems.

⁵⁹Ibid., 41-42. For an example of the heavenly state being experienced immediately at death, see Lefebvre, *Inscriptiones Christianae*, inscription 423. Kajanto also finds the presupposition of the separation of body and soul at death in the Pauline phrase, ἐκδημῆσαι ἐκ τοῦ σώματος καὶ ἐνδημῆσαι πρὸς τὸν κύριον, found in 2 Cor. 5.8.

⁶⁰The viewpoint alluded to earlier (Chapter IV, pp. 184-85) that the use of the passive voice (ἐκοιμήθη or κοιμηθέντας in 1 Thess. 4.14) could possibly reflect the Pauline intention of suggesting that Christians were divinely "put to sleep" at death was definitely the case if Christian tombstone epigraphy is any indication. For representatives examples of the "ἐκοιμήθη ἐν Χριστῷ" and "ἐκοιμήθη ἐν κυρίῳ" epitaphs, see Appendices J and K respectively.

⁶¹These inscriptions were found in Attica and Macedonia respectively, most likely of the third century A.D.

kings sleeping in relation to each other, even though κοιμητήριον does not appear in the LXX.

Although later inscriptions reflected some tendency to dissolve the intermediate state in favor of the immediate delight of Heaven, the majority of the references reflect the eschatological belief that Christians who had died were "asleep in Christ" until the time of the resurrection. Those inscriptions which reveal a tendency to leapfrog the interim state might be explained by the delayed parousia from their point of view. If the delay caused a problem then, how might the even longer delay experienced by contemporary Christians affect eschatology? One must still wonder if there is no intermediate state, what merit can the parousia possibly retain?

Conclusion

The post-biblical consideration of the sleep of death as exemplified by κοιμάομαι is well attested, even though the first few centuries of the Christian era were the only ones treated with any detail in this work. Early Christian response to death was marked by an intense use of the sleep-of-death metaphor. Like the New Testament, it was no longer a euphemistic deception. The resurrection had a great impact on the early church in that Jesus' feat signalled the death of death. So much did the resurrection impress the early Christians that κοιμάομαι became a *terminus technicus* for the death event which was ontologically connected with an intermediate state. To depict the death event as a sleep was a bold statement of faith and hope expressed by the early Christians who believed in an eschatological resurrection which concluded the interim period. This belief not only was exhibited unashamedly in their writings but also was carved in the tombstones of their loved ones.

CONCLUSION

The Meaning of Κοιμάομαι in the New Testament

Of great importance is the fact that κοιμάομαι was chosen in the New Testament in most of the death contexts that have been examined in this study. If it were the case that only stock terms for death were chosen, (e.g., ἀπέθανεν) then one may be inclined to dismiss the possibility of an intermediate state. Whether or not an intermediate state exists, however, goes far beyond the realm of grammar. Even if New Testament writers had categorically chosen to avoid any kind of sleep-of-death metaphor, there still would not be sufficient grounds for the exclusion of the intermediate state from discussions pertaining to the major doctrine of Christian eschatology. Even though the New Testament does not refer to an intermediate state per se, there are substantial indirect statements already discussed which point strongly to its ontological reality. Logically, one must wonder about the feasibility of a bodily resurrection on the last Day if there is no interim state and all believers are already in heaven to live forever with the Lord immediately after their death. The resurrection was a hallmark for Jesus; so it will be for all Christians.

Three different postmortem options have been presented. Philosophically, in relation to death, one must be some kind of monist or dualist in the ontological sense. It is worth remembering that this monist/dualist debate has been raging for years with no firm resolution. This writer believes, however, that monism is not a requirement for the possibility of an intermediate state. It is unfortunate that the term "dualism" has been used, although rightfully so, to describe Platonic, Marcionitic, Gnostic, and Cartesian systems. Why? It is because not everything named dualistic is evil. Similarly, everything that fits into a synthetic framework is not Hegelian. Many well-meaning theologians, scholars, and teachers have desired to avoid dualism only later to contradict themselves.[1] Sadly, many pastors have preached funeral messages which have simultaneously comforted the bereaved and paid at least nominal obeisance to Plato by incorporating some kind of hybrid form of the immortality of the soul into the biblical witness. Although charged with this flaw, Cullmann admits of at least a slight "leaning" toward a Greek concept.[2] This writer believes the main problem with the Platonic system, the Aristotelian form/matter model, or Gnostic dualism is that they all demean the body and glorify the soul, not that they maintain separability of soul and body. Something certainly continues after death for the Christian, but it is not an immortal soul finishing its tireless cycle.

With what kind of duality then can the Christian be comfortable in this interim period and at the same time be biblically grounded? Granted, the New Testament is not exhaustive on the subject. The version of dualism for this writer is not only biblically warranted but also is intended by the use of κοιμάομαι, bound up in the already/not yet tension of salvation in which the ontic spheres of eternity and temporality merge. Eternity reaches out and touches the Christian in the salvation process (2 Cor. 5.17, Gal. 2.20). The postconversion Christian is ἐν Χριστῷ during life and σὺν Χριστῷ during death. Corporate existence and communion with Christ, and most likely with others who are κοιμημένοι, continue between death and resurrection awaiting the parousia of Christ. This writer aligns himself

---

[1]For several examples such as Herman Ridderbos and G. C. Berkouwer, see Cooper, *Body, Soul, & Life Everlasting*, 174-75.

[2]Cullmann, *Immortality of the Soul or Resurrection of the Dead?*, 83.

with the wholistic dualism model advocated by Cooper and referred to at various points throughout this discussion. During life the human is an integrated whole, not a person with inherent, independently functioning elements. Only one distinction needs to be made in reference to the postmortem state. Actually, this concept is probably something with which Cooper would not disagree. While retaining the basic anthropological/thanatological framework of his work, this writer will change the name to "Christological Dualism." This title merely reflects the added emphasis of Christ's involvement in the intermediate state, not a reference to Christ's ontological disposition. Cooper certainly believes in Christ's involvement in the interim period, but referring to Christ in the model's title says something crucial about the reason for and the condition of the intermediate state. The definition of dualism for this study means nothing more than, at the time of biological death, something survives the experience. During life, though, the human is a functioning, integrated whole.

Earlier the writer issued a warning about accepting the idea of theological development in Paul which portrays him correcting an earlier, mistaken eschatological view. The kind of development with which one can safely engage is that one which is the direct result of progressive revelation—that is, the progression that Jesus refers to in Matt. 5.17-20. Although the Old Testament does not fully correct misinformed paganism about death and the post-mortem state, it began to do so. True, the Old Testament is not sufficiently clear about the resurrection, but there is no mistake about its idea of the interim state. For the Hebrew, Sheol was dark, dank, and ontologically precarious. In the Old Testament, the interim state was an open-ended equation. But Jesus' defeat of death, as πρωτότοκος, signalled the proper closure for the eschatological frame. Jesus' resurrection provided an eschatological perspective in the New Testament through which to view the Old Testament. With Jesus, the reinterpretation of κοιμάομαι was accomplished. Didactically and functionally, Jesus converted the concept of the sleep of death from a reality-camouflaging euphemism to a hope-filled metaphor. This is the brand of development that is welcomed and to which this writer subscribes.

Monists make too little of the death experience. For them, Christians do survive death, but they survive it instantaneously either by means of an immediate resurrection or a temporary (although phenomenologically-experienced), time-warping extinction recreation model. These two views are eschatologically deficient in that they juggle the events of salvation history. Simply, the parousia is given, at best, a diminished prominence in their systems. For them, the intermediate state is not a necessary precursor to the resurrection. The pressing question is: "If Christians know they are redeemed and going to heaven, why is there so much consternation over an intermediate state?" This writer is not far removed from the thanatological model advocated by E. Earle Ellis. Disagreement enters, though, in relation to his phenomenological explanation of the experience of time. Even if time is not a factor in eternity, some-"thing" passes even though it passes indefinitely. If events associated with eternity occur instantaneously, then eternity becomes ontologically empty or undefined. Even if the intermediate state is experienced phenomenologically, time is nevertheless passing—that is, many "ticks on the clock" elapse. Eschatological sleep is not necessarily "sleep" in the sense of "unconscious ignorance."

Metaphorically and functionally, κοιμάομαι marks a transitory stage from the temporal to the eternal. Part of the temporal remains because it is pre-parousia, and part of the eternal is pulling because it is posthumous and post-conversion. There is an "eschatological friction" operative in this parenthetical stage of salvation history. Both are overlapping regions about which the Bible sheds little light. As long as the parousia, therefore, has not occurred, οἱ κοιμώμενοι are existing with Christ waiting for the final parenthesis to be added, the resurrection. In fact, two groups, those "awake" and those "asleep," await the parousia. So, one can go to heaven in one of two ways—by resurrection of the body or by translation of the living. Either way, the parousia is the catalyst for both.

Κοιμάομαι as eschatological sleep announces the demise of the monist viewpoints. Κοιμάομαι means that the Christian journey is incomplete at death. Temporality is being swallowed up and is thrust toward the eternal during death. Even during physical life the temporal sphere is surrounded by eternity. What survives death is that which has been transformed by God in the salvation process. At the resurrection, sanctification gives way to the ultimate glorification of the Christian and the eternal damnation of the unrepentant.

It is the intention of the New Testament to depict death, especially with the use of κοιμάομαι, as an event through which the Christian passes accompanied by Christ. Later, the event of the parousia will provoke the bodily resurrection and transformation of all believers. Κοιμάομαι also includes the idea of relief from the earthly struggles associated with sin and from the difficulties in being a servant of Jesus Christ.

For the Christian, the only real fear in death is the aspect of the unknown. What helps counteract this anxiety is the theological ramifications of κοιμάομαι. Also built into the concept of eschatological sleep is the hope of the resurrection. Eschatological sleep is not eternal sleep. Paul did not express concern in 2 Cor. 5.4 about the death event itself. Rather, Paul was bemoaning the sudden realization that he might not be alive at the parousia and therefore have to go through the intermediate state. Quite possibly, the thorn in Paul's flesh could have been an epistemological distancing (2 Cor. 12.7) which prevented him from fully understanding the ontological status of the interim period. God was the *passivum divinum* behind this event in Paul's life.[3] Paul did not know the explicit details of the intermediate state, but he knew it would be there and that Jesus would be the Lord over it.

Some discussion has been entertained about the disciples' collective confusion concerning Jesus' description of the plight of Lazarus in John 11. The same kind of confusion was exhibited by the witnesses of the death of Jairus' daughter in the

---

[3]For a discussion of the "thorn in the flesh," see Ralph P. Martin, *2 Corinthians*, 410-16.

Synoptic tradition. This writer believes that the puzzlement concerning the use of κοιμάομαι or καθεύδω as the eschatological sleep of death can be ascribed to the scriptural deficiency and weak thanatology of Jesus' hearers. For example, one must conclude that the disciples knew very little of the Old Testament or they would have associated Jesus' sleep-of-death talk with either the "Regnal Obituaries" appearing in Kings and Chronicles, the sleep-of-death passages in Job, or in Psalmic thanatology. One must judge the disciples' mind-set by their response to Jesus. Jesus had had little time to teach them about the totality of the Christian faith, only what they needed to know for the continuation of their mission. Now if the disciples had responded in John 11.14 in a negative tone, as in "If Lazarus is asleep (in death), then he has no hope," reflecting pagan despair, one could rightly conclude that they at least knew of the pagan use of κοιμάομαι. This is not the case either. Basically, the pre-Pentecostal understanding of κοιμάομαι differs greatly from the post-Pentecostal. The theological import, therefore, of κοιμάομαι is tied inextricably to Jesus' death and resurrection. That Peter came to understand the difference is seen not only in the Lukan defense speech in Acts 2, but also by his employment of κοιμάομαι in 2 Pet. 3.1-7. They responded to Jesus as though he spoke literally, just as Nicodemus responded literally to Jesus about "being born again" in John 3.

Theologically, Jesus' intermediate state was his Incarnation. By this event, the eternal ruptured the temporal order thus proving that the antithetical spheres could cohabit. He who understands, therefore, the Incarnation can also understand the intermediate state. The mystery which surrounds John 1.14 equally shrouds 1 Thess. 4.13 and John 11.11. Because of the limitation of revelation both the Incarnation and the intermediate state are not completely understandable, but that does not mean they are not legitimate ontological categories.

The Meaning of Κοιμάομαι for Contemporary Christians

What disturbed the Thessalonians still disturbs us today. One of their questions pertained to the whereabouts of their deceased brothers and sisters in

Christ. That which the pastoral Paul addressed in his day must still be addressed today. In fact, this issue could possibly be the most important and most difficult topic for the pastor to grapple with constantly. Doubt is not attached to the certainty or uncertainty of the attainment of eternal life. Timing on the eschatological calendar is the real issue which causes so much concern among Christians. Practically, it is not just a one-time issue. As long as Christians continue to die, the pastor will continually be called upon to preach funerals. Granted, each funeral takes on differing levels of difficulty depending upon the age, spiritual condition, and the circumstances of death of the decedent. Regardless of these aspects, though, the parishioner still will launch the inevitable query: "The text you used was so meaningful as were your consoling words. But where is _____ now?" Gabriel Fackre has charted some familiar responses:

(a) "His soul is with God while his body is in the ground."
(b) "Her soul is with God, her body is in the ground, but the two will be united at the resurrection."
(c) "He died right into the world to come and therefore now has a resurrected body, because there is no time in eternity."
(d) "We do not know or need to know the particulars, but only that all will be well."
(e) "Well, we just don't know."
(f) "She has been making a long journey, transmigrating we hope to a higher plane or better next life in this world."
(g) "I don't know, but there is this medium on Route 88 that may be able to put you in touch with him. . ."[4]

While the New Testament emphasizes the "not yet" aspect of eschatology, which is the resurrection, Scripture does appear to recognize time, "with no clear foreshortened resurrection that dissociates our fulfillment from that of a transfigured world."[5] In communicating the truth of what the New Testament says about death, it is abundantly clear that all its spokesmen emphasize the uninterrupted fellowship we have with Christ, beginning with the initial experience of our conversion and continuing through the death experience. The funeral message should always reflect the Pauline dictum that nothing has the power to

---

[4]Gabriel Fackre, "I Believe in the Resurrection of the Body," 50.

[5]Ibid.

separate the Christian from Christ, not even death, the most foreboding of all earthly experiences (Rom. 8.31-39). So, rightfully, the stress should be placed upon the ultimate destination of the Christian rather than on the penultimate intermediate state, albeit without denying the existence of the real measurable interim between death and resurrection.

Training God's people in eschatology involves a great deal more than equipping one to decide what kind of millenarian viewpoint to hold. An honest investigation of κοιμάομαι as the sleep of death in the New Testament should be one of the main elements involved in equipping Christians to cope with the experience of the death of loved ones and friends and, barring the advent of the parousia, our own impending deaths.

Falling asleep at night and waking in the morning is a clear and natural foreshadowing of our own deaths and subsequent resurrections. This writer does not believe, however, that the deceased Christian is necessarily unconscious. Monists have tried to alleviate this fear by saying that this interim condition is not experienced ontologically, but phenomenologically. This proposed solution does not solve the problem. No matter how it is experienced, time is elapsing. An interim state, therefore, is not only plausible but a biblical reality. If this is the case, then a phenomenologist would not object to the idea of "soul sleep."

Κοιμάομαι for the Christian is also a term of alleviation. It is a promise that what has already been effected in the Christian's life, salvifically, will be embellished all the more upon death. It simply has not been revealed how this intermediate state is related to heaven. Although one cannot be totally certain, it is at least plausible to say that eternity includes the intermediate state. Perhaps the grave is where eternity and the finite order intersect. After death, the next important event to occur in the lineup of salvation history is the parousia. Hardly any scholar would deny this statement unless one thinks that the parousia occurs at death. Ontologically, then, the parousia is an event similar to the Incarnation in that the eternal will again rip into the temporal order bringing about its

173

destruction in an expedient manner.[6] Christological dualism, therefore, would allow the Christian to be part of both the temporal and eternal until and during death. All who have died in Christ are in the pre-parousia configuration known as the intermediate state in conscious fellowship with the one who is still the "first and only born of the dead."

Significance for a Christian Understanding of Death

As has been seen through the diachronic and synchronic evaluations of κοιμάομαι as the sleep of death from the Homeric period into the dawn of the post-biblical era, the death event required a response. Very early in the history of its usage, κοιμάομαι and other synonymous terms were variously employed to communicate a soothing idea or a warm feeling to those who observed death and were shaken by its apparent finality. Diachronically, the concept gradually evolved from a term of despair clouded by euphemism in the Homeric period to a bold metaphor reflecting a confident hope in a future resurrection in the New Testament. While the seeds of the hope of the resurrection were present in the Old Testament, the doctrine would not fully bloom until Jesus reinterpreted κοιμάομαι, not only by assigning it to a deceased person, such as Lazarus, but also by exemplifying this new message through the resuscitation of the same.

Because of Jesus, κοιμάομαι now carries a Christian meaning. The dead-end "iron sleep" of Homer has been corrected to the apocalyptically open-ended "death sleep" of Jesus, which he himself experienced briefly and is in full control of today. The message of the hope of the resurrection is still the calling card of Christianity. The framers of the New Testament initiated it through the inspiration of the Holy Spirit, and Christians are called upon to perpetuate the main theological implication that surrounds κοιμάομαι; there will be an eschatological arousal of "all who are in the tombs and hear his voice (John 5.28, 29)." To be

---

[6]The writer does recognize that one's millenarian disposition will alter the timeframe of these events. The end result, however, is the same.

asleep in Christ means to be in the grave, to be in the intermediate state, and to be in the immediate, conscious presence of Christ awaiting the parousia. Let the reader understand, though, that a significant problem still exists with all thanatologies because they are all before the actual experience of death. Accordingly, the Christian is forced to rely upon the Holy Spirit's illumination of the scriptural attestation of life, death, and the beyond.

APPENDIX A

THE SEMANTIC RANGE OF THE SLEEP-OF-DEATH METAPHOR IN THE NEW TESTAMENT

Reference	Sleep of Death	Physical Sleep	Spiritual Laxity
Matt. 1.24 γ		*	
Matt. 8.24 β		*	
Matt. 9.24 β	*		
Matt. 13.25 β		*	
Matt. 25.5 β			*
Matt. 26.40 β		*	
Matt. 26.43 β		*	
Matt. 26.45 β		*	
Matt. 27.52 α	*		
Matt. 28.13 α		*	
Mk. 4.27 β		*	
Mk. 4.38 β		*	
Mk. 5.39 β	*		
Mk. 13.36 β			*
Mk. 14.37 β		*	
Mk. 14.37 β		*	
Mk. 14.40 β		*	
Mk. 14.41 β		*	
Lk. 8.52 β	*		
Lk 9.32 γ		*	

Reference	Sleep of Death	Physical Sleep	Spiritual Laxity
Lk 22.45 α		*	
Lk 22.46 β		*	
Jn. 11.11 α	*		
Jn. 11.12 α		*	
Jn. 11.13 γ		*	
Jn. 11.13 δ		*	
Acts 7.60 α	*		
Acts 12.6 α		*	
Acts 13.36 α	*		
Acts 20.9 γ		*	
Acts 20.9 γ		*	
Rom. 13.11 γ			*
1 Cor. 7.39 α	*		
1 Cor. 11.30 α	*		
1 Cor. 15.6 α	*		
1 Cor. 15.18 α	*		
1 Cor. 15.20 α	*		
1 Cor. 15.51 α	*		
Eph. 5.14 β	*		
1 Thess. 4.13 α	*		
1 Thess. 4.14 α	*		
1 Thess. 4.15 α	*		
1 Thess. 5.6 β			*
1 Thess. 5.7 β		*	
1 Thess. 5.7 β		*	

Reference	Sleep of Death	Physical Sleep	Spiritual Laxity
1 Thess. 5.10 β	*		
2 Pet. 3.4 α	*		

Legend

α = κοιμάομαι β = καθεύδω
γ = ὕπνος δ = κοίμησις

APPENDIX B

KOIMAOMAI AS THE SLEEP OF DEATH IN THE LXX

Reference	Hebrew/Aramaic Equivalent	Occasion
Gen. 47.30	שָׁכַב	death of Jacob[1]
Deut. 31.16	שָׁכַב	impending death of Moses
Jg. 5.27	שָׁכַב	death of Sisera
2 Sam. 7.12	שָׁכַב	Nathan's allusion to David's death
1 Kg. 1.21	שָׁכַב	Bathsheba's allusion to David's death
1 Kg. 2.10	שָׁכַב	death of David
1 Kg. 11.21	שָׁכַב	Hadad hears of death of David
1 Kg. 11.43	שָׁכַב	death of Solomon
1 Kg. 14.20	שָׁכַב	death of Jeroboam
1 Kg. 14.31	שָׁכַב	death of Rehoboam
1 Kg. 15.8	שָׁכַב	death of Abijam
1 Kg. 15.24	שָׁכַב	death of Asa
1 Kg. 16.6	שָׁכַב	death of Baasha
1 Kg. 16.28	שָׁכַב	death of Omri

---

[1] The first occurrence also implements a standard form which varies slightly only in tense in all the references to the death of the Hebrew kings. This formula which occurs throughout 1 and 2 Kings is known as a "regnal summary" which bears close resemblance to Luke's summary statements in Acts. The recurring formula in 1 and 2 Kings is καὶ ἐκοιμήθη (X) μετὰ τῶν πατρῶν αὐτοῦ = וַיִּשְׁכַּב (X) עִם־אֲבֹתָיו.

Reference	Hebrew/Aramaic Equivalent	Occasion
1 Kg. 22.40	שָׁכַב	death of Ahab
1 Kg. 22.50	שָׁכַב	death of Jehoshaphat
2 Kg. 4.32	שָׁכַב	Shunnamite woman's son
2 Kg. 8.24	שָׁכַב	death of Joram
2 Kg. 9.16	שָׁכַב	reference to Joram's death
2 Kg. 10.35	שָׁכַב	death of Jehu
2 Kg. 13.9	שָׁכַב	death of Jehoahaz
2 Kg. 13.13	שָׁכַב	death of Joash
2 Kg. 14.16	שָׁכַב	death of Jehoash
2 Kg. 14.22	שָׁכַב	death of Amaziah
2 Kg. 14.29	שָׁכַב	death of Jeroboam
2 Kg. 15.7	שָׁכַב	death of Azariah
2 Kg. 15.22	שָׁכַב	death of Menahem
2 Kg. 15.38	שָׁכַב	death of Jotham
2 Kg. 16.20	שָׁכַב	death of Ahaz
2 Kg. 20.21	שָׁכַב	death of Hezekiah
2 Kg. 21.18	שָׁכַב	death of Manasseh
2 Kg. 24.6	שָׁכַב	death of Jehoiakim
1 Chr. 17.11	הָלַךְ	Nathan's allusion to David's death
2 Chr. 9.31	שָׁכַב	death of Solomon
2 Chr. 16.13	שָׁכַב	death of Asa
2 Chr. 21.1	שָׁכַב	death of Jehoshaphat
2 Chr. 26.2	שָׁכַב	death of Amaziah
2 Chr. 26.23	שָׁכַב	death of Uzziah

Reference	Hebrew/Aramaic Equivalent	Occasion
2 Chr. 27.9	שָׁכַב	death of Jotham
2 Chr. 28.27	שָׁכַב	death of Ahaz
2 Chr. 32.33	שָׁכַב	death of Hezekiah
2 Chr. 33.20	שָׁכַב	death of Manasseh
2 Chr. 36.8	only in LXX	death of Jehoiakim
Job 3.13	שָׁכַב	Job probes possible death at birth
Job 14.12	שָׁכַב	Jobian thanatology
Job 20.11	שָׁכַב	Zophar's thanatology
Job 21.13	נָחַת	Jobian Sheol talk
Job 21.26	שָׁכַב	Jobian thanatology
Job 27.19	שָׁכַב	Jobian thanatology
Job 27.20	only in LXX	Jobian thanatology
Ps. 41(40).8	שָׁכַב	death from plague
Is. 14.8	שָׁכַב	prophecy of the King of Babylon's death
Is. 14.18	שָׁכַב	all kings lying dead in glory
Is. 43.17	שָׁכַב	Chaldeans' death
Jer. 49.23-27 (30.12-16)	Hebrew is uncertain	impending death of Damascenes
Lam. 2.21	שָׁכַב	jeremiad about death of males
Ezek. 31.18	שָׁכַב	death in Sheol
Ezek. 32.19	שָׁכַב	death in Sheol
Ezek. 32.19(20)	only in LXX	death with uncircumcised
Ezek. 32.21(20)	שָׁכַב	mighty warriors in Sheol

Reference	Hebrew/Aramaic Equivalent	Occasion
Ezek. 32.27	שָׁכַב	death of uncircumcised
Ezek. 32.28	שָׁכַב	death with uncircumcised
Ezek. 32.29	שָׁכַב	death with Edomites
Ezek. 32.30	שָׁכַב	death with princes of north and Sidonians
Ezek. 32.32	שָׁכַב	death with Pharoah and his army
2 Macc. 12.45	only in LXX	those who rest in godliness
Sir. 46.19[2]	מִשְׁכָּב	Samuel approaching end of life
Sir. 48.13	מִשְׁכָּב	Samuel prophesying while dead
1 Kg. 3.20[3]	שָׁכַב	woman of ill repute crushed son at night
1 Kg. 17.19[4]	שָׁכַב	laying the dead son on the bed[5]
2 Kg. 4.21	שָׁכַב	laying the dead son on the bed[6]
2 Kg. 4.32	שָׁכַב	dead child lying on the couch[7]

[2] The noun form κοίμησις is used in both citations from Sirach.

[3] The verb κοιμίζειν is translated "placed" and is in semantic relationship with τεθνηκότα, "dead".

[4] Alternate form κοιμίζειν used as a *double entendre* for death and being laid down.

[5] Elijah and the widow of Zarephath's dead son.

[6] Elisha and the Shunammite woman's dead son.

[7] Τὸν υἱὸν αὐτῆς τὸν τεθνηκότα ἐκοίμισεν.

Reference	Hebrew/Aramaic Equivalent	Occasion
2 Chr. 16.14[8]	שָׁכַב	Asa lying dead in the death vault
Nahum 3.18	נָוּם[9]	the officers lying to rest in death

---

[8] Κοιμίζειν.

[9] Κοιμάομαι = נומ in this reference. The poetic parallelism of the next line equates נומ (sleep) with יִשְׁכֹּן (at rest).
 "Your shepherds are asleep,
 O king of Asshur.
 Your mighty ones are at rest" (Nahum 3.18a, b, c).

APPENDIX C

ὙΠΝΟΩ AS THE SLEEP OF DEATH IN THE LXX

Reference	Hebrew/Aramaic Equivalent	Occasion
Job 14.12[1]	שֵׁנָה	Jobian thanatology
Ps. 76(75).5[2]	שֵׁנָה	battle dead
Jer. 51(28).39	שֵׁנָה	Babylon's death
Job 3.13	יָשֵׁן	Jobian death wish
Ps. 13(12).3	נוּם	David's cry for help
Ps. 76(75).5[3]	יָשֵׁן	death of stouthearted
Jer. 51(28).39	יָשֵׁן	Babylon's death
Jer. 51(28).57	יָשֵׁן	Babylon's death
Sir. 46.20	יָשֵׁן	Samuel's death

[1] The first three references in the appendix use the noun form, ὕπνος. Variations of the verb form, ὑπνόω, are in the remaining six.

[2] Numbers within parentheses represent LXX references. As is the case with the Masoretic text, Septuagintal references are slightly altered in the translation process in quite a few places due to the presence of alternate text types.

[3] The double references of Ps. 76(75).5 and Jer. 51(28).39 occur because both the noun and verb forms of the same word appear. Numbers inside of parentheses indicate the LXX reference.

APPENDIX D

ΚΑΘΕΥΔΩ AS THE SLEEP OF DEATH IN THE LXX

Reference	Hebrew/Aramaic Equivalent	Occasion
Ps. 87(88).5	שָׁכַב	the slain in the grave
Is. 51.20	שָׁכַב	the death of the sons of Jerusalem
Dan. 12.2	יָשֵׁן	the resurrection of those asleep in the dust

APPENDIX E

SYNONYMY CORRESPONDENCE BETWEEN GREEK AND HEBREW SLEEP-OF-DEATH TERMINOLOGY

	שָׁכַב	יָשֵׁן	נוּם	שֵׁנָה	הָלַךְ	נָחַת	LXX
κοιμάομαι	64	—	1	—	1	1	5
καθεύδω	2	1	—	—	—	—	—
ὑπνόω	—	4	1	3	—	—	—

APPENDIX F

KOIMAOMIA AS PHYSICAL SLEEP IN THE HOMERIC PERIOD

Author	Source	Incidents
Aesopicus	*Fabulae*	9
Anacreon	*Fragmenta*	2
Aristophanes	*Vespae* 8,1.2	2
	Lysistrata 757,58	1
Aristoteles	*Historia animalium*	2
Comica Adespota	*Dubia*	2
Epimenides	*Testimonia*	3
Euripides	*Andromacha*	1
Hippocrates	*De morbis popularibus*	48
	De diaeta acutorum	1
	De affectionibus	2
	De morbis i.-iii.	1
	Prognosticon	2
	De natura muliebri	1
	De mulierum affectibus i.-iii.	3
	De diaeta i.-iv.	1
	De affectionibus interioribus	3
Homer	*Iliad*	12
	Odyssey	27
Plato	*Symposium*	1

Author	Source	Incidents
Plato	*Euthydemus*	1
	Republic	2
	Leges	3
	Axiochus	1
	Phaedrus	1
	Epigrammata	1
Xenophon	*Hellenica*	2
	Memorabilia	2
	Anabasis	4
	Cyropaedia	12
	Agesilaus	2
	Symposium[1]	2
Various Authors	*Anthologia Graeca*	18
Orphica	*Hymni*	1
	Argonautica	1

---

[1] One example in *Symposium* 2.24.3,4-25.1 is interesting because it approaches a death-and-resurrection motif. "So far as drinking is concerned, you have my hearty approval; for wine does of a truth 'moisten the soul' and lull our griefs to sleep (κοιμίζει) just as the mandragora does with men, at the same time awakening (ἐγείρει) kindly feelings as oil quickens a flame." Translation in G. P. Goold, ed. *Xenophon*, vol. 4, trans. O. J. Todd, Loeb Classical Library (Cambridge: Harvard University Press, 1979), 555.

APPENDIX G

KOIMAOMAI AS THE SLEEP OF DEATH IN APOSTOLIC AND PATRISTIC WORKS

Author	κοιμάομαι	κοίμησις	κοιμητήριον
Amphilochius	4	-	-
Asterius	3	-	-
Athanasius	33	4	3
Athenaeus	6	-	-
Basilius	23	4	-
Clement of Alexandria	8	-	-
Clement of Rome	3	-	-
Epiphanius	46	4	3
Eusebius	92	10	5
Gregory Nazianzenus	5	2	2
Gregory Nyssenus	22	2	-
Hermas	8	1	-
Ignatius of Antioch	4	2	-
John Chrysostom	202	25	4
Justin Martyr	6	-	-
Pseudo-Justin Martyr	7	1	-
Macarius	9	3	-
Marcellus	1	-	-
Origen	71	10	1

APPENDIX H

ΚΟΙΜΗΣΙΣ IN THE "BOSOM OF ABRAHAM" EPITAPH[1]

✢ ✢ ✢

ὁ θεὸς ὁ παντοκράτωρ
ὁ ὢν προὼν καὶ μέλλων,
Ἰησοῦς ὁ Χριστὸς ὁ υἱὸς τοῦ
θεοῦ τοῦ ζῶντος, μνήσθητι
τῆς κοιμήσεως καὶ ἀναπαύσεως
τῆς δούλης σου Ζωνεήνης
τῆς εὐσεβεστάτης καὶ (leaf)
φιλεντόλου· καὶ αὐτὴν
καταξίωσον κατασκηνῶσε
διὰ τοῦ ἁγίου σου καὶ φωταγωγοῦ
ἀρχανγέλου Μιχαηλ
εἰς κόλπους τῶν ἁγίων πατέρων
Ἀβρααμ Ἰσακ καὶ Ἰακωβ· ὅτι σοῦ ἐστιν
ἡ δόξα καὶ τὸ κράτος εἰς τοὺς αἰῶνας
τῶν αἰώνων ἀμην. ἔζησε δὲ
μακαρίως ἔτη ο̅ζ̅. ἔστιν δὲ
ἡ μνήμη αὐτῆς Φαμενωθ κ̅γ̅
μετὰ τὴν ὑπατίαν Βάσσου καὶ Φιλίππου.

---

[1]Inscription found in G. Lefebvre, *Inscriptiones Graecae Aegypti*, 5:48.

APPENDIX I

JEWISH EPITAPHS FOUND IN THE NECROPOLIS[1]

183

☦ εκοιμηθ
η ο μικροσ
στρατηγ
ισ παυνι
α αρχ(ησ) γ ιν
δ(ικτιωνοσ) ☦

184

[εκοιμηθη ο μακαρι]
οσ φ[οιϵ]
αμμων
εν μηνι
αθυρ κς
ινδ(ικτιωνοσ) ιγ ·

189

μαρια θυ
γατηρ φ
αμσωθισ
ετων λε
εν ειρηνη
η κοιμη
σισ σου

190

☦ στεφα
νοσ ιατροσ
εκοιμηθη
παχων ιδ̄
ινδι(κτιωνοσ) ιϛ̄
☦

---

[1] Inscriptions found in G. Lefebvre, *Inscriptiones Graecae Aegypti*, 5:183, 184, 189, and 190.

APPENDIX J

THE "'ΕΚΟΙΜΗΘΗ ΕΝ ΧΡΙΣΤΩ" ΕΡΙΤΑΡΗ[1]

4

☩ εκοιμηθη εν χριστω
ο αδελφοσ ϊωαν
νησ ο του αϐϐα σερη
νου του ιατρου μηνι
τυϐη : κ : ινδ(ικτιωνοσ) ιδ : διο
κλητιανου ☩ σνϛ ☩

5

☩ χμγ ☩
εκοιμηθη εν χριστω
ο αδελφοσ ϊουλι
ανοσ ο του αδελφ(ου)
ϊωαννου του κη
πορ(ου) του κοινοϐ(ιου)
του αϐϐα ευσταθ(ιου)
μη(νι) παυνι η ϊνδ(ικτιωνοσ) ιε
διοκλητ(ιανου) συγ ☩

9

☩ εκοιμηθη εν χριστω
ο αδελφοσ επι
μαχοσ ο του κοι
νοϐιου του αϐϐα
ϊωαννου μηνι
μεσορη κγ ινδ(ικτιωνοσ) ιγ
ετου διωκλητι
ανου σπϛ
☩ χμγ ☩

10

☩
☩ εκοιμηθη εν χριστω
ο εν αγιοισ αδελ
φοσ τιμοθεοσ
ο τησ περιστερασ
ο του κοινοϐιου
του αϐϐα σαλαμα
μηνι παχων κγ ινδ(ικτιωνοσ) ιϐ
ετουσ διοκλητι
ανου σϙδ ☩ ☩ ☩

---

[1]Inscriptions found in G. Lefebvre, *Inscriptiones Graecae Aegypti*, 5:4, 5, 9, and 10.

APPENDIX K

THE "ἘΚΟΙΜΗΘΗ ΕΝ ΚΥΡΙΩ" EPITAPH[1]

7

✠ ☉ ✠
εκοιμηθη εν
κυριω ο μακαριοσ
αββα σωφρονι
οσ ο θεοδωρου
και υσχυριων
οσ μηνι επιφη
κε ινδ(ικτιωνοσ) α ετουσ
διοκλητιανου συγ

8

✠ εκοιμηθη εν κυριω
ο αδελφοσ μη
νασ ο του αββα
ηρακλιου μηνι
τυβη δ ινδ(ικτιωνοσ) ε διο
κλητιανου ετ(ουσ)
συη ✠

11

✠ εκοιμηθη εν
κυριω ο μακαριοσ
ημων αδελφοσ
στεφανοσ ο μα
θητησ του αββα ζα
χαριου ο του κοι
νοβ(ιου) του αββ(α) ευστα
θιου " μη(νι) ' θωθ " ι " ινδ(ικτιωνοσ) ιγ
διοκλητ(ιανου) σμς ✠

12

ω ✠ εκοιμηθη
εν κυριω αββα ιου
λιανοσ ο ωτασ
ο μαθητησ του
αββα θεοδωρου
πρεσβυτερου
μονησ ζαστων
μηνι αθυρ θ ινδ(ικτιωνοσ) η
ετουσ διοκλη
τιανου τς ✠

✠ ✠ ✠

---

[1]Inscriptions found in G. Lefebvre, *Inscriptiones Graecae Aegypti*, 5:7, 8, 11, and 12.

SELECTED BIBLIOGRAPHY

Books

Abbey of Maredsous, Centre Informatique et Bible, ed. *A Concordance to the Apocrypha/Deuterocanonical Books of the Revised Standard Version.* Grand Rapids: Eerdmans, 1983.

Aland, Kurt., ed. *Synopsis Quattuor Evangeliorum: Locis parallelis evangeliorum apocryphorum et patrum adhibitis.* 13th rev. ed. Stuttgart: Württembergische Bibelanstalt, 1990.

Allen, T. W. *Homeri Ilias.* Vols. 2-3. Oxford: Clarendon Press, 1931.

Andrews, C. *Egyptian Mummies.* Cambridge: Harvard University Press, 1984.

Bailey, L. *Biblical Perspectives on Death.* Philadelphia: Fortress Press, 1979.

Barr, James. *The Semantics of Biblical Language.* Oxford: Oxford University Press, 1961.

Bauer, J. B., ed. *Clavis Librorum Veteris Testamenti Apocryphorum.* Repr. ed. Graz: Akademische Druck- und Verlagsanstalt, 1972.

Beckby, H., ed. *Anthologia Graeca.* 4 vols. 2d ed. Munich: Heimeran, 1965, 1968.

Beach, Waldo and Richard Niebuhr, eds. *Christian Ethics: Sources of the Living Tradition.* 2d ed. New York: The Ronald Press Co., 1973.

Biblia Patristica: Index des Citations et Allusions Bibliques dans la Littérature Patristique. Paris: Centre National de la Recherche Scientifique, 1975, 1977.

Blanc, C., ed. *Origène. Commentaire sur saint Jean*. 3 vols. Sources chrétiennes. Paris: Cerf, 1966-1975.

Blomberg, Craig. *Interpreting the Parables*. Downers Grove, IL: InterVarsity Press, 1990.

Bornkamm, Günther. *Paul*. Translated by D. M. G. Stalker. New York: Harper & Row, 1971.

Brandon, S. G. F. *The Judgement of the Dead*. London: Weidenfeld and Nicolson, 1967.

Bright, John. *The Authority of the Old Testament*. Grand Rapids: Baker Book House, 1967.

Bruce, F. F. *New Testament History*. Garden City, NY: Doubleday & Co., 1972.

_____. *The New Testament Development of Old Testament Themes*. Grand Rapids: Eerdmans, 1968.

_____. *The Speeches in the Acts of the Apostles*. London: The Tyndale Press, 1942.

Buck, R. S. *Plato's Phaedo*. New York: Bobbs-Merrill, 1955.

Budge, E. A. T. W. *Osiris and the Egyptian Resurrection*. 2 vols. London: Warner, 1911.

Bultmann, Rudolf. *Theology of the New Testament*. 2 vols. Translated by Kendrick Grobel. London: SCM Press, 1952, 1955.

Burnet, J., ed. *Platonis opera*. Vol. 1. Oxford: Clarendon Press, 1900; reprint, 1967.

Cadoux, Cecil J. *The Early Church and the World*. Edinburgh: T. & T. Clark, 1925.

Camelot, P. T., ed. *Ignace d'Antioche. Polycarpe de Smyrne. Lettres. Martyre de Polycarpe*. 4th ed. Sources chrétiennes 10. Paris: Cerf, 1969.

Capps, E., T. E. Page, and W. H. D. Rouse, eds. *The Greek Anthology*. Vols. 2-3. Translated by W. R. Paton. Loeb Classical Library. New York: G. P. Putnam's Sons, 1925.

Carey, George. *I Believe in Man*. Grand Rapids: Eerdmans, 1977.

Cavallin, H. C. C. *Life after Death: Paul's Argument for the Resurrection of the Dead in 1 Corinthians: Part 1; An Enquiry into the Jewish Background*. Lund: Gleerup, 1974.

Charles, R. H. *A Critical History of the Doctrine of a Future Life*. London: A. & C. Black, 1913.

Charlesworth, James H. *The Old Testament Pseudepigrapha*. Vol. 1. Garden City, NY: Doubleday & Co., 1985.

Cohn, L., ed. *Philonis Alexandrini opera quae supersunt*. Vols. 1, 4. Berlin: Reimer, 1896; reprint, De Gruyter, 1962.

Collignon, Maxine. *Les Statues funéraires*. Paris: Leroux, 1911.

Cooper, John W. *Body, Soul, & Life Everlasting: Biblical Anthropology and the Monism-Dualism Debate*. Grand Rapids: Eerdmans, 1989.

Cotterell, Peter, and Max Turner. *Linguistics and Biblical Interpretation*. Downer's Grove, IL: InterVarsity Press, 1989.

Cranford, Lorin L. *Exegeting the New Testament: A Seminar Working Model*. Fort Worth: Scripta Publishing Inc., 1989.

Cullmann, O. *Christ and Time: The Primitive Christian Conception of Time*. Rev. ed. Translated by Floyd V. Filson. Philadelphia: Westminster Press, 1964.

_____. *Immortality of the Soul or Resurrection of the Dead? The Witness of the New Testament*. London: Epworth Press, 1958.

Dahl, M. E. *The Resurrection of the Body*. Studies in Biblical Theology 36. London: SCM Press, 1962.

Dain, A., and P. Mazon, eds. *Sophocle*. 3 vols. Paris: Les Belles Lettres, 1955; reprint, 1967.

Davies, W. D. *St. Paul and Rabbinic Judaism: Some Rabbinic Elements in Pauline Theology*. London: S.P.C.K., 1958.

Defarrari, Roy Joseph, gen. ed. *The Fathers of the Church.* Vol. 10, *Tertullian: Apologetical Works and Marcus Felix Octavius.* Translated by Rudolph Arbesmann, Emily Joseph Daly, and Edwin A. Quain. Washington, DC: The Catholic University of America Press, 1950.

Deissner, Kurt. *Auferstehungshoffnung und Pneumagedanken bei Paulus.* Naumberg: Lippert & Co., 1912.

de Saussure, Ferdinand. *Course in General Linguistics.* New York: McGraw-Hill, 1966.

Dibelius, Martin. *Die Reden der Apostelgeschichte und die antike Geschichtsschreibung.* Heidelberg: Vandenhoeck & Ruprecht, 1949.

Diels, H. and W. Kranz, eds. *Die Fragmente der Vorsokratiker.* 6th ed. Vol. 1. Berlin: Weidmann, 1951; reprint, Dublin: 1966.

Dittenberger, W., ed. *Orientis Graecae Inscriptiones.* Supplementum Sylloges inscriptionum graecarum. Leipzig: S. Hirzel, 1903-1905.

Dodd, C. H. *The Apostolic Preaching and Its Developments.* New York: Harper & Row, Publishers, 1964.

_____. *The Parables of the Kingdom.* London: Nisbet, 1935.

Dupont, Jacques. *ΣΥΝ ΧΡΙΣΤΩ: L'union avec le Christ suivant St. Paul.* Bruges: Editions de l'Abbaye de Saint-André, 1952.

Eichrodt, Walther. *Man in the Old Testament.* Translated by K. and R. Gregor Smith. London: SCM Press, 1961.

_____. *Theology of the Old Testament.* 2 vols. Translated by J. A. Baker. Philadelphia: Westminster Press, 1967.

Elliger, K., and W. Rudolph, eds. *Biblia hebraica stuttgartensia.* Stuttgart: Württembergische Bibelanstalt, 1954.

Ellis, E. Earle. *Paul and His Recent Interpreters.* Grand Rapids: Eerdmans, 1961.

Epstein, I., ed. *Hebrew-English Edition of the Babylonian Talmud.* Translated by Maurice Simon. 7 vols. London: The Soncino Press, 1960.

_____. *The Babylonian Talmud.* Translated by I. Epstein. 6 pts. London: Soncino Press, 1948.

Erickson, Millard J. *Does It Matter What I Believe? What the Bible Teaches and Why We Should Believe It.* Grand Rapids: Baker Book House, 1992.

Fee, Gordon. *New Testament Exegesis: A Handbook for Students and Pastors.* Philadelphia: The Westminster Press, 1983.

Fillion, L. *La Sainte Bible commentée d'après la vulgata.* 8th ed. Paris: Letouzey, 1925.

Finé, H. *Die Terminologie der Jenseitsvorstellungen bei Tertullian.* Bonn: P. Hanstein, 1958.

Fortna, Robert T. *The Fourth Gospel and Its Predecessors.* Philadelphia: Fortress Press, 1988.

_____. *The Gospel of Signs.* Cambridge: Cambridge University Press, 1970.

Funk, F. X., and F. Diekamp, eds. *Patres apostolici.* Vol. 2. 3d ed. Tübingen: Laupp, 1913.

Gard, Donald H. *The Exegetical Method of the Greek Translator of the Book of Job.* SBLMS. Philadelphia: Society of Biblical Literature, 1952.

Gardiner, A. H. *The Attitude of the Ancient Egyptians to Death and the Dead.* Cambridge: Cambridge University Press, 1935.

Geisler, N. *The Battle for the Resurrection.* Nashville: Nelson, 1989.

Gibson, Elsa. *The "Christians for Christians" Inscriptions of Phrygia.* Missoula, MT: Scholar's Press, 1978.

González, Justo. *A History of Christian Thought.* Vol. 1. Nashville: Abingdon Press, 1970.

Goodspeed, E. J., ed. *Die ältesten Apologeten.* Göttingen: Vandenhoeck & Ruprecht, 1915.

_____. *Index Apologeticus.* Leipzig: Hinrichs, 1912.

_____. *Index Patristicus.* Rev. ed. Naperville, IL: Allenson, 1960.

Goold, G. P., ed. *Cicero.* Vol. 18. Translated by J. E. King. Loeb Classical Library. Cambridge: Harvard University Press, 1989.

_____. *Euripides.* Vol. 4. Translated by Arthur S. Way. Loeb Classical Library. Cambridge: Harvard University Press, 1978.

_____. *Lucretius.* Translated by W. H. D. Rouse. Loeb Classical Library. Cambridge: Harvard University Press, 1982.

_____. *Xenophon.* Vol. 4. Translated by O. J. Todd. Loeb Classical Library. Cambridge: Harvard University Press, 1979.

Gow, A. S. F., ed. *Theocritus.* 2d ed. Vol. 1. Cambridge: Harvard University Press, 1952; reprint, 1965.

Gowan, Donald. *Bridge between the Testaments.* Pittsburgh: Pickwick Press, 1976.

Greenup, A. W. *Sukka, Mishna and Tosefta.* London: SPCK, 1925.

Grossfeld, Bernard. *The Targum Onqelos to Deuteronomy.* The Aramaic Bible. Wilmington, DE: Michael Glazier, Inc., 1988.

Gundry, R. H. *The Use of the Old Testament in St. Matthew's Gospel.* Leiden: E. J. Brill, 1967.

Gutiérrez, Gustavo. *On Job: God-Talk and the Suffering of the Innocent.* Translated by Matthew J. O'Connell. Maryknoll, NY: Orbis Books, 1988.

Hanhart, Karel. *The Intermediate State in the New Testament.* Franeker: T. Wever, 1966.

Harris, Murray J. *From Grave to Glory.* Grand Rapids: Zondervan Publishing Co., 1990.

_____. *Raised Immortal: Resurrection and Immortality in the New Testament.* Grand Rapids: Eerdmans, 1983.

Hatch, E., and H. A. Redpath, eds. *A Concordance to the Septuagint and Other Greek Versions of the Old Testament.* Graz-Austria: Akademische Druck- und Verlaganstalt, 1954.

Hathorn, Richard Y. *Greek Mythology.* Lebanon: The American University of Beirut, 1977.

Hayes, John H., and Carl R. Holladay. *Biblical Exegesis.* Rev. ed. Atlanta: John Knox Press, 1987.

Headlam, C. *The Miracles of the New Testament.* London: Murray, 1923.

Heater, Homer. *A Septuagint Translation Technique in the Book of Job.* CBQMS. Washington, DC: The Catholic Biblical Association of America, 1982.

Heidel, A. *The Gilgamesh Epic and Old Testament Parallels.* Chicago: University of Chicago Press, 1946.

Henneberry, Brian H. *The Raising of Lazarus (John 11.1-44): An Evaluation of the Hypothesis That a Written Tradition Lies behind the Narrative.* Ann Arbor, MI: University Microfilms, 1984.

Hennecke, E., and W. Schneemelcher, eds. *New Testament Apocrypha.* 2 vols. Translated by R. McL. Wilson. London: Lutterworth Press, 1963.

Henze, Helen Rowe, ed. *The Odes of Horace.* Norman, OK: University of Oklahoma Press, 1961.

Higgins, A. J. B. *The Historicity of the Fourth Gospel.* London: Lutterworth, 1960.

Hoffmann, Paul. *Die Toten in Christus: Eine religionsgeschichtliche und exegetische Untersuchung zur paulinischen Eschatologie.* Münster: Aschendorff, 1966.

Holladay, Carl R. *Theios Aner in Hellenistic Judaism.* Missoula, MT: Scholars Press, 1977.

Horsley, G. H. R. *New Documents Illustrating Early Christianity: A Review of the Greek Inscriptions and Papyri Published.* 5 vols. Macquarie University: The Ancient History Documentary Research Centre, 1981-1989.

Hull, John M. *Hellenistic Magic and the Synoptic Tradition.* Naperville, IL: Allenson Press, 1974.

Irion, Paul E. *The Funeral: Vestige or Value?* Nashville: Abingdon Press, 1966.

Isaacs, M. E. *The Concept of the Spirit: A Study of Pneuma in Hellenistic Judaism and Its Bearing on the New Testament.* London: Heythrop, 1976.

Jacob, Edmond. *Theology of the Old Testament.* Translated by Arthur W. Heathecote and Philip J. Allcock. New York: Harper & Row, Publishers, 1958.

James, E. O. *The Tree of Life.* Leiden: E. J. Brill, 1966.

Jaubert, A., ed. *Clément de Rome. Epître aux Corinthiens.* Sources chrétiennes 167. Paris: Cerf, 1971.

Jean-Baptiste, P. *Corpus Inscriptionum Judaicarum: Jewish Inscriptions from the Third Century B.C. to the Seventh Century A.D.* Vol. 1. New York: Ktav Publishing House Inc., 1975.

Jensen, C., ed. *Hyperidis orationes sex.* Leipzig: Teubner, 1917; reprint, Stuttgart: 1963.

Kahle, P. E. *Recent Progress in Biblical Scholarship.* Boars Hill, Oxford: Lincombe Research Library, 1965.

Kaibel, G., ed. *Epigrammata Graeca ex lapidibus conlecta.* 3 vols. Berlin: G. Reimer, 1878.

Kaiser, Otto, and Eduard Lohse, eds. *Death and Life.* Translated by John E. Steeley. Nashville: Abingdon Press, 1981.

Kassovsky, Haim Joshua. *'Otsar Leshon ha-mishna, Concordantiae totius Mischnae.* 2 vols. Frankfurt: Y. Kauffmann, 1927.

Kelly, J. N. D. *Early Christian Creeds.* 3d ed. Essex, UK: Longman Group, 1972.

_____. *Early Christian Doctrines.* Rev. ed. New York: Harper & Row, Publishers, 1978.

Kennedy, H. A. A. *St. Paul's Conceptions of the Last Things.* London: Hodder & Stoughton, 1904.

Kertelge, K. *Die Wunder Jesu im Markusevangelium: Eine redaktionsgeschictliche Untersuchung. Studien zum Alten und Neuen Testament.* Munich: Kösel, 1970.

King, J. E., ed. *Cicero.* Vol. 18. Cambridge: Harvard University Press, 1927; reprint, 1989.

Knibb, M. A. *The Ethiopic Book of Enoch.* Vol. 2. Oxford: Clarendon Press, 1978.

Knobel, Peter S. *The Targums Of Job, Proverbs, Qohelet.* The Aramaic Bible. Collegeville, MN: The Liturgical Press, 1991.

Knox, W. L. *St. Paul and the Church of the Gentiles.* Cambridge: Cambridge University Press, 1939.

Kock, T., ed. *Comicorum Atticorum fragmenta*. Vols. 2-3. Leipzig: Teubner, 1884, 1888.

Koetschau, P., ed. *Origenes Werke*. Vol. 2. Die griechischen christlichen Schriftsteller. Leipzig: Hinrichs, 1899.

Kraft, H., ed. *Clavis Patrum Apostolicorum*. Darmstadt: Wissenschaftliche Buchgesellschaft, 1963.

Kroll, W., ed. *Historia Alexandri Magni*. Vol. 1. Berlin: Weidmann, 1926.

Kuhn, K. G. *Konkordanz zu den Qumrantexten*. Göttingen: Vandenhoeck & Ruprecht, 1960.

Ladd, G. E. *A Theology of the New Testament*. Grand Rapids: Eerdmans, 1974.

Lang, F. G. *2 Korinther 5, 1-10 in der neueren Forschung*. BGBE 16. Tübingen: J. C. B. Mohr, 1973.

Lauenstein, U. von, ed. *Der griechische Alexanderroman. Rezension γ*. Buch I. Beiträge zur klassischen Philologie 4. Meisenheim am Glan: Hain, 1962.

Lefebvre, G. *Inscriptiones Graecae Aegypti*. Vol. 5: *Inscriptiones Christianae Aegypti*. Repr. ed. Chicago: University of Chicago Press, 1978.

Lisowsky, Gerhard. *Konkordanz zum Hebräischen Alten Testament*. 12th ed. Stuttgart: Württembergische Bibelanstalt, 1958.

Lods, A. *La Croyance à la Vie Future et le Culte des Morts dans l'Antiquité Israélite*. Vol. 1. Paris: Fischbascher, 1906.

Long, H. S., ed. *Diogenis Laertii vitae philosophorum*. 2 vols. Oxford: Clarendon Press, 1964; reprint, 1966.

Louw, Johannes P., and Eugene A. Nida, eds. *Greek-English Lexicon of the New Testament Based on Semantic Domains*. 2d ed. 2 vols. New York: United Bible Societies, 1989.

Macleod, M. D., ed. *Lucian*. Vol. 7. Cambridge: Harvard University Press, 1961.

Maehler, H., ed. *Pindari carmina cum fragmentis*. 5th ed., Part 1. Leipzig: Teubner, 1971.

Mandelkern, S. *Veteris Testamenti Concordantiae.* Repr. ed. Tel Aviv: Schocken, 1969.

Martin-Achard, Robert. *From Death to Life.* Translated by John Penney Smith. Edinburgh: Oliver and Boyd, 1960.

Martini, E., ed. *Parthenii Nicaeni quae supersunt.* Leipzig: Teubner, 1902.

Matera, F. J. *Passion Narratives and Gospel Theologies.* New York: Paulist Press, 1986.

Mattill, *Luke and the Last Things.* Dillsboro, NC: Western North Carolina Press, 1979.

Mayer, G. *Index Philoneus.* Berlin: de Gruyter, 1974.

McNamara, Martin. *Targum and Testament.* Grand Rapids: Eerdmans, 1972.

_____. *The New Testament and the Palestinian Targum to the Pentateuch.* Rome: Pontifical Biblical Institute, 1966.

Meineke, A., ed. *Fragmenta comicorum Graecorum.* Vol. 4. Berlin: Reimer, 1841; reprint, De Gruyter, 1970.

Menoud, Philippe H. *Le sort des trépassés.* Neuchatel: Delachaux & Niestle, 1945.

Mette, H. J., ed. *Die Fragmente der Tragödien des Aischylos.* Berlin: Akademie, 1959.

Migne, Jacques-Paul, ed. *Patrologia cursus completus.* Series graeca. Vols. 12, 23, 27, 29, 49. Paris: Cerf, 1857-1887.

Miller, F. J., ed. *Seneca's Tragedies.* Loeb Classical Library. Cambridge: Harvard University Press, 1979.

Milne, J. G., ed. *Inscriptiones Graecae Aegypti.* Vol. 1, *Inscriptiones nunc Cairo in museo.* Oxford: Oxford University Press, 1905; reprint, Chicago: University of Chicago Press, 1976.

Mondésert, C., ed. *Clément d'Alexandrie. Le protreptique.* 2d ed. Paris: Cerf, 1949.

Montefiore, C. G., and H. Loewe. *A Rabbinic Anthology.* London: Macmillan, 1938.

Moore, C. H. *Ancient Beliefs in the Immortality of the Soul.* London: Harrap, 1931.

Moule, C. F. D. *Idiom Book of New Testament Greek.* Cambridge: Cambridge University Press, 1953.

Moulton, J. H., ed. *Prolegomena.* Vol. 1 in *A Grammar of New Testament Greek.* 3d ed. Edinburgh: T. & T. Clark, 1906.

Murray, G., ed. *Aeschyli tragoediae.* 2d ed. Oxford: Clarendon Press, 1955.

_____. *Euripidis fabulae.* Vol. 1. Oxford: Clarendon Press, 1902; reprint, 1966.

Nestle, E., and K. Aland, eds. *Novum Testamentum Graece.* 27th ed. Stuttgart: Deutsche Bibelgesellschaft, 1993.

Neusner, Jacob. *A Midrash Reader.* Minneapolis: Fortress Press, 1990.

_____. *Genesis Rabbah: The Judaic Commentary on Genesis. A New American Translation.* Vol. 3. Atlanta: Scholars Press for Brown Judaic Studies, 1985.

_____. *Mekhilta Attributed to R. Ishmael: An Analytic Translation.* Vol. I, *Pisha, Beshallah, Shirata, and Vayassa.* Atlanta: Scholars Press for Brown Judaic Studies, 1988.

Nickelsburg, Jr., George. *Jewish Literature between the Bible and the Mishnah.* Philadelphia: Fortress Press, 1981.

_____. *Resurrection, Immortality, and Eternal Life in Intertestamental Judaism.* Cambridge: Harvard University Press, 1972.

Niese, B., ed. *Flavii Iosephi opera.* Vols. 1-4, 6. Berlin: Weidmann, 1885-1890; reprint, 1955.

Noth, Martin. *The History of Israel.* Translated by Stanley Godman. New York: Harper & Row, 1958.

Owen, D. R. G. *Body and Soul.* Philadelphia: The Westminster Press, 1956.

Page, D. L., ed. *Select Papyri.* Vol. 3. Cambridge: Harvard University Press, 1941; reprint, 1970.

Page, T. E., E. Capps, and W. H. D. Rouse, eds. *Philo.* Vols. 3, 10. Translated by F. H. Colson and G. H. Whitaker. Loeb Classical Library. New York: G. P. Putnam's Sons, 1930, 1929.

Patterson, R. L. *Plato on Immortality.* University Park, PA:Pennsylvania State University, 1965.

Pedersen, Johannes. *Israel: Its Life and Culture.* 2 vols. London: Oxford University Press, 1926.

Peek, E. *Griechische Grabgedichte.* Berlin: Akademie, 1960.

Pfeiffer, R. H. *Introduction to the Old Testament.* 2d ed. New York: Harper Books, 1948.

Pinnock, Clark, and Delvin Brown. Theological Crossfire: An Evangelical-Liberal Dialogue. Grand Rapids: Zondervan Publishing House, 1990.

Pringle-Pattison, A. S. *The Idea of Immortality.* Oxford: Clarendon Press, 1975.

Quell, G. *Die Auffasung des Todes im Alten Testament.* Leipzig: Hinrichs, 1925.

Rahlfs, A. *Lucians Rezension der Königsbücher.* Göttingen: Vandenhoeck & Ruprecht, 1911.

_____. *Septuaginta.* 8th ed. 2 vols. Stuttgart: Württembergische Bibelanstalt, 1965.

_____. *Septuaginta—Studien: I, Studien zu den Königsbücher.* Göttingen: Vandenhoeck & Ruprecht, 1904.

Reichenbach, Bruce. *Is Man the Phoenix? A Study of Immortality.* Washington, DC: Christian University Press, 1978.

Rengstorf, K. H., ed. *A Complete Concordance to Flavius Josephus.* 2 vols. Leiden: E. J. Brill, 1973, 1975.

Ridderbos, H. *Paul: An Outline of His Theology.* Translated by John Richard de Witt. Grand Rapids: Eerdmans, 1975.

Riesenfeld, Harald. *The Resurrection in Ezekiel xxxvii and in the Dura Europos Paintings.* Uppsala, Lundequistska, 1948.

Ringgren, Helmer. *Israelite Religion.* Translated by David E. Green. Philadelphia: Fortress Press, 1966.

Roberts, A., and J. Donaldson, eds. *The Ante-Nicene Fathers*. Vol. 1. Grand Rapids: Eerdmans, 1979.

Roberts, Robert E. *The Theology of Tertullian*. London: Epworth Press, 1924.

Robertson, A. T. *Word Pictures in the New Testament*. 6 vols. Nashville: Broadman Press, 1930.

Robinson, H. Wheeler. *Corporate Personality in Ancient Israel*. Philadelphia: Fortress Press, 1964.

_____. *The Religious Ideas of the Old Testament*. New York: Scribner's, 1913.

Robinson, John A. T. *The Body: A Study in Pauline Theology*. Chicago: Henry Regnery Co., 1952.

Rochais, Gérard. Les récits de résurrection des morts dans le Nouveau Testament. SNTSMS 40. Cambridge: Cambridge University Press, 1981.

Rohde, E. Psyche. *The Cult of the Souls and the Belief in Immortality among the Greeks*. 8th ed. London: Kegan, 1925.

Roscher, Wilhelm Heinrich, ed. *Ausführliches der griechischenund römischen Mythologie*. Vol. 1. Pt. 2. Leipzig: B. G. Teubner, 1884. S.v. "Hypnos," by B. Sauer.

Russell, D. S. *Between the Testaments*. Philadelphia: Fortress Press, 1960.

_____. *The Method & Message of Jewish Apocalyptic: 200 B.C. - A.D. 100*. The Old Testament Library. Philadelphia: The Westminster Press, 1964.

_____. The Old Testament Pseudepigrapha: Patriarchs & Prophets in Early Judaism. Philadelphia: Fortress Press, 1987.

Sanders, E. P. *Judaism: Practice and Belief, 63 b.c.e - 66 c.e.* Philadelphia: Fortress Press, 1992.

_____. *Paul and Palestinian Judaism*. Philadelphia: Fortress Press, 1977.

Sandmel, Samuel. *Judaism and Christian Beginnings*. New York: Oxford Press, 1978.

Santos Otero, A. de, ed. *Los evangelios apócrifos: Colección de textos griegos y latinos, versión crítica, estudios introductorios, comentarios e ilustraciones.* 3d ed. BAC 148. Madrid: Edica, 1975.

Schweitzer, A. *Paul and His Interpreters: A Critical History.* Translated by William Montgomery. London: A. & C. Black, 1912.

_____. *The Mysticism of Paul the Apostle.* Translated by William Montgomery. New York: Seabury Press, 1968.

Schermann, T., ed. *Prophetarum vitae fabulosae.* Leipzig: Teubner, 1907.

Silva, Moisés. *Biblical Words & Their Meaning: An Introduction to Lexical Semantics.* Grand Rapids: Zondervan Press, 1983.

Solmsen, F., ed. *Hesiodi opera.* Oxford: Clarendon Press, 1970.

Spiro, F., ed. *Pausaniae Graeciae descriptio.* 3 vols. Leipzig: Teubner, 1903; reprint, Stuttgart: 1967.

Stein, Robert H. *The Method and Message of Jesus' Teachings.* Philadelphia: The Westminster Press, 1978.

Stemberger G., and Hermann L. Strack, eds. *Introduction to the Talmud and Midrash.* Translated by Marcus Bockmuel. Edinburgh: T. & T. Clark, 1991.

Stendahl, Krister. *The School of St. Matthew and Its Use of the Old Testament.* Lund: C. W. K. Gleerup, 1954.

Strack, Hermann L. *Introduction to the Talmud and Midrash.* Atheneum, NY: The Jewish Publication Society of America, 1931.

Strawson, William. *Jesus and the Future Life: A Study in the Synoptic Gospels.* Philadelphia: Westminster Press, 1959.

The Septuagint Version of the Old Testament, With an English Translation and with Various Readings and Critical Notes. London: S. Bagster and Sons, 1950.

Theissen, Gerd. *The Miracle Stories of the Early Christian Tradition.* Translated by F. McDonagh. Philadelphia: The Fortress Press, 1983.

Thistleton, Anthony C. *The Two Horizons: New Testament Hermeneutics and Philosophical Description.* Grand Rapids: Eerdmans, 1980.

Tromp, Nicholas. *Primitive Conceptions of Death and the Nether World in the Old Testament.* Rome: Pontifical Biblical Institute, 1969.

Turabian, Kate L. *A Manual for Writers of Term Papers, Theses, and Dissertations.* 5th ed. Revised and expanded by Bonnie B. Honigsblum. Chicago: University of Chicago Press, 1987.

Urbach, E. E. *The Sages—Their Concepts and Beliefs.* Translated by Israel Abrahams. Jerusalem: The Magnes Press, 1975.

Vermes, G. *The Dead Sea Scrolls in English.* 2d ed. Baltimore, MD: Penguin Books, 1975.

Wahlde, Urban C. von. *The Earliest Version of John's Gospel: Recovering the Gospel of Signs.* Wilmington, DE: Michael Glazier, 1989.

Warmington, E. H., ed. *Sophocles.* Vol. 2. Translated by F. Storr. Loeb Classical Library. Cambridge: Harvard University Press, 1967.

Wendland, P. *Philonis Alexandrini opera quae supersunt.* Vol. 3. Berlin: Reimer, 1898; reprint, 1962.

Whitelocke, Lester T., ed. *An Analytic Concordance of the Books of the Apocrypha.* 2 vols. Washington, DC: University Press of America, 1978.

Wolff, Hans Walter. *Anthropology of the Old Testament.* Translated by Margaret Kohl. Philadelphia: Fortress Press, 1974.

Articles and Essays

Alexander, Desmond. "The Old Testament View of LIfe after Death." *Themelios* 11 (1986): 41-46.

Alfrink, A. "L'Expression נאסף אל עמיו." *Oudtestamentische Studiën* 5 (1948): 118-31.

_____. "L'Expression שכב עם אבותיו." *Oudtestamentische Studiën* 2 (1945): 106-18.

Askwith, E. H. "The Eschatological Section of 1 Thessalonians." *Expositor* 8,1 (1911): 62-63.

Bailey, E. "Is 'Sleep' the Proper Biblical Term for the Intermediate State?" *Zeitschrift für die neutestamentliche Wissenschaft* 55 (1964): 161-67.

Bailey, Lloyd R. "Death As a Theological Problem in the Old Testament." *Pastoral Psychology* 22 (1971): 29-30.

Barnard, L. W. "Justin Martyr's Eschatology." *Vigiliae Christianae* 19 (1965): 86-98.

Berry, Ronald. "Death and Life in Christ: The Meaning of 2 Corinthians 5.1-10." *Scottish Journal of Theology* 14 (1961): 60-76.

Birkeland, Harris. "The Belief in the Resurrection of the Dead in the Old Testament." *Studia Theologica* 3 (1949): 60-78.

Blackburn, Barry L. "Miracle Working 'ΘΕΙΟΙ ΑΝΔΡΕΣ' in Hellenism and Hellenistic Judaism." Chap. in *Gospel Perspectives*, eds. David Wenham and Craig Blomberg, 185-218. Sheffield: JSOT Press, 1986.

Block, D. I. "Beyond the Grave: Ezekiel's Vision of Death and Afterlife." *Biblical Archaeologist Reader* 2 (1992): 112-41.

Brandscheidt, R. "Psalm 102. Literarische Gestalt und theologische Aussage." *Trierer theologische Zeitschrift* 96 (1987): 51-87.

Bruce, F. F. "Paul on Immortality." *Scottish Journal of Theology* 24 (1971): 457-72.

Brown, Raymond. "The Problem of Historicity in John." *Catholic Biblical Quarterly* 24 (1962): 1-14.

Bultmann, Rudolf. "New Testament and Mythology." Chap. in *Kerygma and Myth*, ed. Hans W. Bartsch. Translated by Reginald Fuller, 1-44. Vol. 1. London: S.P.C.K., 1953.

Craig, William L. "The Problem of Miracles: A Historical and Philosophical Perspective." In *Gospel Perspectives*. Vol. 6: *The Miracles of Jesus*, eds. David Wenham and Craig Blomberg, 9-48. Sheffield: JSOT Press, 1986.

Dahood, M. "Hebrew-Ugaritic Lexicography VII." *Biblica* 50 (1969): 337-56.

Day, John. "טַל אוֹרֹת in Isaiah 26.19." *Zeitschrift für die alttestamentliche Wissenschaft* 90 (1978): 264-69.

Delebecque, Edouard. "Lazare est mort (note sur Jean 11, 11-15." *Biblica* 67 (1986): 89-97.

Delius, Walter. "Ps.-Justin: 'Über die Auferstehung.'" *Theologia Viatorum* 14 (1952): 181-204.

Driver, G. R. "Plurima Mortis Imago." Chap. in *Studies and Essays in Honor of Abraham A. Neuman*. Leiden: E. J. Brill, 1962.

Dunkerley, R. "Lazarus." *New Testament Studies* 5 (1958-59): 321-27.

Edgar, Thomas R. "The Meaning of 'Sleep' in 1 Thessalonians 5.10." *Journal of the Evangelical Theological Society* 22 (1979): 345-49.

Ehrmark, E. "Transmigration in Plato." *Harvard Theological Review* 50 (1957): 1-20.

Ellis, E. E. "II Corinthians v.1-10 in Pauline Eschatology." *New Testament Studies* 6 (1960): 211-24.

_____. "Sōma in First Corinthians." *Interpretation* 44 (1990): 132-44.

Fackre, Gabriel. "I Believe in the Resurrection of the Body." *Interpretation* 46 (1992): 42-52.

Faw, C. E. "Death and Resurrection in Paul's Letters." *Journal of Bible and Religion* 27 (1959): 297-304.

Féret, R. P. "La mort dans la tradition biblique." Chap. in *Le mystère de la mort et sa célébration*. Paris: Editions du Cerf, 1952.

Feuillet, A. "Le drama d'amour du Cantique des Cantiques remis en son contexte prophétique." *Nova et Vetera* (1987): 81-127.

Fishbane, M. "Jeremiah iv:23-26 and Job iii:3-13." *Vetus Testamentum* 21 (1971): 151-67.

Foretell, I. T. "I Am the Resurrection and the Life." In *Contemporary New Testament Studies*, ed. Rosalie Ryan, 100-101. Collegeville, MN: The Liturgical Press, 1965.

Gard, Donald H. "The Concept of a Future Life according to the Greek Translator of the Book of Job." *Journal of Biblical Literature* 73 (1954): 137-38.

Gehman, H. S. "The Theological Approach of the Greek Translator of Job 1-15." *Journal of Biblical Literature* 68 (1949): 231-40.

Geisler, N. "'I Believe . . . in the Resurrection of the Flesh.'" *Christian Research Journal* 12 (1989): 20-22.

_____. "The Apologetic Significance of the Bodily Resurrection of Christ." *Bulletin of the Evangelical Philosophical Society* 10 (1987): 15-37.

_____. "The Battle for the Resurrection." *Fundamentalist Journal* (1989): 12-15.

_____. "The Significance of Christ's Physical Resurrection." *Bibliotheca Sacra* 146 (1989): 148-70.

Gese, Hartmut. "Death in the Old Testament." Chap. in *Essays on Biblical Theology*. Translated by Keith Crim. Minneapolis: Augsburg Publishing House, 1981.

Gonzáles-Ruiz, J. M. "Should We De-Mythologize the 'Separated Soul'?" In *The Problem of Eschatology*, eds. Edward Schillebeeckx and Boniface Wilkens, 82-96. New York: Paulist Press, 1969.

Grassi, J. "Ezekiel XXXVII. 1-14 and the New Testament." *New Testament Studies* 11 (1965): 162-64.

Harris, M. J. "2 Cor. 5:1-10: A Watershed in Paul's Eschatology?" *Tyndale Bulletin* 22 (1971): 32-57.

_____. "The New Testament View of Life after Death." *Themelios* 11 (1986): 47-52.

Harris, M. L. "The Meaning Of *Sheol* as Shown by Parallels in Poetic Passages." *Journal of the Evangelical Theological Society* 4 (1961): 129-35.

Harrison, Jane Ellen. "Orphic Eschatology." Chap. in *Prolegomena to the Study of Greek Religion*. New York: Arno Press, 1975.

Hettlinger, R. F. "2 Corinthians 5.1-10." *Scottish Journal of Theology* 10 (1957): 174-94.

Hick, John. "The Resurrection of the Person." Chap. in *Death and Eternal Life*. San Francisco: Harper & Row, 1976.

Hoffmann, Paul. "4. Das Bildwort vom Todesschlaf." Chap. in *Die Toten in Christus: Eine religionsgeschichtliche und exegetische Untersuchung zur paulinischen Eschatologie*. Münster: Aschendorff, 1966.

Howard, Tracy L. "The Meaning of 'Sleep' in 1 Thessalonians 5.10—A Reappraisal." *Grace Theological Journal* 6 (1985): 337-48.

Jacob, Edmond. "Death and the Future Life." Chap. in *Theology of the Old Testament*. Translated by Arthur W. Heathecote and Philip J. Allcock. New York: Harper & Row, Publishers, 1958.

Jaeger, W. "The Greek Ideas of Immortality." *Harvard Theological Review* 52 (1959): 135-47.

Jones, D. M. "The Sleep of Philoctetes." *The Classical Review* 63 (1949): 83-5.

Kajanto, I. "Im gremio Abraham." *Arctos* 12 (1978): 27-53.

Key, Andrew F. "The Concept of Death in Early Israelite Religion." *The Journal of Bible and Religion* 32 (1964): 239-47.

Lang, F. C. "Auferstehung im Tod und Anderung der Eschatologie." Chap. in *2 Korinther 5, 1-10 in der neuren Forschung*. BGBE 16. Tübingen: J. C. B. Mohr, 1973.

Laughton, E. "Subconscious Repetition and Textual Criticism." *Classical Philology* 45 (1950): 75-85.

Lautenschlager, Markus. "Εἴτε γρηγορῶμεν εἴτε καθεύδωμεν." Zum Verhältnis von Heiligung und Heil in 1 Thess 5,10." *Zeitschrift für die neutestamentliche Wissenschaft* 81 (1990): 39-59.

Le Déaut, R. "Targumic Literature and New Testament Interpretation." *Biblical Theology Bulletin* 4 (1974): 243-89.

Lindenberger, James M. "Daniel 12.1-4." *Interpretation* 39 (1985): 181-86.

Martin, James P. "History and Eschatology in the Lazarus Narrative: John 11.1-44." *Scottish Journal of Theology* 17 (1964): 332-43.

McNaspy, Clement J. "Sheol in the Old Testament." *The Catholic Biblical Quarterly* 6 (1944): 326-33.

Méhat, A. "Apocatastase." *Vigiliae Christianae* 10 (1956): 196-214.

Merlier, O. "Note sur deux passages du quatrième Évangile." *Bulletin de Correspondence Hellénique* 54 (1930): 228-40.

Meyer, B. F. "Did Paul's View of the Resurrection of the Dead Undergo Development?" *Theological Studies* 47 (1986): 363-87.

Michel, Otto. "Zur Lehre vom Todesschlaf." *Zeitschrift für die neutestamentliche Wissenschaft* 35 (1936): 285-90.

Mitchell, T. C. "The Old Testament Usage of nšmh." *Vetus Testamentum* 11 (1961): 177-87.

Molland, E. "Clement of Alexandria on the Origin of Greek Philosophy." *Symbolae Osloenses* 15/16 (1936): 57-85.

Moore, Michael S. "Resurrection and Immortality: Two Motifs Navigating Confluent Theological Streams in the OT (Dan. 12.1-4)." *Theologische Zeitschrift* 39 (1983): 17-34.

Moule, C. F. D. "The Meaning of 'Life' in the Gospels and Epistles of St. John: A Study in the Story of Lazarus, John 11.1-44." *Theology* 78 (1975): 114-25.

Müller, G. "Origenes und die Apokatastasis." *Theologische Zeitschrift* 14 (1958): 174-90.

Noack, B. "Das Zitat in Eph 5,14." *Studia Theologica* 5 (1952): 52-64.

O'Donoghue, N. D. "The Awakening of the Dead." *Irish Theological Quarterly* 56 (1990): 49-59.

Ogle, Marbury B. "The Sleep of Death." *Memoirs of the American Academy in Rome* 11 (1933): 81-117.

Orlinsky, Harry M. "Some Corruptions in the Greek Text of Job." *Jewish Quarterly Review* 26 (1935-36): 133-45.

_____. "Studies in the Septuagint of the Book of Job." *Hebrew Union College Annual* 28 (1957): 53-74; 29 (1958): 229-71; 30 (1959): 153-67; 32 (1961): 239-68; 33 (1962): 119-51; 35 (1964): 57-78.

_____. "The Hebrew and Greek Texts of Job 14.12." *Jewish Quarterly Review* 28 (1937-38): 57-68.

Osei-Bonsu, Joseph. "Anthropological Dualism in the New Testament." *Scottish Journal of Theology* 40 (1987): 571-90.

_____. "Does 2 Cor. 5.1-10 Teach the Reception of the Resurrection Body at the Moment of Death?" *Journal for the Study of the New Testament* 28 (1986): 81-101.

_____. "The Intermediate State in the New Testament." *Scottish Journal of Theology* 44 (1991): 169-94.

Pollard, T. E. "The Raising of Lazarus (John xi)." In *Studia Evangelica*, vol. 6, ed. Elizabeth A. Livingstone, 436-37. Berlin: Akademie, 1973.

Rad, Gerhard von. "Alttestamentlichee Glaubensaussagen von Leben und Tod." *Allgemeine evangelische-lutherische Kirchenzeitung* 4 (1938): 826-28.

Robert, J. and L. "Bulletin épigraphique, 756, no. 7." *Revue des études grecques* 89 (1976): 415-595.

Robinson, H. Wheeler. "Hebrew Psychology." In The People and the Book, ed. A. S. Peake, 353-82. Oxford: The Clarendon Press, 1925.

Schneiders, Sandra M. "Death in the Community of Eternal Life: History, Theology, and Spirituality in John 11." *Interpretation* 41 (1987): 44-56.

Schwertner, S. "Erwägungen zu Moses Tod und Grab in Dtn. 34.5-6." *Zeitschrift für die alttestamentliche Wissenschaft* 84 (1972): 25-46.

Senior, D. "The Death of Jesus and the Resurrection of the Holy Ones (Mt. 27.51-53)." *Catholic Biblical Quarterly* 38 (1976): 312-29.

Sevenster, J. N. "Einige Bemerkungen über den 'Zwischenzustand' bei Paulus." *New Testament Studies* 1 (1955): 291-96.

Sheler, Jeffrey L. "Hell's Sober Comeback." *U.S. News & World Report* 110/11 (1991): 56-90.

Smith, E. J. "Death- and Burial-Formulas in Kings and Chronicles Relating to the Kings of Judah." Chap. in *Biblical Essays*, Proceedings of Die Outestamentiese Werkemeenskap. South Africa: Potchefstroom, 1966.

Stauffer, E. "Historische Elemente in Vierten Evangelium." *Homiletica en Biblica* 22 (1963): 1-7.

Stenger, Wilhelm. "Die Auferweckung des Lazarus (John 11.1-45)." *Trierer theologische Zeitschrift* 83 (1974): 17-37.

Thomson, J. G. S. S. "Sleep: An Aspect of Jewish Anthropology." *Vetus Testamentum* 5 (1955): 421-33.

Welten, Peter. "Die Vernichtung des Todes und die Königsherrschaft Gottes." *Theologische Zeitschrift* 38 (1982): 129-46.

Wenham, J. "The Resurrection Narratives in Matthew's Gospel." *Tyndale Bulletin* 24 (1973): 42-46.

_____. "When Were the Saints Raised? A Note on the Punctuation of Matthew xxvii.51-53." *Journal of Theological Studies* 32 (1981): 150-52.

Wijngaards, J. "Death and Resurrection in Covenantal Context." *Vetus Testamentum* 17 (1967): 226-39.

Wilkens, Wilhelm. "Die Erweckung des Lazarus." *Theologische Zeitschrift* 15 (1959): 23-28.

Wischnitzer-Bernstein, R. "The Conception of the Resurrection in the Ezekiel Panel of the Dura Synagogue." *Journal of Biblical Literature* 60 (1941): 43-55.

Wright, Addison G. "The Literary Genre Midrash." *Catholic Biblical Quarterly* 28 (1966): 105-38, 417-57.

Yeivin, S. "The Sepulchres of the Kings of the House of David." *Journal of Near Eastern Studies* 7 (1948): 3-45.

York, Anthony D. "The Dating of Targumic Literature." *Journal for the Study of Judaism* 5 (1974): 49-62.

Commentaries

Alden, Robert L. *Job*. New American Commentary. Nashville: Broadman & Holman, 1993.

Andersen, Francis I. *Job*. Tyndale Old Testament Commentaries. Downers Grove, IL: InterVarsity Press, 1976.

Barclay, William. *The Letters of James and Peter*. The Daily Study Bible. Philadelphia: The Westminster Press, 1976.

Barrett, C. K. *The Gospel according to John*. Philadelphia: The Westminster Press, 1978.

Beasley-Murray, G. R. *John*. Word Biblical Commentary. Waco: Word Books, 1987.

Best, Ernest. *The First and Second Epistles to the Thessalonians*. Repr. ed. Black's New Testament Commentary. Peabody, MA: Hendrickson Publishers, 1986.

Blomberg, Craig. *Matthew*. The New American Commentary. Nashville: Broadman Press, 1992.

Bruce, F. F. *1 & 2 Thessalonians*. Word Biblical Commentary. Waco, TX: Word Books, Publisher, 1982.

Brooks, James. *Mark*. The New American Commentary. Nashville: Broadman Press, 1991.

Brown, Raymond. *The Gospel according to John I-XII*. 2d ed. The Anchor Bible. Garden City, NY: Doubleday, 1966.

Bultmann, Rudolf. *Das Evangelium des Johannes*. 16th ed. Göttingen: Vandenhoeck & Ruprecht, 1959.

_____. *The Gospel of John*. Translated by R. W. N. Hoare and J. K. Riches. Philadelphia: Westminster Press, 1971.

Conzelmann, Hans. *1 Corinthians*. Translated by James W. Leitch. Hermeneia. Philadelphia: Fortress Press, 1975.

Cooper, Lamar. *Ezekiel*. New American Commentary. Nashville: Broadman & Holman, 1994.

Craigie, Peter C. *The Book of Deuteronomy*. The New International Commentary on the Old Testament. Grand Rapids: Eerdmans, 1976.

Dhorme, E. *A Commentary on the Book of Job*. Translated by H. Knight. Repr. ed. Nashville: Nelson Press, 1984.

Dobschütz, E. von. *Die Thessalonicherbriefe*. Repr. ed. Kritisch-Exegetischer Kommentar. Göttingen: Vandenhoeck & Ruprecht, 1974.

Dodd, C. H. *The Interpretation of the Fourth Gospel*. Cambridge: Cambridge University Press, 1953.

Dunn, James D. G. *Romans 1-8*. Word Biblical Commentary. Dallas: Word Books, 1988.

_____. *Romans 9-16*. Word Biblical Commentary. Dallas: Word Books, 1988.

Ellis, E. Earle. *Gospel of Luke*. Rev. ed. The New Century Bible. Greenwood, SC: Attic Press, 1977.

Fitzmyer, Joseph A. *The Gospel according to Luke X-XXIV*. The Anchor Bible. Garden City, NY: Doubleday & Co., 1985.

Frame, J. E. *The Epistles of St. Paul to the Thessalonians*. International Critical Commentary. Edinburgh: T. & T. Clark, 1912.

Furnish, Victor. *II Corinthians*. The Anchor Bible. Garden City, NY: Doubleday & Company, 1984.

Gnilka, Joachim. *Das Matthäusevangelium*. Vol. 2. Herders Theologischer Kommentar zum Neuen Testament. Freiburg: Herder, 1988.

Gray, John. *The First Book of Kings*. 2d. rev. ed. The Old Testament Library. Philadelphia: The Westminster Press, 1970.

Grundmann, Walter. *Das Evangelium nach Matthäus*. Theologischer Handkommentar zum Neuen Testament. Berlin: Evangelische Verlagsanstalt, 1971.

Guelich, Robert A. *Mark 1-8:26*. Word Biblical Commentary. Dallas: Word Books, 1989.

Gundry, R. H. *Matthew: A Commentary on His Literary and Theological Art*. Grand Rapids: Eerdmans, 1982.

Habel, Norman C. *The Book of Job*. The Old Testament Library. Philadelphia: The Westminster Press, 1985.

Haenchen, Ernst. *The Acts of the Apostles: A Commentary*. Translated by B. Noble and G. Shinn. Philadelphia: The Westminster Press, 1971.

Hartley, John E. *The Book of Job*. The New International Commentary on the Old Testament. Grand Rapids: Eerdmans, 1988.

Hawthorne, Gerald. *Philippians*. Word Biblical Commentary. Waco: Word Books, 1983.

Hertzberg, Hans W. *I & II Samuel*. Translated by J. S. Bowden. The Old Testament Library. Philadelphia: The Westminster Press, 1964.

Jones, G. H. *1 and 2 Kings*. Vol. 1. The New Century Bible Commentary. Grand Rapids: Eerdmans, 1984.

Keil C. F. *The Twelve Minor Prophets*. Translated by James Martin. Vol. 10. Pt. 2. Commentary on the Old Testament. Grand Rapids: Eerdmans, 1978.

Kidner, Derek. *Psalms 1-72*. Tyndale Old Testament Commentaries. Downers Grove, IL: InterVarsity Press, 1973.

Klostermann, Erich. *Das Matthäusevangelium*. Handbuch zum Neuen Testament. Tübingen: J. C. B. Mohr, 1971.

Lincoln, Andrew T. *Ephesians*. Word Biblical Commentary. Dallas: Word Books, 1990.

Long, Burke O. *1 Kings: With an Introduction to Historical Literature*. Grand Rapids: Eerdmans, 1984.

Lumby, J. Rawson. *The Acts of the Apostles*. Cambridge Greek Testament for Schools and Colleges. Cambridge: University Press, 1894.

Marshall, I. Howard. *1 and 2 Thessalonians*. The New Century Bible Commentary. Grand Rapids: Eerdmans, 1983.

_____. *Commentary on Luke*. International Greek Testament Commentary. Grand Rapids: Eerdmans, 1978.

Martin, R. P. *2 Corinthians*. Word Biblical Commentary. Waco, TX: Word Books, Publisher, 1986.

_____. *Philippians*. Rev. repr. ed. Tyndale New Testament Commentaries. Grand Rapids: Eerdmans, 1987.

Melick, Jr., Richard R. *Philippians, Colossians, Philemon*. The New American Commentary. Nashville: Broadman Press, 1991.

Milligan, George. *St. Paul's Epistles to the Thessalonians*. Grand Rapids: Eerdmans, 1953.

Morris, Leon. *The First and Second Epistles to the Thessalonians*. Rev. ed. The New International Commentary on the New Testament. Grand Rapids: Eerdmans, 1991.

Nolland, John. *Luke 1-9:20*. Word Biblical Commentary. Dallas: Word Books, 1989.

O'Brien, Peter T. *The Epistle to the Philippians*. New International Greek Testament Commentary. Grand Rapids: Eerdmans, 1991.

Polhill, John B. *Acts*. The New American Commentary. Nashville: Broadman Press, 1992.

Pope, Marvin. *Job*. 3d ed. The Anchor Bible. Garden City, NY: Doubleday & Co., 1983.

Rad, Gerhard von. *Genesis*. Rev. ed. Translated by John H. Marks. The Old Testament Library. Philadelphia: The Westminster Press, 1961.

Richardson, Alan. *The Gospel according to Saint John*. Torch Commentaries. London: SCM Press, 1959.

Robinson, J. *The First Book of Kings*. The Cambridge Bible Commentary. Cambridge: Cambridge University Press, 1972.

Schnackenburg, Rudolf. *The Gospel according to John*. Vol. 2. Translated by Cecily Hastings, et al. Herder's Theological Commentary New York: Seabury Press, 1980.

Schweizer, Eduard. *The Good News according to Matthew*. Translated by David E. Green. Atlanta: John Knox Press, 1975.

Silva, Moisés. *Philippians*. Baker Exegetical Commentary on the New Testament. Grand Rapids: Baker Book House, 1992.

Smith, Ralph. *Micah-Malachi*. Word Biblical Commentary. Waco: Word Books, Publisher, 1984.

Tasker, R. V. G. *The Gospel according to John*. Tyndale New Testament Commentaries. Grand Rapids: Eerdmans, 1975.

Taylor, Vincent. *The Gospel according to St. Mark.* 2d ed. New York: St. Martin's Press, 1966.

Vaughan, Curtis. *Acts.* Grand Rapids: Zondervan Publishing House, 1974.

Würthwein, Ernst. *Das Erste Buch der Könige.* Das Alte Testament Deutsch. Göttingen: Vandenhoeck & Ruprecht, 1977.

Reference Works

Baab, Otto. *IDB.* S.v. "Father."

Balz, Horst. "Ὕπνος," *TDNT.* 8:545-56.

Balz, Horst, and Gerhard Schneider, eds. *Exegetical Dictionary of the New Testament.* 2 vols. Grand Rapids: Eerdmans, 1991. S.v. "Καθεύδω," by M. Völkel.

Bauer, Walter, ed. *A Greek-English Lexicon of the New Testament and Other Early Christian Literature.* 2d ed. Translated by W. F. Arndt and F. W. Gingrich. Revised and augmented by F. W. Gingrich and F. W. Danker. Chicago: University of Chicago Press, 1979.

Berkowitz, Luci, and Karl A. Squitier, eds. *Thesaurus Linguae Graecae Canon of Greek Authors and Works.* 2d ed. Oxford: Oxford University Press, 1986.

Boisacq, E. *Dictionnaire étymologique de la langue Grecque.* 2d ed. Heidelberg: C. Winter, 1923.

Breuggemann, Walter. *IDB.* Supplementary Volume. S.v. "Death, Theology of."

Brown, Francis, S. R. Driver, and C. A. Briggs. *A Hebrew and English Lexicon of the Old Testament.* Oxford: Clarendon Press, 1979.

Bultmann, Rudolf. "Θάνατος." *TDNT.* 3:7-25.

Enslin, M. S. *IDB.* S.v. "Peter, Gospel of."

Harder, Günther. "Φθείρω." *TDNT.* 9:93-106.

Jastrow, Marcus, ed. *A Dictionary of the Targum, the Talmud Babli and Yerushalmi, and the Midrashic Literature.* 2 vols. New York: Pardes Publishing House, Inc., 1950.

Jeremias, Joachim. "῎Αδης." *TDNT*. 1:146-49.

Köhler, Ludwig, and Walter Baumgartner, eds. *Lexicon in Veteris Testamenti Libros*. Leiden: E. J. Brill, 1958.

Lampe, G. W. H. ed. *A Patristic Greek Lexicon*. Oxford: Clarendon Press, 1961-1968.

Levy, Jacob. *Neuhebräisches und Chaldäisches Wörterbuch über die Talmudim und Midrashim*. Leipzig: F. A. Brockhaus, 1876.

Liddell, H. G., and R. Scott, eds. *A Greek-English Lexicon*. Based on the German work of Francis Passow. New York: Harper & Brothers, Publishers, 1858. S.v. "Κρυβήτης."

Oepke, Albrecht. "Καθεύδω." *TDNT*. 3:431-37.

Schniewind, Julius. "᾽Επαγγέλλω." *TDNT*. 2:576-86.

Schüpphaus, J. "יָשֵׁן." *TDOT*. 6:438-41.

Shepherd, Jr., M. H. *IDB*. S.v. "Apostolic Fathers."

Thesaurus Linguae Graecae. CDROM database. Version C. Irvine, CA: University of California at Urvine, 1987.

Webster's New World Dictionary. 3d ed. New York: Simon & Schuster, 1988.

Unpublished Works

Bailey, R. E. "Life after Death: A New Testament Study in the Relation of Body and Soul." Ph.D. diss., University of Edinburgh, 1962.

Cranford, Lorin L. "A Study of II Corinthians 5:1-10 in the Light of Various Interpretations of Pauline Eschatology." Th.D. diss., Southwestern Baptist Theological Seminary, 1975.

Huey, F. B. "The Hebrew Concept of Life after Death in the Old Testament." Th.D. diss., Southwestern Baptist Theological Seminary, 1961.

Hutton, Delvin D. "The Resurrection of the Holy Ones (Mt. 27:51b-53): A Study of the Matthean Passion Narrative." Th.D. diss., Harvard University, 1970.

Long, William Rudolf. "The Trial of Paul in the Book of Acts: Historical, Literary, and Theological Consideration." Ph.D. diss., Brown University, 1982.

Osei-Bonsu, J. "Soul and Body in Life after Death: An Examination of the New Testament Evidence with Some Reference to Patristic Exegesis." Ph.D. diss., University of Aberdeen, 1980.

INDEX OF ANCIENT SOURCES

Old Testament

Genesis
45, 158
1.1-2.4, 57
1.26-27, 67
2.17, 71
2.21, 157
20.3, 26
20.6, 26
31.10, 26
31.11, 26
31.24, 26
40.9, 26
41.17, 26
41.22, 26
47.30, 76,
47.30 [LXX], 15, 44, 178

Exodus
22.17, 47

Leviticus
19.31, 47
20.6, 47
20.27, 47

Deuteronomy
50
31.16, 76
31.16 [LXX], 44, 50, 178
32.50, 50
34.6, 50

Judges
3.30, 58
5.27 [LXX], 51, 178

1 Samuel
28, 47, 51
28.3, 47
28.9-13, 47
28.15, 48

2 Samuel
51
3.31, 59
7.12 [2 Kings 7.12-LXX], 51, 178
13.5, 75
14.14, 47

1 Kings
15, 44, 51, 52, 54, 76, 78, 128
13, 54
1.21 [LXX], 178
2.10 [LXX], 178
2.11 [LXX], 51
3.19 [LXX], 55
3.20 [LXX], 55, 181
11.21 [LXX], 178

11.43 [LXX], 178
13.22, 54
14.20, 52
14.20 [LXX], 178
14.31 [LXX], 178
15.8 [LXX], 178
15.24 [LXX], 178
15.26, 53
15.27, 53
16.6 [LXX], 178
16.9-10, 53
16.10, 53
16.13, 53
16.28 [LXX], 178
17.17 [LXX], 56
17.17-24 [LXX], 56
17.19 [LXX], 181
17.21 [LXX], 56
17.22 [LXX], 56
18.27, 78
19.5, 78
22.40, 52
22.40 [LXX], 179
22.50 [LXX], 179
22.52, 53

2 Kings
15, 44, 51, 52, 54, 76, 78, 128
11, 75
20, 117
1.1-16, 53
2.1-11, 32
4.8-37 [LXX], 56
4.21 [LXX], 181
4.21, 75
4.32 [LXX], 56, 179, 181
8.24 [LXX], 179
8.27, 53
9.15, 53
9.16 [LXX], 179
9.27, 53
10.35 [LXX], 179
11.4, 75
11.9, 75

11.20, 53
13.9 [LXX], 179
13.13 [LXX], 179
14.16 [LXX], 179
14.22 [LXX], 179
14.29 [LXX], 179
15.7 [LXX], 179
15.9, 53
15.10, 53
15.14, 53
15.15, 53
15.22, 52
15.22 [LXX], 179
15.24, 53
15.25, 53
15.28, 53
15.30, 53
15.38 [LXX], 179
16.20, 76
16.20 [LXX], 179
17.6, 53
20.1, 117
20.21, 52
20.21 [LXX], 179
21.18, 52
21.18 [LXX], 179
21.23, 53
23.34, 53
23.39, 53
24.15, 53
24.6 [LXX], 179
25.7, 53

1 Chronicles
44, 52, 76, 78, 128
17.11 [LXX], 179

2 Chronicles
44, 52, 76, 78, 128
9.31 [LXX], 179
16.13 [LXX], 179
16.14, 59, 60, 75
16.14 [LXX], 60, 182
21.1 [LXX], 179

26.2 [LXX], 179
26.23 [LXX], 179
27.9 [LXX], 180
28.27, 76
28.27 [LXX], 180
32.33 [LXX], 180
33.20 [LXX], 180
36.8 [LXX], 180

Job
44, 57, 61, 62, 63, 64, 71
1-15, 62
1.21, 33
3.1-13 [LXX], 57
3.13, 58, 80
3.13 [LXX], 57, 60, 62, 180, 183
3.17 [LXX], 58
3.23a [LXX], 62, 63
14.12, 61, 62, 118
14.12 [LXX], 61, 62, 180, 183
14.12b [LXX], 61
14.13, 118
14.14, 62, 118
14.14 [LXX], 62, 119
19.25-26 [LXX], 147
19.25-27, 102
20.11, 62
20.11 [LXX], 62, 180
21.13, 62, 64
21.13 [LXX], 62, 64, 180
21.13b, 63
21.13b [LXX], 63
21.26, 62
21.26 [LXX], 180
26.5, 82
27.13-23, 63
27.19, 63, 64
27.19 [LXX], 63, 180
27.20 [LXX], 63, 180
38.7, 79
38.37, 74

Psalms
44, 66, 128

3.5 [LXX], 66
3.6 [LXX], 147, 149, 153
4.8 [LXX], 66
13.3, 80, 157
13.3 [LXX], 183
13.3b, 66
13.3b [LXX], 66
16.9, 82
16.10, 39, 127
41.8b [LXX], 66, 180
76.5, 81
76.5 [LXX], 81, 183
76.5a [LXX], 66
87.5 [LXX], 184
87.6 [LXX], 108
88.5, 108
88.5ab [LXX], 66
88.6, 79
88.12, 79
90.5-6, 80
94.17, 82
139.9, 82
143.3, 79

Proverbs
20.20, 80
21.16 [LXX], 58

Isaiah
14, 94
23, 106
38, 117
4.6, 80
8.19, 47
14.8 [LXX], 180
14.18 [LXX], 180
19.3, 47
23.14, 106
25.4, 80
26.19, 61, 79, 81, 86, 101
28.2, 80
29.4, 47
30.30, 80
32.2, 80

38.1, 117
40.5, 158
43.17 [LXX], 180
51.20 [LXX], 184
57.2, 58, 60
57.2 [LXX], 58, 60
57.2 [Vulgate], 59

Jeremiah
66
4.23-26, 57
49.23-27 [LXX], 180
51.39, 78
51.57, 78
51.39 [28.39—LXX], 65, 183
51.57 [28.57—LXX], 65, 183

Lamentations
2.21 [LXX], 180

Ezekiel
44, 100, 101, 102
31, 59
32, 15, 59, 94
30.2, 106
30.2 [LXX], 106
31.18 [LXX], 180
32.19 [LXX], 180
32.21 [LXX], 180
32.25, 59, 60
32.27 [LXX], 181
32.28 [LXX], 181
32.29 [LXX], 181
32.30 [LXX], 181
32.32 [LXX], 181
37.1-14, 100, 101, 102

Daniel
66
8.17 [LXX], 111
8.19 [LXX], 111
11.35 [LXX], 111
11.40 [LXX], 111
12.1-4, 81

12.2, 61, 69, 79, 81, 86, 101, 108
12.2 [LXX], 65, 79, 184
12.13 [LXX], 58

Hosea
6.2, 78

Joel
2.28, 158

Amos
8.9, 101

Micah
6.8, 109

Nahum
22
3.18, 81
3.18 [LXX], 67, 81, 182

New Testament

Matthew
22, 101, 103, 105
1.24, 175
4.5, 102
5.8, 48
5.17, 3
5.17-20, 167
8.24, 175
9.18-19, 104
9.23-26, 104
9.24, 105, 106, 175
10.23, 141
12.38-42, 157
13.25, 175
17.1-13, 124
25.5, 175
26.40, 175
26.43, 175
26.45, 175
27.45-54, 100
27.50, 102, 103

27.51, 103
27.51-53, 102, 103
27.51a-53, 100
27.51b-53, 101
27.52, 4, 103, 149, 154, 155, 160, 175
27.53, 103, 104
27.54, 100
27.57-61, 102
28.13, 175

Mark
90, 105
3.6, 112
4.27, 175
4.38, 175
5.21-24a, 9, 57, 90
5.21-24, 104
5.35, 107
5.35-43, 9, 25, 57, 90, 104
5.38, 105
5.39, 105, 175
5.40, 106
9.2-8, 105
10.17-31, 105
11.8, 112
13.30, 141
13.36, 175
14.37, 175
14.40, 175
14.41, 175

Luke
105, 123
16, 49, 50
19, 49, 90
6.25, 106
7.11-17, 57
7.14, 59
8.40-42, 104
8.49, 107
8.49-56, 104
8.52, 105, 175
8.53, 90, 107

8.55, 107
9.32, 175
14.7-14, 100, 124
16.19-31, 16, 48, 98, 124, 162
20.35, 123
20.38, 124
23.42, 6
22.45, 176
22.46, 176
23.42-43, 124
23.43, 98, 125
23.46, 122

John
19, 115, 116, 120
1-12, 116
3, 170
11, 9, 16, 26, 49, 112, 114, 169
1.1-18, 5
1.14, 170
2.1-11, 113
4.23, 111
5.1-15, 113
5.25, 111, 154
5.28-29, 65, 69, 100, 173
7.32, 112
11.1, 113
11.1-44, 9, 112, 114, 117
11.1-45, 114
11.3, 113, 114
11.4-5, 117
11.5-6, 113
11.11, 4, 31, 86, 110, 117-19, 170, 176
11.11-12, 113, 155
11.11-13, 118
11.11-14, 9, 12, 57, 111, 114
11.11-15, 117
11.12, 86, 176
11.13, 26, 118, 176
11.14, 118, 170
11.14-15, 113
11.17, 114
11.17-19, 113

11.24-26, 119
11.25, 119
11.26, 120
11.33, 119, 120
11.33-34, 114
11.33-39, 113
11.38, 120
11.38-39, 114
11.41a, 114
11.43-44, 113, 114
16.20, 106

Acts
121, 122, 125
2, 39, 127, 170
13, 141
2.27-31, 157
2.29, 128
2.31, 127
7.59, 122
7.60, 4, 176
12.6, 176
13.16-41, 126
13.34, 127
13.36, 4, 127, 128, 176
17.16-34, 21, 27, 143
20.7-12, 57
20.9, 26, 176
24.15, 100

Romans
7, 137
11, 153
1.13, 130
5.12-21, 157
7.14-25, 137
8.18-27, 3
8.31-39, 172
8.35-39, 140
8.38, 6, 126
10.6-7, 157
10.7, 157
11.25, 130
13.11, 110, 176

13.11-14, 110
13.12, 110
14.8-9, 5

1 Corinthians
19, 68, 128, 158
5, 8, 11
15, 3, 97, 127, 129, 133-38, 160
3.16, 127
3.17, 158
7.39, 4, 133, 148, 176
10.1, 130
11.30, 133, 176
12.1, 130
13.1, 105
15.1-2. 133
15.6, 4, 133, 176
15.18, 4, 133, 155, 163, 176
15.20, 4, 133, 134, 149, 155, 176
15.20-28, 104
15.42, 96
15.50-55, 3
15.50-57, 97
15.51, 4, 133, 176
15.51-57, 6
15.51-58, 136
15.52, 96, 133
15.53, 96

2 Corinthians
8, 132, 137, 169
5, 3, 6, 97, 99, 111, 129, 134-38, 140
1.8, 130
5.1-4, 137
5.1-5, 97
5.1-10, 2, 3, 5, 6, 16, 133-40
5.2, 137
5.2-4, 3, 134
5.2-5, 3
5.4, 137, 169
5.5, 137
5.6-10, 137
5.8, 163

5.11-21, 136
5.14-15, 120
5.17, 96, 120, 166
12.1-4, 138
12.2-4, 125
12.7, 169

Galatians
2.20, 120, 166
6.17, 158

Ephesians
4.9, 151
5.8-14, 110
5.8a, 108
5.8b, 108
5.14, 108, 109, 176
5.15, 108

Philippians
3, 129
1.21, 139
1.21-24, 139
1.23, 6, 111
3.10-11, 140
3.20-21, 136

Colossians
1.18, 157

1 Thessalonians
85, 128, 132, 158
4, 3, 97, 129, 138, 160
1.10, 97
2.19, 97
3.13, 97
4.13, 4, 34, 129, 131, 159, 170, 176
4.13-18, 110, 129, 136, 149
4.14, 4, 131, 155, 163, 176
4.15, 4, 97, 176
5.6, 176
5.6-7, 109, 110
5.7, 176
5.10, 5, 108, 110, 132, 177

5.23, 97

2 Thessalonians
85, 132

1 Timothy
6.6-10, 33

Hebrews
1.1-2, 3

James
4.9, 106
5.1, 106

1 Peter
3, 153
4, 127
3.18-20, 125
3.19, 151, 157

2 Peter
3.1-7, 127, 141, 170
3.4, 4, 16, 142, 177
3.5-7, 142
3.9, 142
3.10, 142
3.11-13, 142
3.14-18, 142

1 John
2.18, 111

Revelation
2.7, 125
3.3, 111
3.10, 111
6.9, 98
6.9-11, 126, 162, 163
6.10, 6
11.18, 127
18.11, 106
18.15, 106
18.19, 106

Josephus

Antiquities
18.1-2, 70

Wars
2.8.2, 70
7.8.7, 70

Philo

De Abrahamos
162.1-2, 71

De Josepho
147.2-3, 71

De mutatione nominum
5.1-2, 71
40.3, 71

De Plantatione
177.2-3, 71

De somnia
70

De vita Mosis
1.185.1-2, 71
1.289.2-3, 71

Legum allegoria
70
1.105-8, 71

Qumran

IQH
6.34, 86
17, 87
19, 87

Apocrypha

2 Maccabees
12.45 [LXX], 60, 181
12.45 [Vulgate], 60, 159

Sirach
46.19, 59, 66
46.19 [LXX], 59, 181
46.20, 60
46.20 [LXX], 60, 183
48.13, 59
48.13 [LXX], 59, 181

Pseudepigrapha

1 Enoch
22.1-14, 49
22.9b, 49
22.10-11, 49
22.12, 49
22.13, 49
100.5, 69
102.4-5, 69

Jubilees
23.31, 69

Sybilline Oracles
67

Life of Adam and Eve
67
3.1-4, 67
42.5-6, 67
42.7-9, 67
42.8, 68

Esdras
7, 68

2 Esdras
78-80, 68
7.32, 69

Talmud and Rabbinic Literature

Genesis Rabbah
s.13, 86
13.6, 101
14.5, 101
96, 91

Leviticus Rabbah
14.9, 101

Deuteronomy Rabbah
7.7, 101

Yalqut Genesis
42, 92

Yalqut Exodus
260, 92

Yalqut Chronicles
1072, 86

Yebamot
46a, 89

Baba Batra
26a, 89
91a, 89

Baba Metzia
73b, 89
85a, 89
86a, 89

Baba Qamma
91b, 89

Ketubot
84b, 89
104a, 89

Erubin
65a, 89

Moed Qatan
27b, 89
28a, 89

Qiddušin
17b, 90
72a, 89

Targum Genesis
26.10, 85

Targum Onq. Leviticus
15.24, 85

Targum Onq. Deuteronomy
24.12, 85

Targum Yer. Deuteronomy
25.5, 84

Targum Ruth
1.8, 84

Targum Qohelet
4.2, 84

Targum Isaiah
13.16, 85

Targum Zechariah
14.2, 85

Yerušalmi Berakot
5.9d, 86

y.Berakot
I.3c, 90

y.Gittin
44d, 91

*b.*Sanhedrin
48b
109b, 85

*y.*Sanhedrin
29b

Mekilta Beshallah
3, 92

Rabbi Johanan b. Zakkai
22

Greco-Roman Literature

Achilles Tatius
22

Aeschrion the Lyricist
Epigramma
7.345.1-2, 31
Fragmenta et titula
4.1-2, 31

Aeschylus
Choephoroe
906, 33

Aesopicus
Fabulae
186

Anacreon
Fragmenta
186

Apollodorus of Corcyra
Fragmenta
1.56.4-5, 42

Aristophanes
Ecclesiazusae
722, 23

Lysistrata
186

Vespae
186

Aristotle
De Anima
21

Historia anaimalium
186

Callimachus
Epigrammata
9.1, 27

Fragments
195.25-26, 23

Carphyllides
Anthologia Palatina
7.260.7-8, 43

Catullus 5.4-6, 34

Comica Adespota
Dubia
186

Diogenes Laertius
Vitae philosophorum
1.109.6-7, 43

Diotimus
Anthologia Palatina
7.173.3-4, 43

Epimenides
Testimonia
186

Euripides
Andromache
186
389-90, 23

Hecuba
470-73, 30

Rhesus
137-38, 23
668-69, 30
825-26, 23

Supplices
531

The Daughters of Troy
593-94, 30

Greek Anthology
187
7.173.3-4, 31
7.183.3-4, 31
7.219.3-4, 32
7.260.7, 27
7.419.1-2, 32
8.59.2, 60.1, 32
9.223.6-7, 32
9.278.pl,1, 31

Heraclitus
Fragments
26, 37

Hesiod
Opera et dies
116, 26

Hesychius of Alexandria
25

Hippocrates
De affectionibus
186

De affectionibus interioribus
186

De diaeta i.-iv.
186

De diaeta acutorum
186

De morbis i.-iii.
186

De morbis popularibus
186

De mulierum affectibus i.-iii.
186

De natura muliebri
186

Prognosticon
186

Historia Alexandri Magni
Recensio α
3.33.8, 41

Recensio γ
33R.137, 41

Homer
Iliad
186
5.685, 55
11.241, 29
14.235-36, 29
14.249-62, 37
14.482, 108
14.482-83, 31
19.32, 55

Odyssey
186
4.574-75, 23
17.296, 55

Horace
Odes and Epodes
1.24.5-6, 34

Hyperides
Epitaphius
41.2-3, 23

Idomeneus
Anthologia Palatina
7.725, 43

Leonidas of Tarentum
Anthologia Palatina
7.408, 43

Lucianus
Dialogus Deorum
5.7-8, 28
5.14-15, 28
10.4.12-13, 28
17.1.12-13, 28

Lucretius
De Rerum Natura
1.102-135, 33
2.45, 33
3.37-93, 33
3.830-1094, 33
3.843-46, 33
3.904-5, 33
3.909-11, 33
6.1182-83, 33
6.1208-12, 33

Moschus
Anthologia Palatina
3.103-4, 43

Orphica
Argonautica
187

Hymni
187

Pausanius
Description of Greece
1.14.4.3-5, 43

Philippus
Anthologia Palatina
7.405.4, 43

Parthenius Nicaenus
Narrationes amatoriae
20.2.4-5, 42

Pindarus
Isthmia
8.21, 23, 28

Plato

Axiochus
187

Epigrammata
187

Euthydemus
187

Leges
187

Phaedo
19, 21

Phaedrus
21, 187

Republic
21, 187

Symposium
186

Theatetus
24

Timaeus
21

Posidippus
Epigrammata
7.170.5-6, 27, 42

Seneca
Hercules Furens
106-9, 34

Socrates
Apologia
40d/e, 24

Sophocles
22
Ajax
673-74, 27
831-32, 30

Antigone
861, 28

Electra
138, 61
508-9, 30

Oedipus Coloneus
621, 108

Philoctetes
827, 37

Statilius Flaccus
Anthologia Palatina
7.290.3, 43

Theocritus
Idyll
4.42, 35
8.65-66, 42

Theophrastus
Historia plantarum
7.5.4.6-7, 23

Timocles
Fragmenta
22.1-2, 43

Virgil
Aenid
6.278, 34
6.522, 34

Xenophon
Agesilaus
187

Anabasis
187

Cyropaedia
187

Hellenica
187

Memorabilia
187

Symposium
187

Early Christian Literature

Athanasius
Expositiones in Psalmos
27.69.42,3-27.521.36,7, 66

Augustine
De civitate Dei
20.20, 159

Basilius
Homiliae super Psalmos
29.296.35-6, 66

Clement of Alexandria
Miscellanies
4.22, 37

Stromata
1.19.92.2, 11
2.9.43.4.2-44.3.3, 153
3.1-4.2, 154
5.14.105.2.2-3.1, 154
6.6.46.5.4-47.1.1, 154

Clement of Rome
1 Clement
24.2.2, 148
26.2.1-2, 147
44.2.2-3, 148

Epiphanius Constantiensis
De prophetarum vita et obitu
4.1t-2t, 55
6.10-11, 55
16.20-17.1, 55

Eusebius of Caesarea
Commentaria in Psalmos
24.72.18-22, 66

Gospel of Peter
41, 151

Gregory of Nyssa
Contra fornicarios oratio
9.215.1-10, 28
9.215.17-18, 28
9.216.2-3, 28

Hermas, Similitude(s)
9.16.5, 151

Ignatius of Antioch
Epistulae spuriae
8.1.3.1-2, 148
12.4.2.1-2, 148

Letter to the Magnesians
9.3, 151

Letter to Polycarp
4.4.2.2-3, 148
7.1.3.1-2, 148

John Chrysostom
22, 147
De coemeterio et de cruce
49.393.1t-394.34, 158

Justin Martyr
Apologia
38.4.3, 149

Dialogus cum Tryphone
5, 151
72.4.3-4, 149
97.1.6-7, 149

Origen
11, 22
Commentarii in evangelium Joannis
13.59.405.8, 155
28.21.183.5, 155

De oratione
11.1.3-31.5.5, 155

Selecta in Psalmos
12.1413.41-2, 155

Oxyrhynchus Papyri
115, 35

Pseudo-Justin Martyr
*Quaestiones et responsiones ad
  orthodoxos*
443.A.8-B.1, 149
443.D.8-9, 149
444.B.4-5, 149
464.C.3-4, 149

Tertullian
22
De anima
50, 157
51, 156, 157

De resurrectione carne
147
5-11, 158

INDEX OF MODERN AUTHORS

Abrahams, I., 70
Aland, K., 17, 106
Alden, R., 118
Alexander, D., 49
Alfrink, A., 53, 76, 77
Allcock, P. J., 32
Andersen, F. I., 61
Andrews, C., 20
Arbesmann, R., 156
Arndt, W. F., 120
Askwith, E. H., 131
Baab, O., 45
Bailey, L. R., 46, 61
Bailey, R. E., 4, 8, 49
Balz, H., 25, 26, 37, 41, 42, 108, 118
Barclay, W., 141
Barnard, L. W., 149
Barr, J., 14
Barrett, C. K., 116
Bartsch, H. W., 13
Bauer, J. B., 15
Bauer, W., 120
Baumgartner, W., 77
Beach, W., 11
Beasley-Murray, G. R., 113, 115, 119, 120
Berkouwer, G. C., 166
Berry, R., 133, 136, 137
Birkeland, H., 78

Bockmuehl, M., 83
Boisacq, E., 24
Blackburn, B. L., 115
Block, D. I., 102
Blomberg, C., 16, 104
Bornkamm, G., 132
Bowden, J. S., 47
Brandon, S. G. F., 20
Brandscheidt, R., 81
Briggs, C. A., 76
Bright, J., 84
Brooks, J., 90
Brown, D., 100
Brown, F., 76
Brown, R. E., 116
Bruce, F. F., 3, 34, 35, 70, 85, 96, 97, 99, 108, 126, 130, 132
Brueggemann, W., 48
Buck, R. S., 21
Budge, E. A. T. W., 20
Bultmann, R., 13, 37, 86, 109, 111, 113, 138
Cadoux, C. J., 146
Capps, E., 31, 32, 71
Carey, G., 99
Cavallin, H. C. C., 68
Charles, R. H., 46
Charlesworth, J. H., 67
Collignon, M., 40, 42
Colson, F. H., 71

Conzelmann, H., 134
Cooke, G. A., 100
Cooper, J. W., 6, 47, 48, 68, 70, 72, 73, 81, 95, 98, 99, 124, 125, 126, 130, 133, 139, 141, 143, 166, 167
Cooper, L., 102
Cotelier, J. B., 146
Cotterell, P., 22, 38, 76
Craig, W. L., 104
Craigie, P. C., 50
Cranford, L., 16, 138
Crim, K., 49
Cullmann, O., 1, 2, 4, 5, 7, 8
Dahl, M. E., 8, 13
Dahood, M., 63
Daly, E. J., 156
Danker, F. W., 120
Davies, W. D., 5, 136
Day, J., 79
Defarrari, R. J., 156
Deissner, K., 8
Delebecque, E., 117
Delius, W., 149
de Santos Otero, A, 151
de Saussure, F., 14
Dessau, H., 42
de Witte, J. R., 8
Dhorme, E., 64
Diehl, E., 42
Dibelius, M., 126
Dittenberger, W., 66
Dodd, C. H., 113, 126, 127, 150
Donaldson, J., 147
Driver, G. R., 76
Driver, S. R., 76
Dunkerley, R., 112
Dunn, J. D. G., 110, 137
Dupont, J., 8, 136
Edgar, T. R., 108
Ehrmark, E., 35
Eichrodt, W., 47
Ellis, E. E., 3, 5, 6, 8, 11, 72, 123, 124, 134, 168
Enslin, M. S., 151

Epstein, I., 88
Erickson, M. J., 144
Fackre, G., 98, 140, 171
Faw, C. E., 135
Fee, G., 16
Finé, H., 158
Frame, J. E., 130
Fuller, R., 13
Féret, R. P., 79
Feuillet, A., 81
Fillion, L., 59
Fishbane, M., 57
Fitzmyer, J., 49, 107, 123, 124
Foretell, I. T., 114
Fortna, R. T., 113
Furnish, V., 132, 137
Gard, D. H., 62, 64
Gardiner, A. H., 20
Geffcken, J., 42
Gehman, H. S., 62
Gese, H., 49
Geisler, N., 2
Gibson, E., 14
Gillman, J., 97, 135
Gingrich, F. W., 120
Gnilka, J., 103
Godman, S., 50
González, J., 148, 149, 151, 153, 154, 155
González-Ruiz, J. M., 21
Goold, G. P., 30, 33, 34, 187
Goodspeed, E. J., 17
Gowan, D., 72
Gray, J., 54
Green, D. E., 79, 102
Greenup, A. W., 91
Grobel, K., 109
Grossfeld, B., 84
Grundmann, W., 103
Guelich, R. A., 105
Gundry, R. H., 101, 103
Gutiérrez, G., 57
Habel, N. C., 60, 61, 63
Haenchen, E., 121, 125

Hals, R. M., 101
Hanhart, K., 8, 48, 124
Harder, G., 127
Harris, M. J., 2, 3, 4, 16, 20, 21, 46, 73, 96, 99, 102, 103, 104, 105, 107, 134, 135, 136
Harrison, J. E., 21
Hartley, J. E., 57, 60, 63, 118
Hastings, C., 112
Hatch, E., 15, 63
Hathorn, R. Y., 36
Haussig, H. W., 26
Hawthorne, G., 139
Headlam, C., 104
Heater, H., 62, 63
Heathcote, A. W., 32
Heidel, A., 46
Henneberry, B. H., 114
Hennecke, E., 17, 151
Hertzberg, H. W., 47
Hettlinger, R. F., 136
Hick, J., 99, 133
Higgins, A. J. B., 116
Hofmann, J. B., 25
Hoffmann, P., 29, 41, 135
Holladay, C. R., 115
Horsley, G. H. R., 14, 42, 50, 162
Howard, T. L., 108
Hutton, D. D., 101
Huey, F. B., 79
Hull, J. M., 115
Irion, P. E., 13
Isaac, E., 68
Isaacs, M. E., 122
Jacob, E., 32, 45, 49, 54, 79
Jaeger, W., 35
James, E. O., 95
Jastrow, M., 15, 84, 89, 92
Jean-Baptiste, P., 14
Jeremias, J., 49
Jolles, A., 25
Jones, D. M., 37
Jones, G. H., 51, 54
Kahle, P. E., 95

Kaibel, G., 41
Kaiser, O., 35, 67
Kajanto, I., 162, 163
Kassovsky, H. J., 88
Kaufmann, C. M., 42
Keil, C. F., 82
Kelly, J. N. D., 151, 152, 154, 157, 158
Kennedy, H. A. A., 8
Kertelge, K., 90
Key, A. F., 45
Kidner, D., 128
King, J. E., 34
Klostermann, E., 103
Knibb, M. A., 49
Knight, H., 64
Knobel, P. S., 84
Knox, W. L., 3, 136
Köhler, L., 77
Kraft, H., 17
Kuhn, K. G., 15, 86
Ladd, G. E., 98
Lampe, G. W. H., 17
Lang, F. G., 3, 135
Laughton, E., 108, 110
Lautenschlager, M., 110
Le Déaut, R., 83
Lefebvre, G., 162, 163, 189, 190, 191, 192
Leitch, J. W., 134
Levy, J., 88, 89, 91
Lincoln, A. T., 108, 109
Lindenberger, J. M., 81
Lisowsky, G., 15, 58, 59, 77
Livingstone, E. A., 114
Lods, A., 45
Long, B. O., 52, 53
Long, W. R., 121
Loewe, H., 15
Lohse, E., 35, 67
Louw, J. P., 144
Lumby, J. R., 128
Mandelkern, S., 15
Marks, J., 45

Marshall, I. H., 123, 131
Martin, J., 82
Martin, J. P., 112
Martin, R. P., 3, 8, 132, 139, 169
Martin-Achard, R., 46, 78
Matera, F. J., 102
Mattill, A. J., 49, 123
Mayer, G., 15
McDonagh, F., 57
McL. Wilson, R., 17
McNamara, M., 83
McNaspy, C. J., 79
Méhat, A., 155
Melick, R. R., 140
Menoud, P. H., 8
Meyer, B. F., 3
Michel, O., 8, 24, 25, 29, 69
Milne, J. G., 50, 66
Milligan, G., 130, 131
Mitchell, T. C., 56
Molland, E., 11
Montefiore, C. G., 15
Montgomery, W., 120
Moore, C. H., 21
Moore, M. S., 81
Morris, L., 130, 131
Moule, C. F. D., 117, 131
Moulton, J. H., 131
Müller, G., 155
Neibuhr, R., 11
Neusner, J., 83, 91, 92
Nickelsburg, G., 72, 87, 88
Nida, E. A., 144
Nisetich, F. J., 28
Noack, B., 109
Noble, B., 121
Nolland, J., 90, 105, 106
Noth, M., 50
O'Brien, P. T., 139, 140
O'Connell, M. J., 57
O'Donoghue, N. D., 4, 5
Oepke, A., 24, 25, 27, 33, 146
Ogle, M. B., 29, 31, 33, 35, 40, 41, 42, 56, 60, 66, 147, 151, 155,

158, 162
Orlinsky, H. M., 61, 64
Osei-Bonsu, J., 2, 49, 123
Owen, D. R. G., 13
Page, T. E., 31, 71
Paton, W. R., 31
Patterson, R. L., 21
Pauly, A. F., 25
Peake, A. S., 13
Pedersen, J., 46
Peek, E., 41
Pfeiffer, R. H., 52
Pinnock, C., 100
Polhill, J. B., 122, 125
Pollard, T. E., 114, 116
Pope, M., 61, 63, 118
Pringle-Pattison, A. S., 21
Quain, E. A., 156
Quell, G., 79
Rahlfs, A., 15, 51
Redpath, H. A., 15, 63
Reichenbach, B., 99, 124, 131
Rengstorf, K. H., 15
Richardson, A., 116
Ridderbos, H., 8, 166
Riesenfeld, H., 101
Ringgren, H., 79
Robert, J., 50
Robert, L., 50
Roberts, A., 147
Roberts, R. E., 158
Robertson, A. T., 122
Robinson, H. W., 13, 46, 49
Robinson, J., 54
Robinson, J. A. T., 8, 13
Rochais, G., 114, 119
Rohde, E., 21
Roscher, W. H., 37
Rose, H. J., 26
Rouse, W. H. D., 31, 33, 71
Russell, D. S., 47, 67, 68
Ryan, R., 114
Sanders, E. P., 82, 83
Sandmel, s., 95

Sauer, B., 37
Schillebeeckx, E., 21
Schnackenburg, R., 112
Schneemelcher, W., 17, 151
Schneider, G., 108
Schneiders, S. M., 9, 10
Schniewind, J., 141
Schrader, H., 26
Schüpphaus, J., 77, 78
Schwally, F., 78
Schweitzer, A., 3, 8, 120, 140
Schweizer, E., 102
Schwertner, S., 50
Senior, D., 102
Sevenster, J. N., 8
Sheler, J. L., 100
Shepherd, M. H., 146
Shinn, G., 121
Silva, M., 14, 139, 140
Simon, M., 88
Smith, E. J., 52
Smith, J. P., 46
Smith, K., 47
Smith, R., 67
Smith, R. G., 47
Stalker, D. M. G., 132
Stauffer, E., 116
Steely, J. E., 35
Stein, R. S., 8
Stendahl, K., 101
Stenger, W., 114
Storr, F., 30
Strack, H. L., 83
Strawson, W., 49
Tasker, R. V. G., 112
Taylor, V., 105
Theissen, G., 104
Thiselton, A. C., 12
Thomson, J. G. S. S., 8, 29, 61, 78
Todd, O. J., 187
Tromp, N., 76, 77, 80, 81
Turner, M., 22, 38, 76
Urbach, E. E., 70, 93
Vaughan, C., 122

Vermes, G., 87, 88
Vestal, D. 7
Völkel, M., 108
von Dobschütz, E., 131
von Rad, G., 45, 79
von Wahlde, U. C., 113
Waldo, A., 25
Warmington, E. H., 30, 37
Way, A. S., 30
Welten, P., 81
Wenham, J., 102, 103, 104
Wevers, J. W., 100
Whitaker, G. H., 71
Whitelocke, L. T., 15
Wijngaards, J., 78
Wilkens, B., 21
Wilkens, W., 113
Wischnitzer-Bernstein, R., 101
Wissowa, G., 25
Wolff, H. W., 39, 40
Wright, A. G., 91
Würthwein, E., 52
Yeivin, S., 54
York, A. D., 83
Zimmerli, W., 100

BS
2545
.D45
J33
1996